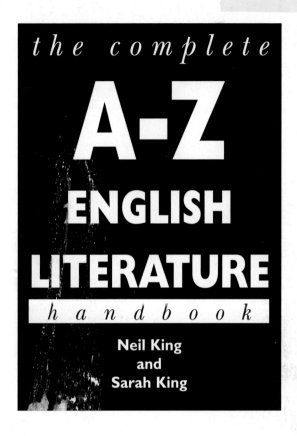

the complete

A-Z
ENGLISH
LITERATURE
handbook

Neil King
and
Sarah King

Hodder & Stoughton

A MEMBER OF THE HODDER HEADLINE GROUP

British Library Cataloguing in Publication Data
A catalogue record for this title is available from The British Library

ISBN 0 340 78291 9

First published 2001

Impression number   10 9 8 7 6 5 4 3 2 1
Year 2005 2004 2003 2002 2001

Typeset by GreenGate Publishing Services, Tonbridge, Kent
Printed in Great Britain for Hodder & Stoughton Educational, a division of Hodder Headline Plc, 338 Euston Road, London NW1 3BH by The Bath Press

HOW TO USE THIS BOOK

It is not intended that this handbook should cover every technical term, concept and writer in English. The aim is to focus upon those which an AS/A or IB Standard/Higher level candidate might encounter, adding a few extra useful terms and writers in order to achieve a reasonable level of 'completeness'. Each entry begins with a straightforward definition, followed by some selected detail. In the interest of clarity there is a good deal of simplification.

One of the most important uses of this handbook is as a cross-referencing tool. Cross-referenced entries are in *italics*, and they have been constructed so that a web of entries inter-relate in order to give an overall picture of areas of interest: for instance, *literary theory* will lead on to entries such as *structuralism* and *post-modernism*, and then into related areas such as the traditional *leavisite* views on *practical criticism*.

A major use of this handbook is to gain a quick handle on writers who may crop up in classroom discussion as related to a set author or topic. Each writer is defined by type, significant preoccupation and/or style, and a selection of notable works. Sometimes collections and selections of a writer's work are listed which, while strictly speaking not 'notable works', help to direct you to useful publications. This handbook covers literature in English, not just English literature, and hence all writers using English and currently set at AS, A or IB level are included. There are a few selected entries devoted to writers in a foreign language who have had a major influence on literature in English.

It is desirable for you in every way possible to imagine your examination script as the examiner will view it. Hence a feature of this handbook is Appendix 1 which covers the terms which examiners use when

- setting English literature examination papers
- discussing examination scripts among themselves.

If you cannot find an entry in the main body of the handbook, try under Appendix 1.

Appendix 2 provides further Hints for examination success. Appendix 3 lists the Assessment Objectives at AS/A and IB Standard/Higher levels. Appendix 4 consists of a Timeline which sets selected authors within the context of their period.

This book is a companion, to be dipped into as the need arises in order to enhance your overall grasp of literature written in English, which in turn will gain you the extra marks which will lift your work into the best grade or level of which you are capable.

Neil King, Sarah King

ACKNOWLEDGEMENTS

We would like to thank Philippa King for her help with background research on various authors; Professor Angus Ross, Liz Whittome and other readers for their helpful suggestions while the work was in progress; Greig Aitken of Hodder for his sensitive editorial assistance; and Neil's Sixth Form English Literature students who kept asking questions which have helped us to clarify what we wanted to write.

Neil King, Sarah King

February 2001

A

abridged: this term indicates when passages of a book have been omitted in order to produce a shortened version of the original.

Abse, Dannie (b.1923): poet, playwright, novelist and autobiographer. Much of his writing is firmly rooted in his own experience as a Jewish, Welsh doctor. Notable works include ASH ON A YOUNG MAN'S SLEEVE (1954), FUNLAND AND OTHER POEMS (1973), WHITE COAT, PURPLE COAT: COLLECTED POEMS 1948–1988 (1989), A POET IN THE FAMILY (1974), THE VIEW FROM ROW C (1990).

abstract can refer to:

- a summary or outline of a piece of writing
- ideas (rather than 'things', which are concrete).

An example of abstract language is 'Hope springs eternal in the human breast' (*Pope*). See *concrete language, concrete poetry*.

Absurd, Theatre and Literature of the, focuses upon a notion that human existence is essentially absurd and meaningless, and that humans are isolated individuals in an alien universe. The Theatre of the Absurd came to prominence in the 1950s, combining *existentialism* with *farce* to provide a type of *black comedy*. Notable among absurd dramatists are *Beckett* (especially WAITING FOR GODOT and ENDGAME), Eugene Ionesco (1900–91), *Pinter*, N.F. Simpson (b.1919). See *surrealism*.

accent: another word for *stress*, particularly in a line of *verse*.

Achebe, Chinua (b.1930): Nigerian novelist. His themes concern such matters as European attitudes towards and impact upon Africa, and African social and political problems. As a critic he argues that the African *novel* must be concerned with local issues and avoid a contrived universality, but at the same time he defends writing in English rather than his native Ibo because he accepts the reality that he must gain as wide an audience as possible for his ideas. Notable works include THINGS FALL APART (1958), NO LONGER AT EASE (1960), ARROW OF GOD (1964), A MAN OF THE PEOPLE (1966), ANTHILLS OF THE SAVANNAH (1987), HOME AND EXILE (2001).

Ackroyd, Peter (b. 1949): novelist, biographer, poet and critic. Most of his *novels* are in the *form* of a mingling of *genres* which explore the relationship between the past and present in a kind of *faction*, and are often located in London. Notable works include POUND (1980), HAWKSMOOR (1985), CHATTERTON (1987), FIRST LIGHT (1989), DAN LENO AND THE LIMEHOUSE GOLEM (1994), THE MYSTERY OF CHARLES DICKENS (2000).

act: a section of a play. Elizabethan and other traditional drama is made up of five acts, which divide very roughly as follows:

- Act I – *exposition*
- Act II – *rising action* or Complication
- Act III – *crisis/ climax/ turning point*
- Act IV – *falling action*
- Act V – *catastrophe, dénouement* and *resolution*.

The German critic Gustav Freytag (1816–95) saw this sequence as pyramid shaped, Act III being the point of the pyramid. Over the past 200 years the number of acts in a play has gradually diminished; nowadays, two acts with one interval is the norm.

action may mean:

- the unfolding of a series of events in a story or play
- the *plot* as a whole.

actual reader: see *implied reader.*

adaptation: any reworking of one medium into another. The most popular kind is the translation of *novels* into films or television scripts, e.g. *Austen's* SENSE AND SENSIBILITY into a film, *Waugh's* BRIDESHEAD REVISITED into a television drama serial. The art of such adaptation can be creative in itself, and if successful can have a stimulating effect upon the sales of the original book. The study of '*text* into pictures' has become popular as coursework in both schools and universities.

Adcock, Fleur (b.1934): New Zealand/English poet. Her *poetry* has been noted for its sensitive yet shrewd observation of contemporary society, unsentimental treatment of relationships, psychological insights and classical themes. Notable works include SELECTED POEMS (1983), THE VIRGIN AND THE NIGHTINGALE (1983), LOOKING BACK (1997).

Addison, Joseph (1672–1719): essayist, journalist, poet and playwright. Associated with *Steele* and *Jonathan Swift*. He founded THE SPECTATOR magazine, which is still published, his many public and political posts influencing his writing. He is best known for his journalism, written in refined, accessible *prose* known as 'middle style' which was acclaimed by *Johnson*. Other notable works include THE CAMPAIGN (1705) and CATO (1713).

Admiral's Men, The: a company of Elizabethan actors managed by *Henslowe*, and rivals to The Lord Chamberlain's Men (later *The King's Men*). *Shakespeare* wrote for both companies at various times.

Aestheticism was a late 19th century European movement, originating principally in France, which advocated the appreciation of 'art for art's sake', reacting among other things to Victorian materialism and *utilitarianism. Ruskin, Swinburne* and *Wilde* were among the foremost proponents of the movement in England. The *poetry* of the *Pre-Raphaelites* is characteristically aesthetic in its sensuousness and striving for musical effect rather than sense; in America *Poe* advocated the importance of 'the *poem* for the poem's sake'. Eventually followers of the movement began to dress, speak and behave in an affected manner, becoming increasingly eccentric in their views and sliding into what became known as *Decadence*. See *aesthetics.*

aesthetic distance: see *distance.*

aesthetics is the appreciation and study of beauty, and is linked to notions of good taste in the arts. See *Aestheticism.*

affectation, in a literary sense, is the use of a pretentious *style* of writing which is unsuited to the *form* or subject-matter.

affective fallacy: the idea that it is inappropriate to judge a *poem* by its emotional or other impact upon the reader, and that *poetry* should be judged by *objective criticism. Reader-response theory* is a reaction to this idea. See *intentional fallacy, New Critics.*

Age of Reason: see *enlightenment*.

Age of Sensibility (or Age of Johnson): generally considered to cover literature written in England between approximately 1745 and 1780.

Age of Transcendentalism: a term sometimes used to cover types of American literature written in New England during the *American Renaissance*. See *transcendentalism*.

Agee, James (1909–55): American novelist, poet, screenwriter and film critic who often brought an objective reporter's eye to his writing. Notable works include LET US NOW PRAISE FAMOUS MEN (1941, a touching account of the plight of Alabama sharecroppers during the 1930s Depression years), AFRICAN QUEEN (1951, film script with John Huston), the semi-autobiographical A DEATH IN THE FAMILY (1957).

agitprop is nowadays used to describe writing which is politically left-wing. The word is a conflation of 'agitation' and 'propaganda' from the Russian word for 'Department of Agitation and Propaganda' which was founded by the Communist Party of Russia in 1920 to make sure that all arts were in line with Communist doctrine. *Brecht* and *Fugard* are among dramatists whose plays may be described as agitprop. See *documentary theatre*.

Agrarians: an early 20th century movement of American writers who favoured the idea of 'back to nature' or 'back to grass roots'.

Aidoo, Ama Ata (b.1942): Ghanaian playwright, novelist, poet, *short story* and children's writer. Her plays offer constructive but uncompromising criticism of Ghanaian society and are often concerned with the position of women in African society as a whole. Notable works include THE DILEMMA OF A GHOST (1964), CHANGES (1991).

Albee, Edward Franklin (b. 1928): American playwright. Influenced by the *Theatre of the Absurd*, his plays often express disillusionment with the values of middle-class America. He claims that his intention as a dramatist has always been 'to offend – as well as to entertain and amuse'. Notable works include THE ZOO STORY (1959), THE AMERICAN DREAM (1961), WHO'S AFRAID OF VIRGINIA WOOLF? (1962), A DELICATE BALANCE (1966).

aleatory writing refers to *poetry* and other arts where the elements (words, in the case of literature) have apparently been put together as if by the throw of a dice. In fact there is nearly always some method behind such apparent randomness. Among others *Ashbery* and *Burroughs* have been described as employing aleatory *techniques*. Jackson Pollock (1912–56) is regarded as having used such techniques in painting, and there are many examples in the field of music.

Alexandrine: another name for *iambic hexameter*. *Pope* considered the line to be clumsy, illustrating it in his ESSAY ON CRITICISM thus:

> A needless Alexandrine ends the song
> That like a wounded snake drags its slow length along

The Alexandrine after the pentameter makes the point, but *Pope* cheats a little by using monosyllabic words, which often create a slowing effect, in the Alexandrine. *Spenser* in THE FAERIE QUEENE and *Keats* in THE EVE OF ST AGNES both use Alexandrines to good effect. See *foot, metre, Spenserian stanza*.

alienation effect: this term refers to stage presentation by means of which, through *devices* such as *songs* which preview or review the *action*, and *heroes* and *heroines* with unattractive *character* traits, the audience is alienated; and thus, unlike more *naturalistic* or realistic *drama*, is prevented from becoming emotionally involved, helped to employ reason rather than emotions, and thus to maintain an objective critical *viewpoint* of the play's subject-matter. This device was evolved by *Brecht* through the work of his Berliner Ensemble. See *brechtian, distance, epic theatre.*

allegory is something which can be read with two *meanings*, an obvious literal meaning and a 'below the surface' meaning. Often there is a point-by-point parallel between the literal and the symbolic meanings. Allegories are a way of conveying comment upon people, moral or religious ideas, historical and/or political events and/or theories. In medieval times a popular *device* was the dream vision whereby the narrator supposes that s/he falls asleep and has an allegorical dream, e.g. *Dante's* DIVINE COMEDY, *Langland's* PIERS PLOWMAN, *Chaucer's* HOUSE OF FAME. *Bunyan's* PILGRIM'S PROGRESS is one of the best known of allegories: it is about a man called Christian and his journey to the Heavenly City, but it represents anyone's struggle through life. Allegories may be of any length from brief *poems* (e.g. those of *Blake*) to a whole book (e.g. *Spenser's* THE FAERIE QUEENE or *Orwell's* ANIMAL FARM). It is closely related to *fable* and parable.

alliteration: the use of repeated consonants in neighbouring words, most often at the beginning of those words, e.g. in Percy *Shelley's* 'O wild west wind'. It is a fundamental device in the alliterative verse of Old English such as BEOWULF (8th century), THE WANDERER and THE SEAFARER, and medieval *poetry* such as SIR GAWAIN AND THE GREEN KNIGHT and *Langland's* PIERS PLOWMAN (both 14th century). It can create a strong effect by introducing pattern into the language. See *assonance, consonance.*

allusion: a reference, sometimes implicit, to any aspect of another piece of literature, art or life in general, e.g. *T.S. Eliot's* THE WASTE LAND is full of allusions, some of which he explains in his notes to the *poem*. Allusiveness can enrich a *text* for a reader who recognises the allusions. See *intertextuality.*

alternate rhyme or **alternate rhyming couplets** is the rhyming of alternate lines of *verse* (abab). See *rhyme, rhyming couplets.*

alternative literature is a term applied to any writing which at the time seems to be outside the mainstream, such as *underground literature*. Such writing as has any merit invariably becomes a part of the mainstream, e.g. significant elements of the *Beat Movement*. See also *subversion.*

Alvarez, A. (b.1929): poet, critic and novelist. Influenced by *Donne* and *Empson*, he rejected *The Movement*, preferring the work of various American poets. His *poetry* is marked by economy of language and tight verse *form*. Notable works include THE SHAPING SPIRIT (1958), THE SCHOOL OF DONNE (1961), THE NEW POETRY (1962).

ambience is another word for *atmosphere*. See also *mood, tone.*

ambiguity, thoroughly explored by *Empson* in his SEVEN TYPES OF AMBIGUITY, is the ability of words and sentences to have more than one *meaning*, deliberately or unintentionally. Sometimes ambiguity is the result of *connotations* of which the individual reader is aware but the writer is unaware. Over-sensitivity to the possibility of ambiguity can lead to *over-reading*. See also *pun.*

ambivalence occurs when the reader has mixed feelings or opposing views towards an event or object, e.g. perhaps towards Lear in the first two *acts* of KING LEAR. An ambivalent attitude can be built up by a writer presenting the *narrative* from more than one *viewpoint* (see *narrator/narrative voice*), e.g. in *Faulkner's* AS I LAY DYING or *Graham Swift's* LAST ORDERS.

American Renaissance: a term sometimes used to cover American literature written between the period 1828–65.

Amis, Kingsley (1922–95): novelist and poet. Associated with *The Movement* and the *Angry Young Men*, his *novels* are often comic and mildly satirical, later writing taking on a darker tone. Notable works include LUCKY JIM (1954), TAKE A GIRL LIKE YOU (1960), THE ALTERATION (1976), JAKE'S THING (1978), THE OLD DEVILS (1986).

Amis, Martin (b.1949): novelist, *short-story* writer, essayist and journalist. Son of *Kingsley Amis*, he is witty, cynical and fiercely satirical, and one of the most stylistically inventive of modern prose writers. Notable works include MONEY (1984), EINSTEIN'S MONSTERS (1987), LONDON FIELDS (1989), NIGHT TRAIN (1997).

amplification is a rhetorical *device* in which language is used to emphasise, magnify or extend. *Dickens* often used the device, most famously in his opening to BLEAK HOUSE in order to create an *atmosphere* of fog, literal and metaphorical. See *palilogy, repetition*.

anabasis is the building towards the *climax* of the action.

anachorism: any aspect of an action, character or scene which is out of sequence, usually as a deliberate part of the structure. See *analepsis, flashback, in media res, prolepsis*.

anachronism: anything which is too early or too late for the given time. It may be a mistake, but more often it is a deliberate ploy in literature or dramatic productions to stress the timelessness of the universe. For instance, *Shakespeare's* reference to a clock in JULIUS CAESAR; or the setting of his HENRY V within the *context* of the Falklands War (as by the English Shakespeare Company in 1987) might give a sense of the play having a contemporary meaning.

anagnorisis means 'recognition', and is the moment when one or more characters, often the *protagonist*, recognises the truth. The word can apply to *tragedy* or *comedy*, but is most often applied to the former, e.g. when in *Shakespeare's* OTHELLO the Moor realises that Iago has practised against him, or in KING LEAR when the king faces the fact that he is 'a very foolish, fond old man'. See *Aristotle, peripeteia*.

analepsis is another term for *flashback*. See also *anachorism, analepsis, flashforward, in media res*.

analogues are stories which have parallels in other cultures, languages and/or literatures. For instance, in medieval literature there are many analogous stories of knights or other *heroes* slaying dragons or monsters.

Anand, Mulk Raj (b.1905): Indian novelist and *short-story* writer. Much influenced by time spent in England, he tries to blend indigenous language rhythms and storytelling methods with contemporary literary *techniques*. He is known for his concern for human rights and realistic and sympathetic portrayal of the Indian poor. Notable works include UNTOUCHABLE (1935), COOLIE (1936), THE VILLAGE (1939), THE SWORD AND THE SICKLE (1942), THE BIG HEART (1945).

anapaest: a single anapaestic *foot*. See also *metre*.

anapaestic: see *metre*.

anaphora: a rhetorical *device* where a word or group of words is repeated in successive clauses. It can be found in many literary *form*s including *song*s, *ballad*s, psalms and *prose*. A famous non-literary example is Winston Churchill's (1874–1965) 'We shall not flag or fail. We shall go on to the end... We shall fight them on the beaches... We shall never surrender.' See *rhetoric, incremental repetition*.

anastrophe: a more extensive changing around of word order than *hyperbaton* by which whole phrases are altered from their normal order for emphatic effect. Used in both *prose* and *poetry*, the impact upon the reader is as often confusion as enlightenment.

anatomy: a thorough examination of a subject, sometimes partly satirical, e.g. *Lyly*'s Euphues, or The Anatomy of Wit, Robert Burton's (1577–1640) Anatomy of Melancholy (1621). Sometimes *fiction* can be part *anatomy*, as in *Melville*'s Moby Dick which is in parts a whaling handbook.

androcentric means 'man-centred', and is used as an alternative term for phallocentric. See also *phallocentric literature*.

anecdote: a short *tale* relating to a single incident told for amusement or gossip, often an entertaining element in biographies.

Angelou, Maya (b.1928): African-American writer and poet, she has also written television documentaries and for stage and screen. She has been a political activist and is a powerful communicator on black American culture. Notable works include I Know Why the Caged Bird Sings (1969) and other autobiographical writings.

Anglo-Saxon Period: see *Old English Period*.

Angry Young Men: a term invented in the 1950s for a group of English writers, musicians and artists, including *Kingsley Amis, Braine, Sillitoe* and, notably, *Osborne* (in his play Look Back in Anger the *anti-hero* Jimmy Porter is the prototypical Angry Young Man). They resented the upper-class lifestyle and superior attitude of the establishment, and their works express their scorn for the hypocrisy of society in post-war Britain where, despite promises and aspirations, working or middle-class educated people were unable to break into influential areas. Their writing was often powerful, sometimes bitter and angry, often humorous, and much of it received critical acclaim.

angst is a constant state of anguish caused by the dread of being responsible for making one's own decisions and choices in life. See *Absurd, Theatre and literature of the, existentialism*.

anisometric: a *stanza* containing lines of unequal length, e.g.

> O sweet spontaneous
> earth how often have
> the
> doting
> (the opening stanza of *e.e.cummings*' 'O Sweet Spontaneous', 1923)

antagonist: the character in a drama who is the main opponent of the *hero* or *protagonist*, e.g. Claudius in Hamlet.

antanaclasis is a figurative *device* (see *figurative language*) whereby a word is repeated in two or more of its senses, e.g. when in *Shakespeare*'s play Othello says:

> Put out the light, and then put out the light   (Act V, Scene 2)

The first 'light' refers to the candle, the second is a *metaphor* for Desdemona's life.

anthology: a *selection* in a single volume of work by different writers (often erroneously used of a selection from the work of a single writer). Sometimes the volume will be of a particular *genre*, e.g. *post-colonial literature, science fiction* or *poetry*; or dedicated to a particular period, e.g. *metaphysical* poetry or The American Short Story. See also *collection*.

Anthony, Michael (b.1932): Trinidadian novelist and *short-story* writer. He is a sympathetic but acute observer of ordinary people, sometimes focusing upon children. Notable works include THE YEAR IN SAN FERNANDO (1965), GREEN DAYS BY THE RIVER (1967).

anthropomorphism is when non-humans are given human abilities to think and, often, speak. Writers of all ages, from Aesop's FABLES through WINNIE THE POOH by A.A. Milne (1882–1956) to *Ted Hughes'* CROW, have used this *device*.

anti-climax refers to any kind of let-down when an anticipated climax is not achieved. It might apply to the plot of a story or play, but is most often applied to intentional *bathos* in a sentence or in *poetry*. *Johnson* described it as 'A sentence in which the last part expresses something lower than the first.' A good example of anti-climax in poetry comes in *Pope*'s 'The Rape of the Lock' when writing about Hampton Court Palace:

> Here Britain's statesmen oft the fall foredoom
> Of foreign tyrants, and of nymphs at home;
> Here thou, Great Anna! whom three realms obey
> Dost sometimes council take – and sometimes tea.
>   [the final word pronounced 'tay' in the 18th century]

Anticlimax is often used in *mock-heroic* writing.

anti-hero: a *protagonist* who displays generally unheroic traits, such as Jimmy Porter in *Osborne*'s LOOK BACK IN ANGER.

antimasque: devised by *Jonson* in 1609, a brief spectacle before or during the *masque* proper, often a *grotesque* burlesque of it. See *burlesque*.

anti-novel: an experimental type of *fiction* which deliberately defies the *convention*s of the traditional *novel*. Some possible aspects include alternative beginnings and endings, lack of clear *plot* or *character* development, diffuse or disconnected episodes, unconventional vocabulary, punctuation and/or syntax, non-sequential use of time; and, at the most extreme, pages which are coloured, blank, detachable, shufflable into different sequences, and/or which contain signs, symbols, drawings or collages. *Sterne*'s TRISTRAM SHANDY is sometimes regarded as the forerunner of the anti-novel. Modern writers who have experimented with aspects of the *genre* include *Joyce, Woolf, Beckett*. See also *avant-garde, fabulation*.

antiphonal describes a *poem*, hymn or prayer which is divided into two parts, one responding to or echoing the other, e.g. *Marvell*'s 'Dialogue Between the Soil and the Body' (1681).

antiphrasis is an ironical, even sarcastic, figure of speech whereby a word is used in a sense opposite to its real meaning, e.g. calling somebody 'clever' who has done something stupid. The device is sometimes used in *litotes*.

anti-play/anti-theatre: drama which deliberately flouts or distorts dramatic convention, as often in *Theatre of the Absurd*.

antistrophe is the changing around of word order to create an emphasis, e.g.

> This hour her Vigil, and her Eve, since this
> Both the year's, and the day's deep midnight is.
> (from Donne's 'A Noctural Upon St Lucy's Day, Being the Shortest Day', 1633)

antithesis is:

- a *rhetorical* term denoting the balancing of two contrasting statements, e.g. 'To err is human; to forgive, divine' (*Pope*); or when Brutus in *Shakespeare*'s JULIUS CAESAR says 'not that I loved Caesar less, but that I loved Rome more.'
- an argument set up in opposition to a *thesis* (as in a parliamentary debate or a court of law).

See also *oxymoron, paradox, parallelism*.

Anyidoho, Kofi (b.1947): Ghanaian poet. A professor of English at the University of Ghana, he is interested in comparative literature and bilingualism, writing in both English and Ewe, his first language. Notable works include HARVEST OF OUR DREAMS (1985).

aphorism: a brief, pithy, sometimes witty saying, close in meaning to *maxim* or proverb, but usually more serious than an *epigram*. A good collection of aphorisms is THE OXFORD BOOK OF APHORISMS (1983) edited by John Gross.

apocryphal, derived from the biblical APOCRYPHA, is a term used to refer to a work of disputed or unknown origin or authorship, e.g. *Shakespeare*'s hand in certain works such as THE TWO NOBLE KINSMEN (see *Fletcher*) or EDWARD III (1596) is so described.

aporia is nowadays a key term in *deconstruction* theory, used to define the point where contradictory meanings in a *text* cause it to 'deconstruct' and no clear meaning can be certain.

aposiopesis: an intentional break in a speech leaving it unfinished. This can have a powerful and threatening effect, e.g. 'if you do that I'll…'; or as in KING LEAR where Lear rails against his daughters Regan and Goneril

> I will have such revenges on you both,
> That all the world shall – I will do such things –   (Act II, Scene 4)

apostrophe is a figure of speech addressing an object, e.g. *Dunn*'s 'Ode to a Paper Clip'; or a person, e.g. *Wordsworth*'s 'Sonnet to Milton'; or an idea e.g. *Milton*'s 'L'Allegro': 'Hence loathed Melancholy!' as if Melancholy exists and can understand. See also *invocation*.

apothegm is the technical word for an *epigram* in *prose*.

archaisms, in a literary sense, are old or obsolete words or syntax which are deliberately used for effect. In THE FAERIE QUEENE *Spenser*, an admirer of *Chaucer*, used archaisms to create a bygone world of courtly *romance*. Thereafter *Milton, Chatterton,*

Keats, Tennyson and others all from time to time used archaisms to evoke another age. In order to give dignity to their writings, the translators of the authorised version of the BIBLE (1611) and others employed archaisms. Their use has always been associated with a notion of *poetic diction*, and such archaic words as 'thee' and 'thou' were accepted usage in *poetry* until well into the 20th century.

Arden, John (b.1930): playwright. Always concerned by social injustice, his themes often involve a clash between rigid authority and anarchic subversion. His recent plays have been more forcefully *polemic* and less intellectually balanced than his much admired earlier ones. Notable works include SERGEANT MUSGRAVE'S DANCE (1959), THE WORKHOUSE DONKEY (1963), ARMSTRONG'S LAST GOODNIGHT (1964).

argument may mean:

- a line of reasoning
- a summary of a *plot*, e.g. that which *Coleridge* provided for 'The Rime of the Ancient Mariner'
- a declaration of purpose at the beginning of an *epic*.

See also *argument* in Appendix 1.

Aristotle (384–322BC): ancient Greek philosopher and writer whose book POETICS is a good introduction to the nature of literature, and who introduced many terms, useful especially in discussing *drama*, such as *anagnorisis, catharsis, peripeteia*.

Armah, Ayi Kwei (b.1939): Ghanaian novelist. His writings tend to reflect continuing African suffering and disillusion with independence, often employing *imagery* of decay and disease. Notable works include THE BEAUTIFUL ONES ARE NOT YET BORN (1968).

Armitage, Simon (b.1963): poet. Sharply observant, witty and popular he uses, among other things, his experiences as a probation officer and his native West Yorkshire settings and manner of speech. Notable works include ZOOM (1989), KID (1992), A BOOK OF MATCHES (1993), DEAD SEA POEMS (1995), CLOUDCUCKOOLAND (1997), LITTLE GREEN MAN (2001), SELECTED POEMS (2001).

Arnold, Matthew (1822–88): English poet and critic. His works are considered by some to be among the best of the *Victorian Age*. The *elegy* 'Dover Beach' (1867) is probably his most acclaimed *poem* in which he uses the ebbing of the tide as a *metaphor* for the diminishing of religious faith in society. His collection of essays CULTURE AND ANARCHY (1869) contains many of his central critical arguments.

Arthurian legend: many versions exist of the semi-historical legend of King Arthur and the Knights of the Round Table. *Malory* collected many of the stories into his MORTE D'ARTHUR, a tale of courtly love and chivalric behaviour which was printed by *William Caxton*, the first English printer.

Ashbery, John (b.1927): American poet. A leading member of the New York school of poets, his interest in art generates strong visual imagery in his *poetry*. Notable works include SELF-PORTRAIT IN A CONVEX MIRROR (1975).

aside: a theatrical *convention*, often leading to *dramatic irony*, whereby a *character* in a play speaks to one side so that the audience may hear (sometimes directly addressing the audience) but, it is supposed, the other characters on stage do not hear.

Nowadays this *device* is used more in *farce* and pantomime than in other kinds of *drama*. See also *soliloquy*.

association: the mental connection between objects and ideas. *Coleridge* writes of this idea in BIOGRAPHIA LITERARIA, and he and *Wordsworth* wrote many conversational poems (see *conversation piece/poem*) and other writings in which a poet's mood and surroundings lead to an *association*, often between the past and the present, and through a natural and freely structured progression of thought, e.g. *Coleridge*'s 'Frost at Midnight', *Wordsworth*'s 'Tintern Abbey'. An interest in rendering into words this free-wheeling process of thought led to the development in the 20th century of the *stream of consciousness* technique. See *connotation*.

assonance, sometimes known as rhyming of vowels, is used to create a melodious effect, more often in *poetry* than *prose*, when similar vowel sounds are repeated, e.g. 'wide' and 'time'. The device only occasionally results in the rhyming of words. It is the vocalic equivalent of *alliteration*, and is far more powerful in creating poetic effects than the more often noted alliteration. See also *consonance, half-rhyme*.

asyndeton: a rhetorical *device* whereby small words such as articles, conjunctions, and possibly prepositions and pronouns, are omitted in order to create a particular effect, often of speed and concision. The *technique* is popular amongst many modern poets such as *Berryman, Auden, Lowell, MacNeice*, e.g.

> World is crazier and more of it than we think,
> Incorrigibly plural. (from 'Snow', 1935)

The opposite is *polysyndeton*.

atmosphere is the feeling or mood evoked by a part or whole of a work of art. For instance, it may be argued that the opening lines of *Shakespeare*'s HAMLET create an *atmosphere* of chill and suspenseful apprehension; or the description of Miss Havisham's house in *Dickens*' GREAT EXPECTATIONS one of gloom, decay and foreboding. See *ambience, mood, tone*.

attitude: see *authorial intention*.

Atwood, Margaret (b.1939): Canadian novelist, poet and *short-story* writer. In her writing there are elements of social *realism* and *satire*, and she tends to adopt a feminist slant. She has spoken of the importance in her work of an individual refusing to be a victim. She sometimes focuses upon the Canadian landscape, for instance in SURFACING (1972), and has an ability to create a strong sense of place. Other notable works include THE HANDMAID'S TALE (1985), CAT'S EYE (1989, remarkable in its depiction of aspects of the behaviour of young girls), THE BLIND ASSASSIN (2000) for which she won the Booker Prize 2000.

Auden, W.H. (1907–73): poet, playwright, critic and editor. Influenced, among others, by *Yeats*, Karl Marx (1811–83) and Sigmund Freud (1856–1939), and friends/collaborator with *MacNeice, Spender, Day-Lewis* and *Isherwood*, his *poetry* is varied in *theme* and *style*, from the left-wing social comment of his early poetry to the interest in religion and Christian viewpoint of later writing. He was skilled in using contemporary language within traditional *verse forms*, and he had considerable influence upon poets who followed him. Notable works include THE DOG BENEATH THE SKIN (1935), THE ASCENT OF F6 (1936), LETTERS FROM ICELAND (1937), NONES (1951),

THE SHIELD OF ACHILLES (1955), HOMAGE TO CLIO (1960), COLLECTED SHORTER POEMS (1966), COLLECTED LONGER POEMS (1968).

Augustan refers in English literature to writers active during the English *Augustan Period* who admired and imitated the *wit*, elegance and *style* of the classical writers, e.g. *Addison, Pope, Steele, Jonathan Swift.* From the stylistic point of view, some critics would include *Dryden*, who wrote before 1700, and *Goldsmith* and *Johnson*, who continued writing into the later 18th century. The term originally referred to such classical writers as Horace (65–8BC), Ovid (43BC–18AD) and Virgil (70–19BC) active during the reign of the Roman Emperor Augustus (27BC– 14AD).

Augustan Period (or The Age of Pope): generally considered to cover literature written in England between approximately 1700 and 1745, although *Goldsmith* confined the period to that which was written during the reign of Queen Anne (1702–14).

Austen, Jane (1775–1817): Often considered England's finest woman novelist. She wrote with great *wit*, humour, *irony* and a keen interest in human nature, creating a precise picture of aspects of her age with characters such as the engaging Elizabeth Bennett, the obsequious Mr Collins and the obnoxiously haughty aristocrat Lady Catherine de Burgh in PRIDE AND PREJUDICE (1813). Her books all deal with ideas of position, etiquette and *tradition*s intrinsic to English society. Other notable works include SENSE AND SENSIBILITY (1811), MANSFIELD PARK (1814), EMMA (1816), NORTHANGER ABBEY (1818), PERSUASION (1818).

Auster, Paul (b.1947): American novelist, poet and essayist. Often his writing is experimental, the *setting* of his stories is New York, and his main subject the process of writing itself. Notable works include IN THE COUNTRY OF LAST THINGS (1987).

author: anyone who produces any kind of written material. *Literary theory* has increasingly questioned the author's place in the appreciation and understanding of literature. See also *deconstruction, death of the author, Marxist criticism, New Critics, poststructuralism, structuralism.*

authorial attitude: see *authorial intention.*

authorial intention/authorial attitude: a phrase used to signify what the author meant when s/he wrote a *text*. Many modern critics believe that what the author may or may not have intended is irrelevant, that there is no fixed meaning in a text, and that an individual reader's interpretation is all-important. They argue that an author may be ambiguous in her or his intentions, and that it is not 'incorrect' if a reader's interpretation was not anticipated by the author. One critic has commented that *poetry* 'is detached from the author at birth and goes about the world beyond his power to intend about it or control it'. The same is applied to a playwright or theatre director's intentions and what the reader/audience read into a play/production. See *death of the author, intentional fallacy.*

authorial voice: see *voice.*

autobiographical memoir: a book dealing with events in the author's life, but not a comprehensive *autobiography*, e.g. *Malan*'s MY TRAITOR'S HEART.

autobiography: a *memoir* of a person's life written by her or himself. Classical writers such as Herodotus (c.480–425BC) wrote works which may be considered autobiographical. Bede (673–735) wrote a short account of his life in his

ECCLESIASTICAL HISTORY (731). By the 17th century diaries had become popular. In the 18th century a link between the *novel* and the autobiography can be found in *Defoe*'s ROBINSON CRUSOE. In the 19th century *Wordsworth* spent much of his time writing and re-writing THE PRELUDE, an autobiography in *poetry* of his early years. Among notable autobiographies are *Twain*'s LIFE ON THE MISSISSIPPI (1883), *Wilde*'s DE PROFUNDIS (1905), *Gosse*'s FATHER AND SON, *Brittain*'s TESTAMENT OF YOUTH. From the 1950s the writing of autobiographies escalated and nowadays anyone who has achieved fame, be they sportsman, popstar, politician, scientist, explorer, military leader or whatever, will write (or more likely have ghost-written) their autobiography, some of scant literary merit. See *biography, diary*.

autoclesis is a rhetorical *device* whereby an idea is mentioned negatively or dismissively in order to arouse interest in the listener, e.g. Mark Antony's treatment of Caesar's will in *Shakespeare*'s JULIUS CAESAR (?1599).

avant-garde is a term used to describe modern works which are at the cutting edge or 'ahead of their time', deliberately setting out to be innovative, and even to shock; and in which the writer (or artist) experiments with new *techniques, forms* and *themes*. The phrase is a French military term meaning 'advance guard' and was initially used by and of certain 19th century French writers and artists.

Awoonor, Kofi (b.1935): Ghanaian poet and novelist who writes in both English and Ewe. Influenced by *Pound* and *Dylan Thomas,* he utilises the oral *poetry* of the Ewes to try to blend European and pre-colonial cultures in order to explore the modern African psyche. Notable works include REDISCOVERY (1964), NIGHT OF MY BLOOD (1971), THIS EARTH, MY BROTHER (1972).

Ayckbourn, Alan (b.1939): prolific playwright in the *comedy of manners* tradition. He explores a multiplicity of aspects of middle-class anxieties and neuroses, writing for his provincial theatre in Scarborough, Yorkshire, and usually transferring his plays to London. He is innovative in his stagecraft and handling of his subject-matter, unusual in one so popular and commercially successful. He is the most performed English playwright apart from *Shakespeare.* Notable works include RELATIVELY SPEAKING (1964), HOW THE OTHER HALF LOVES (1969), ABSURD PERSON SINGULAR (1972), THE NORMAN CONQUESTS (trilogy, 1973), BEDROOM FARCE (1975), JOKING APART (1978), SISTERLY FEELINGS (1979), WAY UPSTREAM (1981), A CHORUS OF DISAPPROVAL (1985), A SMALL FAMILY BUSINESS (1987), THE THINGS WE DO FOR LOVE (1997). Most of his plays are *farces,* but some later work has developed increasingly dark tones.

Bacon, Francis (1561–1626): Best known for his ESSAYS (1597–1625), a collection of brief, pithy pieces on various topics which he reworked as life taught him different lessons and modified his thinking. In Act I, Scene 5 of *Shakespeare*'s play, Hamlet notes down an important observation on life in his 'tables', much as Bacon would have done. A philosopher, scientist and polymath, he also held high government office. It was once fashionable to suggest that he was the true writer of Shakespeare's plays (known as the Baconian Controversy) on the assumption that one from Shakespeare's ordinary background could not have written plays of genius. This theory is today discounted.

Baldwin, James (1924–87): American novelist and essayist. As a black writer from Harlem his work centres on racial and sexual politics, subjects close to home. Notable works include GO TELL IT ON THE MOUNTAIN (1953), GIOVANNI'S ROOM (1956), ANOTHER COUNTRY (1962), JUST ABOVE MY HEAD (1979).

ballad: a *poem* which tells a *story*, usually in the form of four-line *stanza*s or *quatrain*s with lines one and three unrhymed *iambic tetrameter*s, lines two and four *iambic trimeter*s. Thus the opening of arguably the most famous English literary ballad, *Coleridge*'s 'The Rime of the Ancient Mariner', runs:

> It is an ancient mariner
> And he stoppeth one in three
> – 'By thy long grey beard and glittering hand
> Now wherefore stopp'st thou me?'

Sometimes all lines are *tetrameter*s, sometimes the *rhyme* scheme is abcd, abab or aabb. Narrative folk ballads are passed on by word of mouth from generation to generation, especially in rural areas, a traditional *form* of story-telling which still thrives in remote parts of the world. A typical ballad has a swift opening, uses everyday language, and often tells a story of disasters, battles and conflicts in *dialogue* and *action*, sometimes with a *chorus*. Examples are the legends of the rebel Robin Hood, and the Border Ballads telling of skirmishes and bloodshed on the England/Scotland borders. Urban communities have created their own ballads, sometimes referred to as street or broadside ballads. Notable literary ballads include *Keats*' LA BELLE DAME SANS MERCI (1819) and *Wilde*'s THE BALLAD OF READING GOAL (1898). See *lyric, song*.

Banks, Iain M. (b.1954): Scottish novelist. As well as his *science fiction* novels, he has also produced highly imaginative writings, sometimes controversially violent, which explore modern culture. Notable works include THE WASP FACTORY (1984), WALKING ON GLASS (1985), THE BRIDGE (1986), COMPLICITY (1993), AGAINST A DARK BACKGROUND (1993).

Bankside: an area of Elizabethan London to the south side of the River Thames, opposite the City and outside its limits and jurisdiction. There in Elizabethan times thrived theatres, taverns and brothels, all prohibited or disapproved of by the controlling hand of the Puritans within the City. See *Globe Theatre, Rose Theatre*.

Barker, Howard (b.1946): playwright. For a time he acquired something of a cult following, his *post-modernist* plays challenging social and political conventions, and questioning those in power. Notable works include THE HANG OF THE GAOL (1978), NO END OF BLAME (1980), VICTORY (1983), SCENES FROM AN EXECUTION (1984), THE CASTLE (1985).

Barker, Pat (b.1943): novelist. Both her earlier work, which concentrates on the struggles of working-class women, and her more recent writing, which focuses on psychological issues, have a strong historical basis. Notable works include THE MAN WHO WASN'T THERE (1989), REGENERATION TRILOGY (1991), THE GHOST ROAD (1995), BORDER CROSSING (2001).

Barnes, Julian (b.1946): novelist. In his books he often employs *faction*, combining comedy with psychological insight in a *witty* style. Notable works include METROLAND (1981), FLAUBERT'S PARROT (1984), A HISTORY OF THE WORLD IN 10½ CHAPTERS (1989), ENGLAND, ENGLAND (1998).

baroque: a term used to describe a style of architecture, art and music, but it can be used appropriately for writing with similar 17th century features; that is, florid, exuberant, dramatic. *Metaphysical* writing of the 17th century is sometimes so described.

bathos is when a writer, intending to be *pathetic*, over-reaches and descends to the ridiculous. *Pope* established this term in OF THE ART OF SINKING IN POETRY (1727), and gives as an example:

> Ye Gods! Annihilate but Space and Time
> And make two lovers happy.

THE STUFFED OWL (1930), edited by Wyndham Lewis and Charles Lee, is a good collection of pompous bathetic *verse*. Some consider that bathos can cover intentionally absurd effects of this kind, but this is more properly one of the meanings of *anti-climax*.

Baxter, James K. (1926–72): New Zealand poet, dramatist and critic. His largely religious writings cover a wide range of personal experiences. Notable works include BEYOND THE PALISADE (1944), PIG ISLAND LETTERS (1966), THE BAND ROTUNDA (1967), JERSUALEM SONNETS (1970), AUTUMN TESTAMENT (1972).

Beat Movement: a 1950s loose-knit group of American anti-establishment writers sometimes known as the Beat Generation. Down-beat, off-beat, down-and-out, free-wheeling, unconventional and sometimes anarchic in both writing and permissive lifestyle, they deliberately shocked middle-class Americans (whom they called 'squares'). Influenced among other things by jazz and Zen Buddhism, notable writers include *Kerouac* (who is credited with inventing the term 'beat'), *William Burroughs, Ginsberg, Corso, Ferlinghetti*. The movement as such was short-lived, but influenced many who followed, such as *performance poets*. See also *alternative literature, underground literature*.

Beaumont, Francis (1584–1616): playwright. Much admired by *Dryden*, he was reputed to be a shrewd judge of what worked well on the stage, *Jonson* relying upon his advice and judgement in reviewing and correcting his own work. Notable works include THE KNIGHT OF THE BURNING PESTLE (?1607), PHILASTER (1609), THE MAID'S TRAGEDY (?1611), the latter two in collaboration with *Fletcher*.

Beckett, Samuel (1906–89): Irish playwright, novelist, *prose* writer and essayist. He was friendly with and influenced by his fellow-countryman *Joyce*. He has become associated with the *Theatre of the Absurd*, his best known work being WAITING FOR GODOT (1955, originally written in French) where, typical of his plays, stage trappings are *minimalist*, the focus being upon individuals within a stark predicament. He had considerable influence on, among others, *Pinter, Stoppard, Fugard*. Other notable works include ALL THAT FALL (1957), ENDGAME (1958), KRAPP'S LAST TAPE (1958), HAPPY DAYS (1961), NOT I (1973).

Beckford, William (1759–1844): novelist. A wealthy man, his extravagant lifestyle was matched by his highly imaginative writing, his best known work being the *gothic novel* VATHEK (1787). Other notable works include DREAMS, WAKING THOUGHTS, AND INCIDENTS (1784), AZEMIA (1797).

bedlam: a madhouse or lunatic asylum, from St Bethlehem's Hospital in London. At one time begging bedlamites released into the community would have been a common sight, e.g. 'Mad Tom' in *Shakespeare's* KING LEAR.

Beer, Patricia (1919–99): poet. Incorporating many references to the West Country and focusing on mundane scenarios, she creates an individual style which is *witty* and serious. Notable works include LOSS OF THE MAGYAR (1959), MRS BEER'S HOUSE (1968), MOON'S OTTERY (1978).

Behn, Aphra (1640–89): playwright, novelist, poet and translator. She takes material from earlier writers, creating plays which explore with *wit* social issues of the time. She lived an adventurous life, and is credited with being the first Englishwoman to earn her living as a writer. Her *comedy* THE EMPEROR OF THE MOON (1687) uses elements of *commedia dell'arte*, introducing harlequinade and thus possibly the beginnings of pantomime to England. Other notable works include THE TOWN FOP (1676), THE ROVER (1677), THE EMPEROR OF THE MOON (1687), OROONOKO (1688).

Bell, Gertrude (1868–1926): travel writer. Her archaeological pursuits are noted in her writings, which frequently develop an interest in Arabic history. Notable works include THE DESERT AND THE SOWN (1907), AMURATH TO AMURATH (1911).

Belloc, Hilaire (1870–1953) poet, essayist, journalist, novelist, biographer and travel writer. After turning his back on politics he befriended *Chesterton*, whose interests and Roman Catholic religion he shared. Prolific and skilled over a range of material and *forms*, he is best remembered for his humorous *verse*. Notable works include THE PATH TO ROME (1902), CAUTIONARY TALES (1907), SONNETS AND VERSES (1923), PONGO AND THE BULL (1910), EUROPE AND FAITH (1920), BELINDA (1928).

Bellow, Saul (b.1915): American novelist. He writes with richness and humour as his philosophical interests lead him to explore the human soul in various social situations. Notable works include THE ADVENTURES OF AUGIE MARCH (1953), HERZOG (1964), MR SAMMLER'S PLANET (1970).

Bennett, Alan (b.1934): playwright, television and radio writer, and essayist. He is known for his sensitive, often melancholy portrayal of people, and his work frequently has a satirical edge. He does not see himself a committed political playwright like some of his contemporaries, but as 'political' in its widest sense. He sometimes draws upon his North of England roots. Notable works include Forty Years On (1968), Habeas Corpus (1973), Talking Heads (1989), The Madness of King George (1990).

Berryman, John (1914–72): American poet. His unique voice is heard through *poem*s of personal and emotional exploration, which eventually led to his suicide in 1972. Notable works include The Dispossessed (1948), Homage to Mistress Bradstreet (1956), The Dream Songs (1969), Delusions (1972).

bestiaries: *tale*s with a moral about real or imaginary animals. *Collection*s of such tales, sometimes derived from Aesop's fables, were popular in *prose* or *verse* form in the Middle Ages, and writers such as *Chaucer* drew on them, e.g. The Nun's Priest's Tale in The Canterbury Tales, with its cunning fox and vain cockerel.

Betjeman, John (1906–84): poet, critic of architecture, journalist and broadcaster. His *poem*s take a light-hearted and sometimes melancholic look at middle-class society. They are *traditional* in style and at first seem simple, but Betjeman's technique includes excellent *rhyme* and *rhythm*. English landscape and architecture were his passion. He was *poet laureate* from 1972–84. Notable works include Collected Poems (1958, revised 1962) and the autobiographical Summoned By Bells (1960).

Bible: it was once said that an essential requisite for studying western literature is a working knowledge of the Bible, and this is very valuable in order to appreciate and evaluate the *context*s within which much English literature is written and understood.

bibliography: a list of books, articles, *essay*s and other written material which is available on a particular author or subject.

Bierce, Ambrose (1842–c1914): American *short-story* writer and journalist. Much of his writing is based on the bitterness he felt from his experiences in the Civil War. Notable works include Tales of Soldiers and Civilians (1891).

biography: an account of a person's life and personality by another person, e.g. *Boswell*'s The Life of Samuel Johnson (1791), Eminent Victorians (1918) by Lytton Strachey (1880–1932), John Keats (1968) by Robert Gittings (1911–92). See *autobiography, diary, memoir*.

Bird, Isabella (1831–1904): travel writer. Her adventurous spirit comes over in her writings, which inspired the women of her time who were mainly used to a narrow domestic existence. *Churchill* characterises her in Top Girls. Notable works include A Lady's Life in the Rocky Mountains (1879).

Bishop, Elizabeth (1911–79): American poet. Much of her work is influenced by her time in South America and this adds to the strong sense of place in her work. Notable works include North and South/a Cold Spring (1955), Questions of Travel (1965), Geography III (1976).

black comedy is a term used to describe *drama* where potentially horrific situations are treated with amusement and ridicule by both the characters and the audience, as is *Beckett*'s Waiting for Godot. *Pinter, Albee* and *Orton* are among other notable English playwrights of black comedy, whose antecedents go back to *Shakespeare*'s The Merchant of Venice (?1596) and Measure for Measure (?1604), and beyond. The term is also extended to other kinds of literature such as *novel*s, e.g. *Heller*'s Catch-22 or *A.N.Wilson*'s The Healing Art. See also *graveyard school of poetry, sick verse*.

Blake, William (1757–1827): poet, engraver and artist. His radical politics led him to befriend like-minded people such as *Godwin* and Thomas Paine (1735–1809). He admired *Milton* as a great national poet, but in THE MARRIAGE OF HEAVEN AND HELL (1790–3) attacks *Milton*'s PARADISE LOST and displays his unorthodox aversion to Christianity and all organised religions. He illustrated most of his writings with engravings, and much of this work was not discovered until after his death. In some ways a *Romantic* idealist in times of industrial revolution and political unrest, his work demonstrates great depth and range from energetic, scathing attacks to lyrical tenderness. His brand of *Romanticism* is perhaps best summed up in his belief that 'every thing that lives is holy'. Notable works include THE FRENCH REVOLUTION (1791), VISIONS OF THE DAUGHTERS OF ALBION (1793), SONGS OF INNOCENCE AND OF EXPERIENCE (1794).

blank verse is unrhymed *iambic pentameter* (a common mistake is to describe any unrhymed *verse* as 'blank'). It is the most common metrical pattern in English verse, notable users including *Milton* and *Wordsworth*. *Marlowe* and *Shakespeare* did much to make blank verse a flexible and powerful dramatic medium. See *metre*.

Blixen, Karen: see *Dineson*.

Bloomsbury Group: the name given to a group of writers, intellectuals and artists who befriended each other and who between about 1907 and 1939 met in Bloomsbury, London to discuss their mutual views on the arts. Much opposed to the artistic and social constraints of the era, their influence on art and philosophy during and after the First World War was extensive. Often regarded as elitist and dilettante, the group included *Forster*, Lytton Strachey (1880–1932), *Woolf*.

Blunden, Edmund (1896–1974): poet, critic and biographer. His writing includes some of the best of First World War *poetry*. Notable works include UNDERTONES OF WAR (1928).

blurb: publisher's comments printed on the cover of a book, often including an enthusiastic brief summary of the contents and designed to entice the reader.

Boccaccio, Giovanni (1313–75): Italian writer who influenced many subsequent European writers. For instance, *narrative* and other aspects of *Chaucer*'s CANTERBURY TALES owe much to Boccaccio's story-cycle THE DECAMERON (1349–51), in which ten people each tell one story a day over ten days. Writers whom he influenced include *Lydgate, Shakespeare, Dryden, Keats, Longfellow, Tennyson*. Among his output are *prose* romances, and some of his writing in Latin was widely read in England. Other notable works include FILOCOLO, FILOSTRATO, TESEIDA. The dates of most of his writing are uncertain.

Boland, Eavan (b.1944): Irish poet whose writing tends to be preoccupied with contemporary Irish troubles. Notable works include NEW TERRITORY (1967), THE WAR HORSE (1975), IN HER OWN IMAGE (1980), OUTSIDE HISTORY (1990), IN A TIME OF VIOLENCE (1994).

Bolt, Robert (1924–95): playwright and screenwriter, best known for his historical plays. Notable works include A MAN FOR ALL SEASONS (1960).

bombast is pompous, overblown language. Polonius in *Shakespeare*'s HAMLET often speaks bombastically, and when giving his advice to the players Hamlet criticises old-fashioned bombastic actors.

Bond, Edward (b.1934): playwright. A controversial writer whose plays often deal with alienation from society and violence. Several of his works were initially banned. He highlights contemporary issues, the world's injustices and the struggle of good for survival. He uses historical *character*s and *setting*s, and the writings of such as *Clare* and *Shakespeare* (both in his writings and as a person). In the 1970s he said that 'we need an active philosophy – time is running out.' Notable works include SAVED (1966), THE NARROW ROAD TO THE DEEP NORTH (1968), EARLY MORNING (1968), LEAR (1971), THE SEA (1973), BINGO (1972), THE WAR PLAYS (1985).

book of hours: an illustrated prayer book. One of the most exquisite is the Duc de Berry's TRÈS RICHES HEURES (15th century).

Booker McConnell Prize for Fiction: an annual prize awarded since 1969, commonly known as the Booker Prize. Former winners include *Farrell* in 1973 for THE SEIGE OF KRISHNAPUR, *Golding* in 1980 for RITES OF PASSAGE, *Rushdie* in 1981 for MIDNIGHT'S CHILDREN, *Keneally* in 1982 for SCHINDLER'S ARK, *Coetzee* in 1983 for LIFE AND TIMES OF MICHAEL K, *Ishiguro* in 1989 for THE REMAINS OF THE DAY, *Margaret Atwood* in 2000 for THE BLIND ASSASSIN.

Boswell, James (1740–95): *journal* writer and biographer. He left Scotland for London to pursue an ambitious political life where he successfully published several anonymous pamphlets and *verse*s. He then travelled widely, but remained in close contact with the London literary scene including *Johnson* and *Goldsmith*, publishing many works under the name 'Hypochondriack'. His many letters reveal his ambitiousness, countless affairs, and fits of depression. His writing is largely entertaining and readable, telling much of his life and times. Notable works include AN ACCOUNT OF CORSICA (1768), DORANDO (1767), THE JOURNAL OF A TOUR TO THE HEBRIDES (1785), THE LIFE OF SAMUEL JOHNSON LL.D. (1791).

Bradbury, Malcolm (1932–2000): Novelist and critic. Admiring of modern experimental writers, his first three *novel*s were *campus novel*s. His favoured satirical style of work centres on political and modern cultural opinions, which he questions through his frequent use of academic characters. Notable works include WHAT IS A NOVEL? (1969), THE HISTORY MAN (1975), RATES OF EXCHANGE (1983), DOCTOR CRIMINALE (1982), TO THE HERMITAGE (2000).

Bradley, A.C. (1851–1935): critic and renowned Shakespearian scholar. Much of his opinions have been superseded by later scholarship; but his criticism is very readable, and still influential is his SHAKESPEARIAN TRAGEDY (1904), a collection of lectures in which he advances his theory of the *tragic flaw* in each of the *protagonist*s in *Shakespeare*'s major tragedies: in Hamlet it is indecision; King Lear, vanity; Macbeth, ambition; Othello, jealousy.

Bradstreet, Anne (?1612–72): American poet. After emigrating from England at the age of 16, her first work, THE TENTH MUSE LATELY SPRUNG UP IN AMERICA (1650), was published without her knowledge, then republished in 1678 with her corrections under the title SEVERAL POEMS COMPILED WITH A GREAT VARIETY OF WIT. Influenced by Elizabethans such as *Spenser* and *Sidney*, her earlier *poem*s tend to be longer historical works, the later progressing towards a more individual *style* and *form* exploring personal, domestic subjects, such as her family.

Bragg, Melvyn (b.1939): novelist, journalist and playwright. Much of his work is set in his native Cumbria, and he often uses a sense of place as a key to an exploration of social issues. Notable works include FOR WANT OF A NAIL (1965), THE MAID OF BUTTERMERE (1987), CRYSTAL ROOMS (1992), THE SOLDIER'S RETURN (2000).

Braine, John (1922–1986): novelist. He was born out of a working-class background and established himself as one of the *Angry Young Men* of the 1950s. At this time his extreme left-wing views, from which his later writing veers away, criticises capitalist opportunism. Notable works include ROOM AT THE TOP (1957), LIFE AT THE TOP (1962), THE CRYING GAME (1964), THE JEALOUS GOD (1964), THE TWO OF US (1984).

Brand, Dionne (b.1953): Trinidadian poet and *short-story* writer. Having spent much of her life in Canada, she has produced writing based on personal experiences of immigration expressed through imagery of the past and present. Notable works include FORE DAY MORNING (1978), SANS SOUCI AND OTHER TALES (1988), NO BURDEN TO CARRY (1992).

Brathwaite, Edward Kaman (b.1930): Caribbean poet, historian and literary critic who draws upon African roots in order to develop the Caribbean culture. Notable works include RIGHTS OF PASSAGE (1967), MASKS (1968), ISLANDS (1969), WINGS OF A DOVE (1973).

Brecht, Bertolt (1898–1956): German dramatist and poet. Influenced by *expressionism*, he in turn had a major influence upon theatre, breaking free from dramatic *convention*s with his desire to strip the stage of theatrical illusions, aiming to leave the audience feeling as if they had learnt something. Notable works include MAN IS MAN (1927), THE THREEPENNY OPERA (1928), THE LIFE OF GALILEO (1937–9), MOTHER COURAGE (1941), THE CAUCASIAN CHALK CIRCLE (1948). See *alienation effect, brechtian, epic theatre.*

brechtian is a term used to describe plays written or presented according to the theories of *Brecht*. See *alienation effect, epic theatre.*

Brenton, Howard (b.1942): playwright. His very left-wing political drama, heavily influenced by Brecht, explores class and culture. Notable works include CHRISTIE IN LOVE (1969), REVENGE (1969), MAGNIFICENCE (1973), THE CHURCHILL PLAY (1974), THE ROMANS IN BRITAIN (1980).

Brink, André (b.1935): South African novelist, Afrikaans writer and translator. Heavily against the apartheid, he explores the culture and morals of the Afrikaans world, which led to the banning of LOOKING ON DARKNESS (1974) by the South African Government. Other notable works include A DRY WHITE SEASON (1979), A CHAIN OF VOICES (1982), STATES OF EMERGENCY (1988).

Brittain, Vera (1893–1970): novelist, poet and autobiographer, she is a highly acclaimed feminist and pacifist author, and is closely associated with *Holtby*. Notable works include TESTAMENT OF YOUTH (1933), a poignant *elegy* for her generation lost in the First World War, and for her own lost youth.

Brodber, Erna (b.1940): Jamaican novelist. Her early writing is sociological, after which she began to write *novel*s exploring cultural heritage against a modern world, incorporating *stream of consciousness* techniques and drawing on an oral *tradition*.

Notable works include ABANDONMENT OF CHILDREN IN JAMAICA (1974), A STUDY OF YARDS IN THE CITY OF KINGSTON (1975), JANE AND LOUISA WILL COME HOME SOON (1980), MYAL (1988), LOUISIANA (1994).

broken rhyme occurs when a word is split in order to create a rhyme. Rare except in comic *verse*, but sometimes *Hopkins* uses it, e.g.

> I caught this morning morning's minion, king-
> dom of daylight's dauphin, dappled-dawn-drawn Falcon, in his riding
>
> (the opening of 'The Windhover', 1877)

Brontë family: included three female novelists and poets who lived with their father and unstable brother Branwell in the parsonage at Haworth, a remote weaving village on the Yorkshire moors. All read widely, and were particularly influenced by *Byron* and *Walter Scott:*

- Charlotte Brontë (1816–55), whose writing has been remarked upon for its emotional *realism*. Notable works include JANE EYRE (1847), which was immediately acclaimed upon publication, VILLETTE (1853)
- Emily Brontë (1818–48), notable works including WUTHERING HEIGHTS (1847), the *tone* of which Charlotte noted as a 'horror of great darkness' – a blend of realism, *romance* and the *gothic* which did not find favour with the public until after her death. Her *poetry* has achieved increasing critical approval
- Anne Brontë (1820–49), some of whose poetry, influenced by *Cowper*, explores religious doubt. Notable works include THE TENANT OF WILDFELL HALL (1848), which has attracted the attention of *feminist criticism.*

Brooke, Rupert (1887–1915): poet. Sometimes classed as a *Georgian poet*, for some years he was a leading light on the Cambridge literary scene and his travels in Germany, the Americas and the Pacific influenced his *poetry*. His high reputation has now faded, but he is still valued for his lighter *verse*, sometimes written in an accessible, colloquial language and often nostalgic. Notable works include POEMS (1911), 'The Old Vicarage, Granchester' (1912), 'The Dead' (1914), LITHUANIA (1915), NEW NUMBERS (1915, which includes 'The Soldier'), 1914 AND OTHER POEMS (1915).

Browning, Elizabeth Barrett (1806–61): poet. Regarded as the foremost woman poet of her time with liberal social ideas, she was passionately interested in and venturesome with *verse* construction, e.g. MOTHER AND POET (1861). An invalid for much of her life, she secretly married her fellow poet *Robert Browning*. Other notable works include POEMS (1844), SONNETS FROM THE PORTUGUESE (1850), AURORA LEIGH (1856).

Browning, Robert (1812–89): poet, influenced particularly by *Keats, Shelley* and *Byron*. Amongst his prolific output he excelled in *dramatic monologue*, e.g. 'My Last Duchess' (1842), 'Andrea Del Sarto, Fra Lippo Lippi', the latter two included along with *poem*s such as 'Childe Roland to the Dark Tower Came' (1855) in MEN AND WOMEN (1855). Although not as popular in his lifetime as his contemporary *Tennyson*, by the time of his death he had achieved a high critical status which has endured.

Brutus, Dennis (b.1924): South African poet. He draws on his experiences of imprisonment and exile following his resistance to apartheid. Notable works include LETTERS TO MARTHA AND OTHER POEMS FROM A SOUTH AFRICAN PRISON (1968).

Bunyan, John (1628–88): English writer and preacher. Imprisoned for many years in Bedford gaol for preaching without a licence, he began to write. Nearly all of his output has a moral or religious basis, and much is presented in a clear and accessible *style*. Notable works include his famous *allegory* PILGRIM'S PROGRESS (1678), THE LIFE AND DEATH OF MR BADMAN (1680), THE HOLY WAR (1682).

Burgess, Anthony (1917–94): novelist, scriptwriter, biographer, critic and composer. His novels display sharply observed social comment and verbal inventiveness. Notable works include A CLOCKWORK ORANGE (1962), a prophetic vision of the future made into a controversial film in 1971.

burlesque is a term applied to writing which sets out to satirise a subject, work or literary style by making a deliberate mismatch between the *manner* and the matter, usually for satirical purposes. *Lampoon, mock-heroic, mock-epic, parody* are all types of *burlesque*.

Burns, Robert (1759–96): Scottish poet. Even after he became famous he retained a sense of his humble rural background, and this is reflected in his work. Very personal *poem*s sometimes speak of his passionate relationships and financial problems. He is able to write in the *formal* English of the day and the vernacular Scots, sometimes combining the two. He was also an avid collector, writer and re-writer of traditional Scottish songs, most famously 'Auld Lang Syne' and 'Red, Red Rose'. He achieved a cult status during his lifetime and this has endured, making him widely regarded as the Scottish national poet. Notable works include POEMS CHIEFLY IN SCOTTISH DIALECT (1786, including 'The Cotter's Saturday Night' and 'Halloween'), 'Holy Willie's Prayer' (1789), 'Tam O'shanter' (1790).

Burroughs, John (1837–1921): journalist, essayist, literary critic, biographer, philosopher and poet. He also writes much about nature. Notable works include NOTES ON WALT WHITMAN AS POET AND PERSON (1867), WAKE-ROBIN (1871).

Burroughs, William (1914–97): American novelist. One of the *Beat Movement* and friends with *Ginsberg* and *Kerouac*, he writes of his experiences and the culture surrounding his addiction to heroin. Notable works include JUNKIE (1953), NAKED LUNCH (1959), THE SOFT MACHINE (1961), BLADE RUNNER: A MOVIE (1979), QUEER (1984).

Butler, Samuel (1612–80): poet and *prose* writer best known for his satirical *burlesque* poem HUDIBRAS (1663–78).

Butler, Samuel (1835–1902): novelist, poet, satirist, philosopher, composer and art critic. His output is unfocused, a wide variety of subjects being the targets of his *irony* and *satire*. He is best remembered for his semi-autobiographical *novel* THE WAY OF ALL FLESH (1903) which reveals an unhappy childhood. Other notable works include EREWHON (1872).

Byatt, A.S. (b.1936): novelist, *short-story* writer and critic. Her writing is characterised by historical, artistic and literary perspectives, perceptions, and *allusions*. Notable works include THE VIRGIN IN THE GARDEN (1978), STILL-LIFE (1985), SUGAR AND OTHER STORIES (1987), POSSESSION (1990).

Byron, George Gordon, Lord (1788–1824): *Romantic* poet and playwright. Among other qualities his *poetry* expresses by turns lyrical beauty and biting *satire*, and its intense popularity, especially amongst a female readership, became known as

'Byronmania'. Celebrated for his lifestyle as much as his writing, he doubtless played up to Lady Caroline Lamb's image of him as 'Mad, bad, and dangerous to know', and his creation of the *byronic hero* probably had much to do with his perception of himself. A friend of *Shelley* and possessing the same Romantic ideals of freedom and liberty, he embraced the cause of independence for Greece and died there. Notable works include CHILDE HAROLD'S PILGRIMAGE (1812–18), THE PRISONER OF CHILLON (1816), DON JUAN (1819).

byronic hero is a term given to a *hero* figure who displays the characteristics of Childe Harold, Don Juan or other heroes of Byron's *narrative* poems; typically he is a brooding, passionate, outcast, solitary wanderer in wild, remote lands, rebellious and fascinatingly attractive – in other words a typical *Romantic* figure, alone in the world and finding new pathways which owe nothing to social convention. See *Byron*.

byronic stanza: see *ottava rima*.

C

cacophony is the same as *dissonance.*

cadence refers to the musical *rhythm* of language in *prose* or *verse*:
- in a general sense
- in particular towards the end of a sentence, line or short passage, e.g. whether it rises or falls, is questioning or commanding, and so forth. It is a part of a writer's *style*; for instance, the cadences of *Beckett, Dickens* and *Tennyson* are distinctive.

caesura: a natural pause in a line of *verse*, sometimes roughly midway and usually indicated by punctuation. Frequently used in combination with enjambement to give variety in the pacing of verse and to avoid monotonous regularity. For an example see *enjambement.*

Cambridge School of Critics: an umbrella term given to an opinion-forming group of English academics at Cambridge University between the 1920s and 1950s. See *leavisite, Empson, Richards.*

Campbell, Roy (1901–57): South African poet, translator and autobiographer. His reputation was established by THE FLAMING TERRAPIN (1924), a long allegorical *poem.* Sometimes accused of self-congratulatory writing, he took a satirical view of South African intellectuals, attacked the *Bloomsbury Group,* and was influenced by his experiences as a fascist sympathiser fighting for Franco in the Spanish Civil War. Later writing tends to be more calmly contemplative. Other notable works include ADAMASTOR (1930), THE GEORGIAD (1931), THE FLOWERING REEDS (1933), MITHRAIC EMBLEMS (1936), FLOWERING RIFLE (1939), SONS OF THE MISTRAL (1941), LIGHT ON A DARK HORSE (1951), COLLECTED POEMS (1960).

campus novel: a *novel,* often humorous, exploring university life, e.g. *Kingsley Amis'* Lucky JIM, *Bradbury's* THE HISTORY MAN, *Lodge's* CHANGING PLACES.

canon: the notion that there is an accepted list of great literature which constitutes the essential tradition of English (or any other) culture. See *leavisite.*

caricature: a *style* of writing (or drawing) which deliberately exaggerates particular features of its subject, usually for comic and/or satirical effect, e.g. Sir Andrew Aguecheek in *Shakespeare's* TWELFTH NIGHT. The *novels* of writers such as *Fielding, Smollett, Dickens* and *Thackeray* are rich in caricatures.

Caroline Age generally refers to literature written in England during the reign of Charles I (1625–49).

Caroline drama covers plays written during the reign of Charles II (1625–49); however:
- no plays were performed after the closing of the theatres by the Puritans in 1642
- the period 1603–42 is sometimes covered by the term *Jacobean drama*
- the period 1558–1642 is sometimes covered by the overall term *Elizabethan drama.*

carpe diem, meaning 'seize the day', is a phrase coined by the Latin poet Horace suggesting that because life is short one must grasp present pleasures. This *motif* is commonplace in literature, and was especially popular with the Elizabethan lyric poets, e.g. *Herrick*'s 'Gather ye Rosebuds, While ye May', and Feste's song 'O Mistress Mine' in *Shakespeare*'s TWELFTH NIGHT. Other notable examples include *Marvell*'s 'To His Coy Mistress'.

Carter, Angela (1940–92): novelist, *short-story* writer and essayist. Some of her early works are examples of *magic realism*. Her writing is often humorous, feminist and challenges ideas of reality, later work mixing *fantasy* with reality in an accessible *style*. Notable works include THE MAGIC TOYSHOP (1967), HEROES AND VILLAINS (1969), THE BLOODY CHAMBER (1979), THE SADEIAN WOMEN (1979), NIGHTS AT THE CIRCUS (1984), WISE CHILDREN (1991), BURNING YOUR BOATS: COLLECTED SHORT STORIES (1995).

Carter, Martin (b.1927): Guyanese poet. His *poems* are noted for their *rhetoric*, compassion and startling *imagery*; they are sometimes influenced by his political activity, but also show personal concerns. Notable works include HILLS OF FIRE GLOW RED (1951), THE KIND EAGLE (1952), RETURNING (1953), POEMS OF RESISTANCE (1954), POEMS OF SUCCESSION (1977).

Carver, Raymond (1938–88): American *short-story* writer and poet. His reputation rests on the former which are often very short, *minimalist*, tightly written pieces about ordinary people, simple on the surface but containing a concentrated and dark view of lack of communication in the 20th century world. Notable works include WILL YOU PLEASE BE QUIET, PLEASE? (1976), CATHEDRAL (1983), FIRES (1983).

Cary, Joyce (1888–1957): novelist. He uses his experience in Nigeria to write his early *novel*s looking at the ways in which Africans and their British administrators related to each other. He also explores politics, childhood experiences and the British Empire, but most important to him was the world of art. Notable works include AISSA SAVED (1932), AN AMERICAN VISITOR (1933), MISTER JOHNSON (1939), POWER IN MEN (1939), CHARLEY IS MY DARLING (1940), HERSELF SURPRISED (1941), THE HORSE'S MOUTH (1944), NOT HONOUR MORE (1955).

catalexis: catalectic *verse* is where a syllable is omitted from the final *foot* of a line, e.g. as happens quite frequently in *trochaic* verse:

> Through the / forest / I have / gone
>> (Puck in *Shakespeare*'s A MIDSUMMER NIGHT'S DREAM)

> Tiger / Tiger / burning / bright   (from *Blake*'s TIGER)

In these examples the lost syllable creates a *masculine ending*.

catastrophe: the final *climax* of a play or *story* after which the *plot* is resolved. See also *act, dénouement, resolution*.

catharsis: an emotional release experienced by an audience as they witness the fate of a tragic hero. See *Aristotle*.

Cather, Willa (1873–1947): American novelist, poet and *short-story* writer. There are many aspects of the pioneer in her wide-ranging and complex work as a woman writer dealing with issues such as contrary impulses towards life (e.g. adventure/safety) and the American frontier. Notable works include O PIONEERS! (1913), MY ÁNTONIA (1918), DEATH COMES FOR THE ARCHBISHOP (1927), ONE OF OURS (1922).

Causley, Charles (b.1917): poet and children's story writer. Influenced by *Clare*, innocence is a frequent *theme* in his *poetry*. His *diction* is direct, and he often uses the straightforward *rhythm* of *ballad* and popular song. Notable works include COLLECTED POEMS 1951–75 (1975), THE ANIMALS' CAROL (1978), EARLY IN THE MORNING (1986), JACK THE TREACLE EATER (1987), THE GIFT OF A LAMB (1978).

Cavalier is a label given to certain *lyric* poets active during the reign of King Charles I, e.g. Thomas Carew (?1594–1640), *Herrick, Lovelace*, John Suckling (1609–42). Their *verse* is characteristically elegant and *witty love poetry* . The term is also sometimes used of certain court *dramas* of the period.

Caxton, William (?1420–?92): set up the first printing press in England close to Westminster Abbey in ?1471, for the first time making available in print many works including those of the major early English poets such as *Gower, Lydgate* and *Chaucer*.

Celtic Renaissance/Revival/Twilight: all terms associated with the resurgence of Irish literature at the end of the 19th century of which *Yeats* was the leading light.

Chang, Jung (b.1952): Chinese writer best known for WILD SWANS (1992), which might be described as a non-fiction *saga novel*, part *autobiography*, telling of her family's experiences in 20th century China.

Chapman, George (?1559–1634): playwright, poet, translator and collaborator. Friendly with and influenced by *Jonson*, he was highly praised during his lifetime as a writer of comedies, tragedies and masques for the stage, but subsequently did not maintain the status of some of his peers. Perhaps now best remembered for his translation of Homer which was praised by *Keats* in his *sonnet* 'On First Looking into Chapman's Homer' (1816). Other notable works include THE SHADOW OF NIGHT (1594), OVID'S BANQUET OF SENSE (1595), ALL FOOLS (?1599), BUSSY D'AMBOIS (?1604), EASTWARD HO (1605, with *Jonson* and *Marston*), THE REVENGE OF BUSSY D'AMBOIS (?1610).

character: a created person in a play or a story whose particular qualities are revealed by the *action, description* and conversation. Not to be confused with the 'actor' in a play, who represents the character.

characterisation is the method by which *character*s are established in a *narrative* or *drama*. See *flat characters, round characters, showing and telling*.

Chatterton, Thomas (1752–70): poet. The 'marvellous boy', as *Wordsworth* called him, has become an image of lost talent, his youthful suicide being part of his attraction for the Romantics, *Keats* dedicating ENDYMION to him. His *poetry*, written in *Spenserian style* using *archaicisms*, shows a budding talent. Notable works include 'Ethelgar, A Saxon Poem' (1769), ROWLEY POEMS (1777).

Chatwin, Bruce (1940–89): travel writer and novelist. A versatile and sensitive writer, notable works include IN PATAGONIA (1977), ON THE BLACK HILL (1982), THE SONGLINES (1987), UTZ (1989).

Chaucer, Geoffrey (?1340–1400): poet and translator. A superb story-teller, he is generally acknowledged as the greatest English writer of the Middle Ages. He spent much of his life in royal service and this enabled him to travel, his time in Italy bringing him into contact with *Boccaccio* and *Petrarch* by whom his work is much influenced. His decision to write in English rather than Anglo-Norman or Latin did much to establish the former as a literary language. His range moves between the courtly and the earthy, combining philosophy and *realism*, and he is credited with shrewd insights into the enduring traits of human nature. His best-known work is THE CANTERBURY TALES (?1387–1400), a collection of stories in the *manner* of *Boccaccio*, in which pilgrims en route from London to the tomb of Thomas à Becket at Canterbury tell stories ranging from *fabliau* to those of *courtly love* in order to pass the time. Notable works include THE BOOK OF THE DUCHESS (?1370), THE HOUSE OF FAME (?1376), THE PARLEMENT OF FOULES (?1382), THE LEGEND OF GOOD WOMEN (?1384), TROILUS AND CRISEYDE (?1385). See also *courtly love, decasyllabic line, dream visions, exemplum, fabliau, fable, rhyme royal.*

Chaucerian stanza: see *rhyme royal.*

Chaudhuri, N.C. (1897–1999): Indian historian, biographer and autobiographer. Much of his work explores Anglo-Indian relationships. Notable works include THE AUTOBIOGRAPHY OF AN UNKNOWN INDIAN (1951), THY HAND, GREAT ANARCH! (1987).

Chesterton, G.K. (1874–1936): poet, novelist, *short-story* writer, critic, journalist, essayist and autobiographer. His prolific output was invariably coloured by his strong moral and politically left-wing views. He made a marked contribution to *detective fiction* with his Father Brown stories. Notable works include CHARLES DICKENS (1906), THE VICTORIAN AGE IN LITERATURE (1913), THE INNOCENCE OF FATHER BROWN (1911), THE FLYING INN (1914), COLLECTED POEMS (1927), CHAUCER (1932), AUTOBIOGRAPHY (1936).

chiasmus: figure of speech in which the word order of similar phrases is turned round, e.g. adverb-verb-subject is followed by subject-adverb-verb. Used frequently in 18th century *verse*, it is a *form* of *antithesis*. A famous non-literary example is President Kennedy's 'Ask not what your country can do for you, but what you can do for your country'.

Chopin, Kate (1850–1904): American novelist, poet, *short-story* writer and essayist who was influenced by the French writer Guy de Maupassant (1850–93). Notable works include THE AWAKENING (1899) which, like the Norwegian playwright Henrik Ibsen's (1828–1906) THE DOLL'S HOUSE (1879), was regarded as scandalous in its sympathetic depiction of a woman who breaks the traditional constraints of marriage.

choric figures are *characters* within a play or *novel* who comment upon the *action* while being a part of it, e.g. in *Shakespeare*, the Fool in KING LEAR, Enobarbus in ANTONY AND CLEOPATRA, Thersites in TROILUS AND CRESSIDA (1602), Tom in *Tennessee Williams'* THE GLASS MENAGERIE, Alfieri in *Miller's* A VIEW FROM THE BRIDGE. Examples of choric figures in *novels* are the rustics in *George Eliot's* SILAS MARNER or various of *Hardy's* novels, and the use of aged black women and other figures in some of *Faulkner's* works.

chorus: a person or group of people which stand outside the *action* of a *drama* and comment upon it. Most tragedies in ancient Greece had a chorus of citizens or elders who, as virtual representatives of the audience, react to the events of the action but are powerless to affect the course of events. *Shakespeare* occasionally uses choruses of various kinds, as in ROMEO AND JULIET and HENRY V, and among other notable usages are in *Milton's* SAMSON AGONISTES, *T.S. Eliot's* MURDER IN THE CATHEDRAL and *Wilder's* OUR TOWN; but there has not been great use of a chorus in English theatre. See *choric figures.*

chronicle: any kind of sequential historical account such as the Anglo-Saxon chronicle, written in Old English. Edward Hall's THE UNION OF THE NOBLE AND ILLUSTRE FAMILIES OF LANCASTER AND YORK and Raphael Holinshed's CHRONICLES OF ENGLAND,

Scotland and Ireland (1577–87) were important sources for the *chronicle plays* of *Shakespeare* and his contemporary playwrights.

chronicle play: a type of history play which deals with highlighted events from the reign of an English king. Such plays were popular during the closing years of the 16th century, fuelled by patriotic enthusiasm after the defeat of the Spanish Armada in 1588, e.g. *Marlowe*'s Edward II and *Shakespeare*'s two cycles of eight plays covering seven kings in English history from the 1370s to 1485.

Churchill, Caryl (b.1938): playwright. Her work is characteristically left-wing and feminist, but not narrowly so: she ranges with humour and intelligence over a wide range of social, moral, political and other subjects. She has worked closely with small theatre companies such as Monstrous Regiment and Joint Stock Theatre. Notable works include Vinegar Tom (1976), Cloud Nine (1979), Top Girls (1982), Fen (1982), Serious Money (1987).

Cibber, Colley (1671–1757): actor, playwright, adapter and poet. His Love's Last Shift (1696, satirised by *Vanbrugh* in The Relapse – in which, ironically, Cibber played Lord Foppington) began the vogue for *sentimental comedy* which lasted through most of the 18th century, and which encouraged Cibber to adapt several of *Shakespeare*'s plays to suit the taste of the time. His literary merit (much mocked by his contemporaries) is considered doubtful, but his contribution to the theatre is underrated. In his autobiography An Apology for the Life of Mr Colley Cibber, Comedian (1740), he paints a colourful picture of theatre life in his day. He was *poet laureate* from 1730–57. Other notable works include The Careless Husband (1704).

ciceronian style is an elaborate and florid, yet clear and well-ordered, prose *style* (from the Roman writer, politician and orator Cicero (106–43BC). It may be regarded as the opposite of the *senecan style*.

Cisneros, Sandra (b.1945): American poet and novelist. Her work explores poverty, and racial and sexual oppression, drawing on childhood reminiscences and her Mexican/American parentage. Notable works include The House on Mango Street (1983) and My Wicked Wicked Ways (1987).

citizen comedy was popular in the early 17th century, and usually dealt with lower- and middle-class London life. Good examples are *Dekker*'s The Shoemaker's Holiday, *Jonson*'s Bartholomew Fair, *Middleton*'s A Chaste Maid in Cheapside (?1613). *Shakespeare*'s only citizen comedy is The Merry Wives of Windsor (?1598).

Clare, John (1793-1864): poet. Usually categorised as a rural poet, he was much attached to his native village of Helpston where he was an agricultural labourer. He wrote with clarity and truth about the coutryside of his corner of Northamptonshire. His *poetry* was at first fashionable, but a decline in the popularity of 'ploughman poets' contributed to growing insanity, and he spent the last years of his life in Northampton General Asylum. Thanks to the attention of *Blunden*, *Day-Lewis* and others his poetry has once more become known and admired. Notable works include The Village Minstrel (1821), The Shepherd's Calendar (1827), Poems (1935), Prose (1951), Letters (1951).

Clark, Bekederemo J.P. (b.1935): Nigerian poet, playwright and literary critic. His work is rooted in Ijaw culture. Notable works include Song of a Goat (1961),

AMERICA THEIR AMERICA (1964), THE EXAMPLE OF SHAKESPEARE (1970), A DECADE OF TONGUES (1981).

Clarke, Gillian (b.1937): Welsh poet. She can focus upon particular moments, artefacts or incidents, often inspired by her native Wales, handling them and their significance with lyricism and within a controlled *structure*. Notable works include LETTER FROM A FAR COUNTRY (1982), SELECTED POEMS (1985), LETTING IN THE RUMOUR (1989), THE KING OF BRITAIN'S DAUGHTER (1993).

classic as a term has developed three broad meanings when applied to literature:

- works from ancient Greece or Rome (from 'classical' times), whether of high merit or not
- outstanding works from any age
- typical, e.g. *Shakespeare*'s HAMLET might be described as a classic *revenge tragedy*, or *Mary Shelley*'s FRANKENSTEIN as a classic *gothic* novel.

clerihew: a four-line *verse* of two couplets, often comic and sometimes epigrammatic, named after its inventor E. Clerihew Bentley (1875–1956), e.g.

> George the Third
> Ought never to have occurred.
> One can only wonder
> At so grotesque a blunder.

cliché: a word or phrase which when first used has some freshness and originality but which has become worn out through overuse, e.g. 'to turn over a new leaf', 'interface', 'a whole new ballgame', 'over the moon'. *Pope* famously satirised the clichés of *poetasters* in his ESSAY ON CRITICISM:

> Where'er you find "the cooling western breeze",
> In the next line, it "whispers through the trees";
> If crystal streams "with pleasing murmurs creep",
> The reader's threatened (not in vain) with "sleep".

climax is a term sometimes used interchangeably with *crisis* and *turning point* generally to indicate the arrival of any time of crucial intensity in a play or story; but the term is more precisely used to indicate that particular moment when the *rising action* leads to a high point in the fortunes of the *hero* or *heroine*. See *act, anabasis, plot*.

close reading: the focusing upon ways that writers' choices of *form, structure* and language shape meanings. This approach was sometimes disparaged in the 1970s and 1980s, but it is essential to a precise understanding of how writers create their effects. See *explication, intrinsic attitude, leavisite*. By contrast, see *extrinsic attitude*.

closed couplet: a *couplet* of *verse*, common in the *heroic couplet*, where the sense is complete by the end of the second line, e.g.

> Say what strange motive, Goddess! could compel
> A well-bred lord to assault a gentle belle?

(from Pope's THE RAPE OF THE LOCK)

closet drama may best be described as a dramatic *poem*, as it is intended to be read rather than performed, e.g. *Milton*'s SAMSON AGONISTES, *Shelley*'s PROMETHEUS UNBOUND.

closure is a sense of conclusion at the end of:

- a *novel* or *drama* when the *resolution* is clear and there are no loose ends
- a line in *poetry* which is *end-stopped* or a *stanza* which finishes with a full stop.

Clough, Arthur Hugh (1819–1861): poet whose *lyric* ability often conveys characteristic Victorian doubts. Notable works include THE BOTHIE OF TOBER-NA-VUOLICH (1848), AMOURS DE VOYAGE (1858), POEMS (1862), DIPSYCHUS (1865).

cockney school of poetry: a contemptuous and snobbish term which first appeared in the October 1817 edition of the right-wing BLACKMORE'S magazine and used to mock a particular group of London-based poets including *Hazlitt, Keats, Lamb* and *Hunt* who were not considered to be of any social standing.

coda: similar to an *epilogue*, a concluding section which rounds off a piece of literature in some way, e.g. at the end of *Stoppard's* JUMPERS.

code is a term used in *structuralism* to denote the system of *signs* in a language which the reader must understand, or de-code, in order to interpret a *text*. See *hermeneutics, interpretation*.

Coetzee, J.M. (b.1940): South African novelist and literary critic. He is a political writer who is also concerned about the *techniques* of *fiction*. Notable works include IN THE HEART OF THE COUNTRY (1977), WAITING FOR THE BARBARIANS (1980), LIFE AND TIMES OF MICHAEL K (1982), FOE (1986), DISGRACE (1999).

Coleridge, Samuel Taylor (1772–1834): poet, critic and translator. His relationship with *Wordsworth*, especially their collaboration over the LYRICAL BALLADS, affected the direction of English *poetry* and was a keystone in English *Romanticism*. Inventive, imaginative and exciting, his small but brilliant poetic output is shot through with a sense of insecurity. He was an influential critic and thinker, and his theories on such matters as the poetic *imagination, organic form* and the Elizabethan stage contribute much to literary *criticism* in general and our understanding of Romanticism in particular. Notable works include 'Kubla Khan' (1797), 'The Rime of the Ancient Mariner' (1798, published in LYRICAL BALLADS), 'Frost at Midnight' (1798), 'Dejection: an Ode' (1802), BIOGRAPHIA LITERARIA (1817).

collection: a gathering together of all the work of a single writer, usually *poetry* and of a particular period of output, e.g. *Lochhead's* DREAMING FRANKENSTEIN, AND COLLECTED POEMS. Not to be confused with *anthology*. See also *selection*.

Collins, Billy (b.1941): American poet. His accessible *poetry* has achieved both critical and popular acclaim, and he is in demand as a performance poet. He has said that his *poetry* is about dwelling on the interesting side issues which distract us from our planned direction through the day. Notable works include QUESTIONS ABOUT ANGELS (1991), THE ART OF DROWNING (1995), PICNIC, LIGHTENING (1998).

Collins, Wilkie (1824–89): novelist and playwright. A friend of *Dickens* whose advice and *criticism* he respected, he is regarded as one of the first *thriller* writers; his complex plots of crime, mystery and suspense were popular but often criticised for sensationalism. Notable works include THE FROZEN DEEP (1857), THE WOMAN IN WHITE (1860), NO NAME (1862), ARMADALE (1866), THE MOONSTONE (1868). See *novel of sensation*.

Collins, William (1721–59): poet. He wrote much in his short life, including some fine *odes*. He was technically skilful, but perhaps never quite achieved his potential. Notable works include ODES ON SEVERAL DESCRIPTIVE AND ALLEGORICAL SUBJECTS (1746–7), 'Ode on the Popular Superstitions of the Highlands' (1788, published posthumously).

colonial criticism: see *post-colonial criticism*.

Colonial Period: often used to define the period of American literature covering 1607 (the founding of the settlement at Jamestown) until 1775 (the outbreak of the Revolutionary War).

comedy defines a work which is primarily designed to amuse and entertain, and where, despite alarms along the way, all ends well for the characters. The term is usually applied to a play (originally referring to Greek and Roman dramas), sometimes to a *novel*, and very occasionally to *narrative verse*. The *genre* is a wide category covering many different types, and does not necessarily mean that the work intends to provoke laughter.

comedy of humours is a kind of drama where the characters are constructed upon the old physiological theory of *humours*. The *genre* was particularly popular around the time when *Jonson* wrote EVERY MAN IN HIS HUMOUR (1598) and EVERY MAN OUT OF HIS HUMOUR (1599), and several of his contemporaries such as *Chapman, Fletcher, Massinger* and *Middleton* exploited the *form*.

comedy of ideas is a term sometimes applied to plays which debate ideas in a *witty* or humorous way, e.g. several of *Shaw's* such as MAN AND SUPERMAN (1905) or BACK TO METHUSELAH (1922).

comedy of manners refers to a type of drama where the social behaviour of a section of the community is humorously portrayed. *Shakespeare's* LOVE'S LABOUR'S LOST (?1595) and MUCH ADO ABOUT NOTHING may be so described, but some critics consider an essential element to be that the audience is composed of the same social class as that depicted on stage; that is, they are induced to laugh at themselves. Most *Restoration comedy* fulfils this requirement, where upper and upper-middle class behaviour is portrayed. Later examples include the plays of *Sheridan, Wilde* and *Coward*. A good example of a modern writer in the *genre* is *Ayckbourn*, whose comedies depict middle-class behaviour for a middle-class audience.

comedy of menace is a term originating in the 1950s to denote a type of play in which the characters feel, or indeed are, threatened, e.g. *Pinter's* THE BIRTHDAY PARTY.

comic relief is a term given to an episode in an otherwise serious play, even a *tragedy*, in order to provide one or more of the following:

- relief from the intensity of the drama, e.g. the Porter scene in Act II, Scene 3 of *Shakespeare's* MACBETH
- a contrast to the *tone* of the surrounding drama, e.g. the Gravediggers' scene in Act V, Scene 1 of Shakespeare's HAMLET
- a pause before the final *climax* of the drama, e.g. the appearance of the CLOWN in Act V, Scene 2 of Shakespeare's ANTONY AND CLEOPATRA.

Only the MACBETH instance above is not an example of all three cases. Comic relief fails if it is merely that and is not integrated into the scheme of the drama as a whole.

commedia dell'arte: a *form* of comic *drama* developed in Italy during the 16th century and involving stock characters such as a young daughter, a lover, an old father

(Pantaloon), a cunning servant (Harlequin), a hunchback clown (Punch), the *action* being improvised around a standard *plot*. The *genre* influenced Elizabethan writing, e.g. *Shakespeare*'s THE TAMING OF THE SHREW (?1592), and also French playwrights such as Molière (1622–73), and *opera*.

Commonwealth literature is *post-colonial literature* from member countries of the British Commonwealth of Nations.

Commonwealth Period: generally refers to literature written in England between 1649 and 1660 (the Puritan Interregnum).

comparative literature: a study of similarities and parallels in the literature of different cultures and countries.

complaint: a melancholy sub-*genre* of *lyric* poem, typically mourning the loss of a lover or the sad state of the world, e.g. *Chaucer*'s 'A Complaint unto Pity' (14th century), *Wyatt*'s 'They Flee From Me', *Surrey*'s 'Complaint by Night of the Lover not Beloved', Abraham Cowley's (1618–87) *ode* 'The Complaint' (1656). See *dirge, elegy, lament*.

conceit: a clever or *witty* thought, often conveyed by a surprising image. In Elizabethan *poetry* 'conceit' simply referred to a *simile, metaphor* or any extended figure of speech; in later *metaphysical* poetry it increasingly indicated ingenious, striking use of *figurative language*.

concrete language is that which refers to things rather than ideas (which are *abstract*), e.g. 'There is a willow grows aslant a brook' (*Shakespeare*, HAMLET).

concrete poetry is a *form* of *poetry* where the typography and/or the shape of the *poem* on the page creates a pattern or picture which has immediate impact and which is very much a part of the *meaning*. The fashion for such poetry grew in the 20th century, but poets such as *Herbert*, with his pattern poetry, and *Hopkins* had experimented with it in earlier centuries. Good modern examples include John Hollander's 'Swan and Shadow' (1969 – words in the shape of a swan and its reflection in the water) and *McGough*'s '40-Love' (1971). (See page 32.)

confessional literature is a term covering self-revelatory *prose* such as *de Quincy*'s CONFESSIONS OF AN ENGLISH OPIUM EATER and THE PRIVATE MEMOIRS AND CONFESSIONS OF A JUSTIFIED SINNER (1824) by James Hogg (1770–1835). See *confessional poetry*.

confessional poetry is a term used to describe *poetry* which reveals, sometimes in explicit detail, the personal life of the poet. Although *Coleridge, Wordsworth* (THE PRELUDE) and others had written of their personal responses to life, this term is usually applied to the very candid American *narrative* and *lyric* verse which emerged with *Lowell*'s LIFE STUDIES in the late 1950s, partly in reaction against the idea of *T.S. Eliot* and the *New Critics* that poetry should be impersonal. Those who have been classified as confessional poets include *Lowell*, the *Beat Movement* poets, *Plath, Berryman, Rich,* Anne Sexton (1928–74). See *confessional literature*.

Congreve, William (1670–1728): playwright. Considered one of the best writers of *Restoration comedy*, his *comedy of manners* dealing subtlely and humorously with the social tensions of romance and marriage in the upper-class society of his day. Notable works include LOVE FOR LOVE (1695), THE WAY OF THE WORLD (1700).

connotation: an implication, suggestion or *association* which a word or string of words conveys to an individual, or to people in general, beyond the literal, surface *meaning* (or *denotation*) of the word(s). Connotations make metaphors possible. See also *referential language*.

                    Dusk
                Above the
            water hang the
                    loud
                    flies
                    Here
                  O so
                   gray
                   then
            What   A pale signal will appear
            When   Soon before its shadow fades
            Where   Here in this pool of opened eye
         In us   No Upon us As at the very edges
            of where we take shape in the dark air
             this object bares its image awakening
               ripples of recognition that will
                  brush darkness up into light
even after this bird this hour both drift by atop the perfect sad instant now
               already passing out of sight
            toward yet-untroubled reflection
          this image bears its object darkening
            into memorial shades Scattered bits of
         light   No of water Or something across
         water   Breaking up No Being regathered
          soon   Yet by then a swan will have
           gone   Yes out of mind into what
                 vast
                 pale
                 hush
                 of a
                 place
                 past
          sudden dark as
             if a swan
                 sang

Concrete poetry (see page 31)

Conrad, Joseph (1857–1924): novelist considered to be a leading *modernist*. His experience as a sailor inspired his writing. A Pole who loved the English language, the stylistic beauty of his own writing may be a result of his not being a native speaker. *Leavis* considered him one of the greatest novelists in the English language (see *leavisite*). He often explores the psychological and the mythic, although some recent readings of his work tend to focus on *post-colonial* and gender aspects. He constantly criticises colonial powers for their treatment of the Third World; yet HEART OF DARKNESS (1902) has recently been criticised as racist (although it could be read as a trenchant *criticism* of racism). Other notable works include LORD JIM (1900), NOSTROMO (1904), THE SECRET AGENT (1907), UNDER WESTERN EYES (1911).

consonance: repetition of the same consonant sounds before and after a different vowel, e.g. clip-clop, crust crest, stop step, leader loader louder. In *poetry* it is a variety of *half-rhyme*. See also *alliteration, assonance*.

Contemporary Period: sometimes used to cover American literature written from 1939 and the present.

content, in a literary sense, is any theme, idea, argument, action, story or moral message which is contained within a literary *form*.

context: this term has traditionally been used to indicate the placing of a given passage or section of a literary work in relation to the parts which immediately precede and follow it. However, for the wider sense in which the term is currently applied, see *contextuality*.

contextuality: the idea that both writers, readers and *text*s function within personal, biographical, political, social, literary, cultural and/or historical *context*s, and are influenced by the beliefs and assumptions of the times in which they are written and read.

convention: the term is used in two main senses:

- an agreed method of conveying an idea between the writer and reader (or audience). The term is often used when the *manner* of presentation is not realistic. For instance, when watching a play an audience *suspends disbelief*, knowing that what they are watching is only a representation of a certain scene; or accepts the *convention* that in *soliloquy* a character is speaking thoughts aloud (see *suspension of disbelief*)
- any accepted recurrent feature in writing, such as the use of *metre* in *verse*, the *convention* that a *sonnet* has 14 lines, the appearance of certain minor *stock characters* in *fiction* in order to move the *plot* along.

Structuralist critics frequently point out that all literature is written in conventions or *codes* which are not realistic.

conversation piece/poem: writing, usually *blank verse poetry*, which in an informal *style* and *tone* conveys a mood often by association. *Coleridge* and *Wordsworth* wrote many such *poem*s, e.g. respectively 'This Limetree Bower my Prison' and 'Tintern Abbey', and among others who wrote in this *genre* were *Robert Browning, Frost, Auden*.

Cooper, James Fenimore (1789–1851): American novelist best known for his portrayal of American Indian and pioneer life, and for his development of the Leather-Stocking character. Notable works include THE PIONEERS (1826), THE LAST OF THE MOHICANS (1826).

Cope, Wendy (b. 1945): poet. She writes reflective *poetry* on a wide range of topics, and is particularly skilled at *witty*, sensitive and technically clever parodies of other modern poets. Notable works include MAKING COCOA FOR KINGSLEY AMIS (1986), IF I DON'T KNOW (2001).

Copernican revolution: a theory explained by Nicolas Copernicus (1473–1543) in which the earth and other planets revolve round the sun. This superseded the

Ptolemaic idea of astronomy in which the earth was the centre of the universe, making way for modern ideas of cosmology. In THE FIRST ANNIVERSARY (1611) *Donne* wrote that the 'new Philosophy calls all in doubt', and indeed it had a profound effect on *Renaissance* literature. For decades after the *Ptolemaic system* was scientifically accepted as dead, writers often used imaginatively the old cosmology, e.g. *Milton* in PARADISE LOST. Donne blends attachment to the old system with grasp of the new when he begins 'Holy Sonnet 7' (1635) 'At the round earth's imagined corners…'.

correctness is conforming to rules and *conventions*. Seventeenth and eighteenth century writers tended to think that this was a good idea; but in general the English, unlike the French and mindful of *Shakespeare*'s lack of concern with rules such as the *dramatic unities*, have valued appropriateness as more important.

Corso, Gregory (1930–2001): poet, novelist and playwright. He is the best known and most read of the *Beat Movement* poets, and in his prodigious output he aimed at the *rhythm*s of speech. Anarchic in *style* and often politically motivated, his *poem*s are generally more humorous, lighter of touch and sometimes more exuberant than others in the group. Notable works include 'Gasoline' (1958), 'Bomb' (1958, an example of *concrete poetry*), THE HAPPY BIRTHDAY OF DEATH (1960), MINDFIELD: NEW AND SELECTED POEMS (1989).

counterpoint, a term adopted from music, is applied to *verse* to indicate the introduction of metrical variation, e.g. if the *metre* is basically *iambic*, and then *trochaic*, *dactylic* or *anapaestic* variations are introduced, the effect may be said to be counterpoint.

coup de théâtre: a strikingly theatrical twist in the *plot* of a play which changes the direction of the *action*.

couplet: a pair of rhyming lines in *verse*, e.g.

> O body swayed to music, O brightening glance
> How can we know the dancer from the dance?
> (from *Yeats* 'Among School Children', 1928)

courtly love refers to a kind of idealised love portrayed in *poem*s, *romance*s and *song*s of the Middle Ages. The lovers are always of a high social class, and their love is ennobling despite being outside marriage (which was likely to be an arranged marriage of economic and/or political convenience between powerful families, and little to do with love). By *convention* the lady is worshipped by the lover, who suffers constantly in body and mind, at some point making an extended lover's *complaint*, and is tested by a very arduous task or quest on behalf of the beloved. The pattern of courtly love was that of Lancelot for Guinevere in Arthurian legend. It is unlikely that the concept is a realistic picture of medieval love. *Feminist criticism* tends to view it as yet another way of subordinating women to men. Among other works there are aspects of courtly love, and also *criticism* and even mocking of the *convention*, in *Chaucer*'s TROILUS AND CRISEYDE and in several of THE CANTERBURY TALES. *Sidney*, *Spenser* and *Shakespeare* also depict courtly love, especially in their *sonnets*.

Couzyn, Jeni (b.1942): Canadian poet. Her work, much of it introspective, tends to focus with clarity and directness upon various aspects of womanhood, and on the difficulties of living. Notable works include FLYING (1970), CHRISTMAS IN AFRICA (1975), A TIME TO BE BORN (1981), LIFE BY DROWNING: SELECTED POEMS (1985), THAT'S IT (1993).

Coward, Nöel (1899–1973): playwright and lyricist. Characteristically he portrays a society where all are out for pleasure, the sophisticated and the unconventional showing *wit* and elegance, winning the audience's admiration at the expense of the boring, sober and conservatively puritanical. Notable works include THE VORTEX (1924), HAY FEVER (1925), PRIVATE LIVES (1930), DESIGN FOR LIVING (1933), BLITHE SPIRIT (1941), PRESENT LAUGHTER (1942).

Cowleyan ode: see *irregular ode.*

Cowper, William (1731–1800): poet and translator. His *poetry*, often dealing with the helpless isolation of the individual, is by turns direct, simple, quietly *witty* and powerful, pointing towards *Romanticism* through his frequent focus upon rural subjects. Notable works include 'God Moves in a Mysterious Way' (1779, a hymn), THE TASK (1785), THE CASTAWAY (1799).

Crabbe, George (1755–1832): poet. Much of his early *poetry* is *Augustan* in the *manner* of *Pope*, later *narrative verse* being more akin to contemporary Romantics; yet he continued to write in *heroic couplets*. Inspired by the landscape of his native Suffolk, he creates a picture of an often poor and degraded rural life. Among his friends or admirers he numbered *Austen, Byron, Johnson, Walter Scott, Southey, Wordsworth.* Notable works include 'The Village' (1783), 'The Borough' (1810, including 'Peter Grimes').

Crane, Stephen (1871–1900): American novelist, journalist, *short-story* writer and poet. His experiences of travelling as a journalist were used in his writing, although he had not encountered war before he wrote his best known work, THE RED BADGE OF COURAGE (1895), hailed as a masterpiece of *realism*. Conrad and *Henry James* became friends and admirers. Other notable works include MAGGIE (1893), THE BLACK RIDER (1895), THE OPEN BOAT AND OTHER STORIES (1898), THE MONSTER (1898), ACTIVE SERVICE (1899), WAR IS KIND (1900).

crime novel: a very general term covering both *detective fiction* and *police procedural* and other kinds of crime stories. Often the psychological state of the criminal and her or his attempts to elude the law is of prime interest, e.g. in *Highsmith*'s Ripley *novels*.

crisis is used generally to denote any important moment or *turning point* in a play or *story*. Several crises may lead up to a *climax*, and may follow thereafter. For instance, in *Shakespeare*'s HAMLET there may be said to be a crisis when in Act I Hamlet hears from the Ghost of his uncle's guilt, a climax in Act III when he 'proves' that guilt by means of the play-within-the-play, and another crisis soon afterwards when he kills Polonius in mistake for his uncle. However, some critics use the two words interchangeably.

Critical Quarterly: an influential critical review of aspects of English literature published every three months.

critical theory: see *literary/critical theory.*

criticism is a term which refers to the whole business of the analysis, evaluation and interpretation of works of literature. The long history of criticism starts with classical theorists such as *Aristotle, Plato,* Horace (65–8BC) and Cicero (106–43BC). Writers in English who have made important contributions to theories of criticism include *Sydney, Jonson, Dryden, Johnson, Coleridge, Shelley, Poe, Arnold, Bradley, Richards, T.S. Eliot, Leavis, Raymond Williams.* See *extrinsic attitude, intrinsic attitude, leavisite, literary/critical* *theory* (and all the cross-references listed thereunder), *New Critics, objective criticism, practical criticism.* Two Frenchmen, Roland Barthes (1915–80) and Jacques Derrida (b.1930) have made crucial contributions to modern *critical theory.*

critique: a detailed analysis of a work, sometimes adversely critical but implying that this standpoint is carefully reasoned.

Crozier, Lorna (b.1948): Canadian poet. Much of her work is inspired by her native prairies, but her lyricism, passion and humour take her observation of humanity beyond the merely local and onto a universal plane. Notable works include THE WEATHER (1981), THE GARDEN GOING ON WITHOUT US (1983), ANGELS OF FLESH, ANGELS OF SILENCE (1988), INVENTING THE HAWK (1992).

Cruden's Concordance is an invaluable cross-reference source to all the main words used in the *Bible.*

Cruelty, Theatre of: originates from the theories of the French actor and director Artaud (1896–1948) who said that theatre should disturb profoundly so as to release people's subconscious repressions, and that the director should be 'a master of magic'. For him, mime, gesture, scenery and spectacular theatrical effects were all important. THE MARAT SADE (1964) by Peter Weiss is a good example of the *genre.*

cultural materialism: the idea that the time and place in which the *text* is written and being read is vitally important. Cultural materialists argue that gender, race, age, class, educational background, sexual orientation and many other factors influence the writer and the reader. See *hermeneutics, reader-response theory, Shakespeare.*

cummings, e e (1894–1962): American poet. Radical and anti-establishment in subject-matter, he developed his own *style* of *poetry* with his unconventional punctuation and typography as seen in the use of lower case for his name. Influenced by jazz and contemporary slang, his work as a graphic artist stimulated experimentation with the *form* and layout of his poetry. Notable works include THE ENORMOUS ROOM (1922), & (1925), IS 5 (1925).

cyberpunk is a sub-species of *science fiction.* The setting is often located within a virtual reality created by computers. The *character*s are bizarre, whether real or artificial intelligences. The *genre* adapts very well to cinema. Cyberpunk has been seen as an aspect of *post-modernism.*

cycle: another word for a group of linked works, e.g. the cycle of *Mystery* plays from the Creation to the Last Judgment, or *Shakespeare*'s two cycles of history plays from RICHARD II (?1597) to RICHARD III (?1591), or his *sonnet sequence.* Collections such as *Chaucer*'s CANTERBURY TALES may also be classed as a cycle.

D

Dabydeen, David (b.1956): Guyanese poet and novelist. He presents the East Indian colonial legacy in a harsh light, is concerned with the experience of migration, and sometimes writes in Creole dialect. He claims to have been particularly influenced by *Shakespeare*'s THE TEMPEST and *Conrad*'s HEART OF DARKNESS. Notable works include SLAVE SONG (1984), TURNER: NEW AND SELECTED POEMS (1994), THE INTENDED (1990), DISAPPEARANCE (1993). See *D'Aguiar*.

dactyl: a *foot* in *verse* consisting of one stressed syllable followed by two unstressed, thus:

- Cánnon to \ ríght of them,
- Cánnon to \ léft of them

           (from *Tennyson*'s 'The Charge of the Light Brigade', 1854)

dactylic: see *metre*.

D'Aguiar, Fred (b.1960): Guyanese poet, novelist and playwright. His *poem*s are often humorous, compassionate and written in the Creole dialect. Notable works include MAMA DOT (1985), AIRY DOT (1989), A JAMAICAN AIRMAN FORSEES HIS DEATH (1991), DEAR FUTURE (1996). See *Dabydeen*.

Dante, Alighieri (1265–1321): Italian poet whose long *poem* THE DIVINE COMEDY had a considerable influence on European literature.

Davie, Donald (b.1922): poet and literary critic. Influenced as a student by *Leavis*, he was a part of and wrote much for *The Movement*, but was later critical of its English parochialism. Notable works include COLLECTED POEMS (1990).

Davies, John (1569–1626): poet. Notable works include ORCHESTRA: OR, A POEM OF DANCING (1596), which presents a celebration of Elizabethan life as a courtly, well-ordered and harmonious dance. See *Tillyard*.

Davies, Robertson (1913–95): Canadian novelist, playwright and journalist. Heavily influenced by the philosophy of Carl Jung (1875–1961), his works often deal with myth, magic and wonder, or place provincial Canada within the *context* of the psychic imagination of a wider world. Notable works include SALTERTON TRILOGY (1970–75), FIFTH BUSINESS (1970), DEPTFORD TRILOGY (1970–75), HUNTING STUART (1972), CORNISH TRILOGY (1981–88), THE CUNNING MAN (1995).

Day-Lewis, C. (1904–72): poet and writer of *detective fiction* under the *pseudonym* Nicholas Blake. Associated with *Auden, Spender* and *MacNeice*, he is praised mainly for his early verse, in which the *paradox* of Day-Lewis as a Marxist with Romantic tendencies is sometimes evident. After the Second World War he increasingly became one of the literary establishment. He was *poet laureate* from 1967–72. Notable works include A QUESTION OF PROOF (1935), OVERTURES TO A DEATH (1938), THE POEMS OF C. DAY-LEWIS 1925–72 (1977).

de Bernières, Louis (b.1954): novelist. His subjects have ranged from persecution, the drugs trade, gangsterism and terrorism to love, sometimes employing *satire* or *magic realism* and using South America (where he has taught) as a *setting*. Notable works include THE WAR OF DON EMMANUEL'S NETHER PARTS (1990), CAPTAIN CORELLI'S MANDOLIN (1994).

de la Mare, Walter (1873–1956): poet, novelist, literary critic, children's and *short-story* writer associated with the *Georgian* poets. Many of his *poem*s explore childhood and, although sometimes regarded as light-weight, some are enduring. Notable works include PEACOCK PIE: A BOOK OF RHYMES (1913), MEMORY AND OTHER POEMS (1938), THE BURNING GLASS AND OTHER POEMS (1945), THE WINGED CHARIOT (1951).

de Quincey, Thomas (1785–1859): literary critic and journalist who was friends with *Coleridge* and *Wordsworth*. His writing on aspects of the way that the mind works had considerable influence on *Poe*, among others. Notable works include CONFESSIONS OF AN ENGLISH OPIUM EATER (1822).

death of the author, the: a concept advanced by Roland Barthes (1915–80) in his DISCOURSE (1968), as a key aspect of *structuralism*. The idea is that readers respond to *text*s regardless of *authorial intention*. Barthes argues that 'the death of the author' leads to 'the birth of the reader' in the sense that the reader should not be trying to solve the puzzle of what the author means, but should feel free to react with the text in a way which creates a variety of possible and personal interpretations. See *post-structuralism, semiotics*.

Decadence: see *Aestheticism*.

decasyllabic line: a *verse* line containing ten syllables, the most common line in English *metre* and most often found in the *form* of *iambic pentameter*. Sometimes the line is irregular and carries a syllable more or less than ten. *Chaucer*'s discovery of this line from continental sources was vital and led to the development of, among other things, the *sonnet, Spenserian stanza* and *blank verse*, the medium in which *Shakespeare* and his contemporaries mainly wrote.

deconstruction is a central word in *post-structuralist criticism*, and it has taken on many meanings. At its simplest it may be used as a word which implies analysis with the knowledge that all *text*s depend on interpretation and how both writer and reader variously interpret language, and hence with an awareness that the same text is capable of an enormous multiplicity of possible meanings. Where *post-structuralism* differs from *structuralism* is that the later holds, in general terms, that rigorous analysis will ultimately fix upon a definite meaning of a text; the former holds that no fixed meaning can ever be found. The French philosopher Jacques Derrida (b.1930) is the foremost figure in the development of deconstruction.

Defoe, Daniel (1660–1731): novelist, journalist and poet whose output was among the most prolific of all writers in English. His early work consists largely of satirical *poem*s and political *essays* in which, unlike most of his *Augustan* contemporaries, his prose *style* is plain and direct. He later turned to social, moral and historical essays, and then late in life discovered his talent for *narrative*. He is now often regarded as the first English novelist, best known for works such as ROBINSON CRUSOE (1719) and MOLL FLANDERS (1722); at the least he is an important experimenter and innovator in the *genre*, and his lively subject-matter set the pattern of novel writing for years to come. Other notable works include JOURNAL OF THE PLAGUE YEAR (1722) and ROXANA (1724).

Dekker, Thomas (?1570–1632): playwright who collaborated with many of his contemporaries, and pamphleteer. His work is vivid, realistic and, on the whole, cheerful. Notable works include THE SHOEMAKER'S HOLIDAY (1600), THE WITCH OF EDMONTON (1621, in collaboration with *John Ford* and *Rowley*).

Delaney, Shelagh (b.1939): playwright, cinema and television scriptwriter. Notable works include A TASTE OF HONEY (1957) which established her at only 17 years old as one of the new breed of kitchen-sink dramatists. See *kitchen-sink drama*.

DeLillo, Don (b.1936): American novelist, his writing is acclaimed as a notable example of a *post-modern* reading of contemporary American society. Notable works include AMERICANA (1971), GREAT JONES STREET (1974), RUNNING DOG (1979), LIBRA (1988), MAO II (1991), UNDERWORLD (1997).

denotation: the simplest and most literal meaning of a word, without any further *connotation* or *association*. See *referential language*.

dénouement: the final unravelling of the *plot* to the audience or reader's delight or sadness. See also *act, catastrophe, resolution*.

Desai, Anita (b.1937): Indian novelist and *short-story* writer. She often explores the interface between the cultures of the East and the West. Notable works include CRY, THE PEACOCK (1963), FIRE ON THE MOUNTAIN (1977), IN CUSTODY (1984), CLEAR LIGHT OF DAY (1980), BAUMGARTNER'S BOMBAY (1988), FASTING, FEASTING (1999).

description is the word used to denote passages of writing, most often (but by no means always) in *prose*, which are descriptive of places (in order to create *setting*), people, objects, social manners and so forth. Unlike *narrative*, description may not strictly advance the *story*, although it may have an explicit or implicit impact upon it. The selection of descriptive detail may well tell the reader something about the author's *viewpoint*.

desert island fiction: stories in which the *setting* is an isolated wild island. It is a *genre* which includes tales of adventure, exploration, paradise and savagery, e.g. *Defoe's* ROBINSON CRUSOE, *Golding's* LORD OF THE FLIES, *Huxley's* ISLAND.

detachment: see *distance*.

detective fiction is *fiction* in which the mystery is solved by a detective. *Poe* did much to encourage the *genre*, creating the solitary, detached but sharply observant detective Dupin. He was followed by the more down-to-earth figures of *Dickens'* Bucket in BLEAK HOUSE and *Wilkie Collins'* Sergeant Cuff in THE MOONSTONE. Poe's kind of detective was revived by *Arthur Conan Doyle* in the figure of Sherlock Holmes, and thereafter most English detectives were in this mould, from Agatha Christie's (1890–1976) Poirot to *P.D. James'* Dalgleish and Colin Dexter's (b.1930) Inspector Morse (although the latter two, as usual from the mid-20th century onwards, are of the *police procedural* type). Among others Raymond Chandler (1888–1959) and Dashiell Hammett (1894–1961) produced a distinctively American *detective fiction* genre, their detectives becoming known as of the 'hard-boiled' variety – tough, ruthless and 'seen-it-all'.

deus ex machina: when the plot takes an unexpected turn in order to solve a tricky situation, and literally meaning 'the god from the machine'. In *Greek drama* a god was mechanically lowered by means of a crane onto the stage in order to intervene in human affairs and assist in the *resolution* of the plot.

device is a word used to describe any literary *technique*.

dialectics can refer to:

- a question-and-answer method of discussion
- a thematic line of reasoning which runs through and unifies a work or works, e.g. in *Donne's love poetry*
- the German philosopher Georg Hegel's (1730–1831) idea, which draws on the foregoing definitions, that all on-going human thought, ideas and history develop a *thesis,* against which there develops an inevitable rebellion or *antithesis,* a clash which in time develops a synthesis, which in turn becomes the new *thesis*; against which... and so on through history.

dialogue is

- speech between two or more characters in any kind of literature
- a literary *genre* in which characters discuss a *theme. Plato* was one of the earliest writers to use this form. Notable examples in English include *Dryden's* ESSAY OF DRAMATIC POESY (1667), *Hopkins'* ON THE ORIGIN OF BEAUTY (1865), *Wilde's* THE ARTIST AS A CRITIC (1891).

diary (or journal): personal observations of events in the *form* of a day-to-day record, usually not intended for others to read or for publication, but sometimes written with an eye to posterity. Notable examples are those of Samuel Pepys (1633–1703), John Aubrey (1626–97), John Evelyn (1620–1706), *Boswell,* Fanney Burney (1752–1840), and *Dorothy Wordsworth.* The diary form has also been used by novelists as way of telling a *story,* for instance *Richardson's* PAMELA OR VIRTUE REWARDED, or THE DIARY OF A NOBODY (1892) by George Grossmith (1847–1912) and Weedon Grossmith (1852–1919). The *epistolary novel* is another form of the same *genre.* See *autobiography, memoir.*

Dickens, Charles (1812–70): novelist and journalist. Despite or perhaps because of some sensation and sentimentality in his works, Dickens was an immensely popular author during his lifetime, and has since steadily grown in academic approval. In general his early work is full of vitality, vivid *character*s and *caricature*s, and atmospheric *setting*s – all things which gave rise to the adjective 'Dickensian'; his later *novel*s are darker in *tone,* more disciplined and with a greater sense of unity, and of increasing thematic and psychological complexity. His characterisation of women is sometimes regarded as unconvincing. Notable works include THE PICKWICK PAPERS (1836–7), OLIVER TWIST (1837–8), NICHOLAS NICKLEBY (1838–9), A CHRISTMAS CAROL (1843), DAVID COPPERFIELD (1849–50), BLEAK HOUSE (1852–3), LITTLE DORRIT (1855–7), GREAT EXPECTATIONS (1861), OUR MUTUAL FRIEND (1864–5).

Dickinson, Emily (1830–86): American poet, her two thousand *poems* contribute greatly to 19th century American literature. She endured inner torment for much of her life. She described her *poetry* as 'New Englandy', and her subject-matter was influenced by a Puritan outlook. In her poetry simple *imagery* and melancholic themes of death and loss of love have a powerful effect, and her experiments with punctuation, typography, grammar, *metre* and use of *metaphor* influenced 20th century poetry. Notable works include 'I Like a Look of Agone' (1861) and 'I Heard a Fly Buzz – When I Died' (?1866).

diction: a term sometimes used to mean the language in which a *text* is written. See *poetic diction.*

didactic: a term used of writing which aims to instruct, or even preach.

Didion, Joan (b1934): American essayist and novelist. Her *essays* are good examples of *New Journalism* and her *novels* of *post-modernism*, although it is limiting wholly to define her work by such labels. Much of her writing is a powerful critique of aspects of American society. Notable works include RUN, RIVER (1964), SLOUCHING TOWARD BETHLEHEM (1968), THE WHITE ALBUM (1979), SALVADOR (1983), JOAN DIDION: ESSAYS AND CONVERSATIONS (1984), MIAMI (1987).

différance is a term important in *post-structuralism*, coined by the French philosopher Jacques Derrida (b.1930) to indicate the instability of meaning in language. The word does not exist in French, but contains elements of several French words which do exist (différence, différer, différant), generating complications and difficulty in establishing meaning.

digression: a side-tracking from the main *theme* or story, e.g. *Chaucer* frequently breaks up his narrative with the rhetorical *device* of digression.

Dillard, Anne/Annie (b.1945): American novelist, essayist, poet and literary critic who writes in a polished and individual style. Notable works include PILGRIM AT TINKER'S CREEK (1974), the semi-autobiographical AN AMERICAN CHILDHOOD (1987).

dimeter: see *foot.*

Dinesen, Isak (1885–1962): the *nom de plume* of Danish *short-story* writer and essayist *Karen Blixen* who wrote mainly in English and was particularly popular in America. Her skilfully told tales often deal with mental disturbance and grotesque *characters*. Notable works include SEVEN GOTHIC TALES (1934), the autobiographical OUT OF AFRICA (1937, about her life in Kenya and which was made into a successful film), ESSAYS (1965).

dirge: a song of mourning or *lament*, shorter than an *elegy*, e.g. Ariel's song 'Full Fathom Five Thy Father Lies' in *Shakespeare*'s THE TEMPEST. See *monody, threnody.* See also *complaint.*

Dirty Realism: an American *style* of *fiction* typically featuring tough characters speaking terse dialogue and involved in violent action, often in a rural setting. Writers associated with the *genre* include *Carver, Hemingway, Wolff.*

discourse may mean:

- a learned discussion (see *dissertation, thesis, tract, treatise*)
- a specialised language or jargon which is used in any area, from literary *criticism* to football. In this sense the word often crops up in discussions concerning such areas as *linguistics, structuralism* and *post-structuralism.*

discovery is another word for *anagnorisis.*

dissertation: a written discussion, usually scholarly, on some learned topic. See *discourse, thesis, tract, treatise.*

dissonance is the deliberate or inadvertent use in *poetry* or *prose* of discordant or clashing sounds. Examples are frequent in the writings of, among others, *Berryman, Hardy, Ted Hughes, Lowell, Tennyson.*

distance, sometimes referred to as '*aesthetic distance*', is a term used to indicate the detachment from the subject-matter with which either the writer or the reader views a piece of *literature*. For instance, a writer might view her/his *character*s from an objective, disinterested distance, as in *existentialist* literature or *satire* (as opposed to *involvement*). Likewise, a reader may remain detached or emotionally involved in a story. The idea of aesthetic *distance* may be summed up thus:

- in a real fog we are emotionally involved because of the anxiety of coping with a real situation which may be dangerous
- in a fictional fog, such as in the opening to *Dickens'* BLEAK HOUSE, we can enjoy in a detached way Dickens' artistic creation and the *symbolism* of the fog because we are not directly involved.

See *alienation effect*.

document: a written record giving information or evidence, e.g. gazette, *diary*, state paper, will, archive.

documentary novel: fiction based on documentary evidence with the intention of recreating an event from an historical aspect, e.g. *Dreiser*'s AN AMERICAN TRAGEDY. See also *thesis novel*.

documentary theatre: *drama* based on documentary evidence as found in newspapers, diaries, reports and so forth. *Edgar*'s MARY BARNES (1977) and THE JAIL DIARY OF ALBEE SACHS are examples of the *genre*. See *drama of ideas*.

doggerel is poorly constructed, bad light *verse*, sometimes deliberately so for comic effect and usually on a trivial subject. The term may come from 'dog-Latin', which means bad Latin.

domestic comedy: a *form* of *drama* about family life in the higher social classes popular since the 18th century, e.g. *Goldsmith*'s SHE STOOPS TO CONQUER. Modern *dramatists* using this *genre* include *Ayckbourn, Coward, Tennessee Williams*.

domestic tragedy focuses upon middle or lower-middle class family life, as opposed to *tragedy* in the grand manner involving important people (such as Kings)… and great enterprises. Examples from *Elizabethan* and *Jacobean* drama include the anonymous ARDEN OF FEVERSHAM (1592), A WOMAN KILLED WITH KINDNESS (1603) by Thomas Heywood (1573–1641), the anonymous A YORKSHIRE TRAGEDY (1608), *Middleton* and *Rowley*'s THE CHANGELING. The *genre* had some popularity in the 18th and 19th centuries, and it saw a notable revival with some of the plays of *Ibsen* and *Strindberg*, and particularly with 20th century American *dramatists* such as *Miller, O'Neill* and *Tennessee Williams*, who did much to broaden the traditional concept of *tragedy*.

Donne, John (1572–1631): poet, generally regarded as the foremost of the *metaphysicals*. In his early years he wrote mainly *love poetry* which was by turns ironic, passionate, erotic (he was the first writer to use the word 'sex' in its modern sense), psychological, intellectually and syntactically complex; but always vigorous, the direct, colloquial language grabbing the reader's attention. The religious *poetry* of his maturer years, especially after his ordination in 1615, is more reflective, less sure, showing a struggle for faith. His religious *prose* is some of the most effective written in the English language. His reputation has declined in recent years, but he is still counted as one of the most original of English poets. Notable works include DEVOTIONS (1624), COLLECTED POEMS (1633, which contain many but not all of his best-known work such as 'The Good Morrow', 'Go and Catch a Falling Star', 'The Sun Rising', 'The Canonization', 'The Ecstasy', 'The Relic', 'At the Round Earth's Imagined Corners...', 'Death be not Proud'), 'Elegy XIX.' 'To His Mistress Going to Bed' (1669).

double plot is a term used of plays which have a main and a *sub-plot*. Some plays even have triple or multiple plots.

double rhyme is another term for *feminine rhyme*.

Douglass, Frederick (1817–95): Black American writer, a freed slave and famous anti-slavery orator who founded an anti-slavery journal called THE NORTH STAR (1847–64), later renamed FREDERICK DOUGLASS' PAPER. In 1858 he established the *periodical* DOUGLASS' MONTHLY (published until 1863). He was important in American political life, organised two black regiments during the Civil War, and held various public offices. Other notable works include his influential autobiographies MY BONDAGE AND MY FREEDOM (1855) and THE LIFE AND TIMES OF FREDERICK DOUGLASS (1881).

Dove, Rita (b.1952): African–American poet, novelist *short-story* and *verse drama* writer. Her *poetry* is distinguished for its lyrical and *narrative* qualities. Notable works include THOMAS AND BEULAH: POEMS (1987), SELECTED POEMS (1993).

Doyle, Arthur Conan (1859–1930): novelist. Best known as the creator of the amateur detective Sherlock Holmes, he was irritated that the popularity of this *character* obscured his other *historical novels*, *science fiction* and *romances*. Notable works include THE ADVENTURES OF SHERLOCK HOLMES (1892), THE EXPLOITS OF BRIGADIER GERARD (1896), THE HOUND OF THE BASKERVILLES (1902), THE LOST WORLD (1912). See *detective fiction*.

Doyle, Roddy (b.1958): Irish novelist and playwright. Often locating his stories in working-class northern Dublin, his style is invigoratingly free-wheeling and collo- quial, his tone compassionate, his characters memorable. Notable works include THE BARRYTOWN TRILOGY (1992), PADDY CLARKE HA HA HA (1993) in which he memorably captures the world as seen through the eyes of a lively child.

Drabble, Margaret (b.1939): novelist. Her early *novels* focus upon the situation of modern educated young women coming to terms with conflicting needs, demands and aspirations, but more recent work uses a broader canvas. Notable works include THE MILLSTONE (1966), THE WATERFALL (1969), THE NEEDLE'S EYE (1972), THE ICE-AGE (1977), THE RADIANT WAY (1987), THE GATES OF IVORY (1991), THE WITCH OF EXMOOR (1996), editor of THE OXFORD COMPANION TO ENGLISH LITERATURE (1979–2000), THE PEPPERED MOTH (2001).

drama may be described as any kind of performance designed for an audience in some kind of theatre, characteristically showing an *action* by *characters* covering an imagined length of time within a *setting* or settings. The script of a play is like an architect's drawing, only an indication of the real thing, which comes to life when actors adopt characters, and speak the words and perform the actions indicated by the playwright. A reader of a play needs to be 'theatre literate' in order to visualise it successfully in her or his head. Examiners tend to be dismayed when a candidate, in talking of a drama, writes 'the book' rather than 'the play': it is an indication that the candidate has little sense of the piece as something which has reality in performance, involving presentation and action as well as words. Sometimes the word 'drama' is used to indicate a relatively serious play, as opposed to a light piece. See also *unities, dramatic*.

drama of ideas is a term used to define plays which deal with problems, often of a social rather than individual nature. Plays have dealt with social issues over the centuries, but it is the late 19th century with the work of *dramatist*s such as *Ibsen* and *Shaw* that a sense of debate within a *drama* emerges. During the 20th century *Brecht* encouraged explicit debate on stage and had a considerable influence upon drama in the second half of the century. Among notable 'ideas' playwrights since the 1960s are *Howard Barker, Bond, Brenton, Churchill, Edgar, Hare, McGrath* whose concerns have ranged over subjects such as the class system, racism, feminisim, Thatcherism, the press, hypocrisy and political corruption. See *agitprop*.

dramatic irony: in *drama*, where a *character* is unaware of the *irony* of her/his words or situation and other characters on stage or, more especially, the audience are (or soon will become) aware, e.g. in Act II, Scene 5 of TWELFTH NIGHT when Malvolio reads aloud a letter believing it to be a declaration of love from Olivia, the other characters listening to him and the audience knowing that he is being tricked. In *comedy*, this gives rise to mirth; in *tragedy*, to pain. See *tragic irony*.

dramatic monologue: see *monologue*.

dramatis personae: list of *character*s who take part in a play.

dramatisation is any kind of conversion into *drama* from another medium, e.g. the adaptation of Bible stories into *Mystery plays,* or the conversion of *novel*s into television drama or screenplay.

dramatist is another word for 'playwright', sometimes used to cover those who also write *drama* for media other than the stage, e.g. film, radio, television.

dramaturgy is the art of dramatic composition.

drawing-room comedy is a semi-disparaging term for pleasant, often undemanding, *comedy of manners* concerning the English middle classes, the best of which are plays such as *Shaw*'s CANDIDA (1895) and *Coward*'s HAY FEVER.

dream vision refers to a kind of literature, most popular in the Middle Ages, in which a *character* falls asleep, often in pleasant, rural surroundings, and has a dream in which s/he is guided through a landscape. This *genre* often provides a good vehicle for *allegory*. Medieval writers were much influenced by the French 13th century ROMANCE OF THE ROSE, and the Italian *Dante*'s DIVINE COMEDY is a dream vision. Examples in English include *Langland*'s PIERS PLOWMAN, *Chaucer*'s THE BOOK OF THE DUCHESS and THE HOUSE OF FAME; and later examples include *Bunyan*'s THE PILGRIM'S PROGRESS, *Keats*'s 'The Fall of Hyperion: A Dream' (1819). ALICE IN WONDERLAND (1865) by Lewis Carroll (1832–98) is in the same *genre*, as is *Joyce*'s FINNEGAN'S WAKE.

Dreiser, Theodore (1871–1945): American novelist, journalist, playwright, *short-story* writer, poet, essayist and autobiographer. *Sinclair Lewis* considered Dreiser's first *novel* SISTER CARRIE (1900) to be 'the first book free of English literature's influence'. This book and his next, JENNIE GERHARDT (1901), were unpopular on account of their uncompromising *realism*. He became increasingly socialist in outlook. Other notable works include his *documentary novel* AN AMERICAN TRAGEDY (1925).

Dryden, John (1631–1700): poet, playwright, critic and translator. His interests were wide, and his writing often considers philosophical or political questions. A polished, exact and versatile craftsman in *verse, prose* and *drama*, Dryden's reputation is as high as ever, but nowadays he is more admired than read for pleasure. His *poetry* is often noted for his mastery of the *heroic couplet*. He was the first official *poet laureate*. Notable works include ESSAY OF DRAMATIC POESY (1668), MARRIAGE À LA MODE (1672), ALL FOR LOVE (1678, a reworking of *Shakespeare*'s ANTONY AND CLEOPATRA), ABSALOM AND ACHITOPHEL, MAC FLECKNOE (1684).

Du Bois, W.E.B. (1868–1963): Black American historian, essayist and editor, famous for his work on the position of black people in America. Notable works include THE SOULS OF THE BLACK FOLK (1903), THE SUPPRESSION OF THE AFRICAN SLAVE TRADE (1896), BLACK RECONSTRUCTION (1935). From the 1930s his politics grew increasingly radical and in 1960 at the age of 92 he joined the Communist Party and went to live in Ghana.

Duffy, Carol Ann (b.1955): poet and playwright. Her *poems* are at the same time sensitive and unsentimental. Notable works include SELLING MANHATTAN (1987), SELECTED POEMS (1994).

dumb show is a term used to describe a mimed dramatic *action* which is intended to prepare the audience for the main action of the play which follows. It is mainly used in *Elizabethan* and *Jacobean drama*, derived from the tragedies of the Roman Seneca, the most famous example being the dumb show which precedes the play-within-the-play in *Shakespeare*'s HAMLET. Other examples are to be found in *Norton* and *Sackville*'s GORBODUC, *Kyd*'s THE SPANISH TRAGEDY, and in *Webster*'s THE WHITE DEVIL and THE DUCHESS OF MALFI.

Dunbar, William (?1456–?1513): Scottish poet. Sometimes classified with *Henryson* in a group known as Scottish Chaucerians, he wrote in a range of *styles*, humorous and serious, courtly and low, religious and secular. Some of his *poems* are allegories and *satires*. Notable works include THE THRISELL AND THE ROIS (1503), LAMENT FOR THE MAKARIS (1508), DONE IS A BATTLE (?1510).

Dunn, Douglas (b.1942): Scottish poet, *short-story* writer, translator and editor. Influenced by *Larkin*, his *poems* often contain clearly-observed depictions of ordinary people and their lives, and his focus ranges from the local to wider political and aesthetic considerations. Notable works include TERRY STREET (1969), ELEGIES (1985, a commemoration of his wife who died in 1981, and which has been hailed as the finest work of its kind since *Tennyson*'s IN MEMORIAM).

duologue: a conversation between two *characters* in any kind of *literature*.

duple metre occurs when each *foot* is made up of two syllables, as in *iambs* and *trochees*. It is much more common in English *verse* than the *triple metre* of *dactyls* and *anapaests*.

duple rhythm: another term for *duple metre*.

Durrell, Gerald (1925–95): travel and natural history writer, journalist and novelist. His writing is light and readable. Notable works include THE BAFUT BEAGLES (1953), MY FAMILY AND OTHER ANIMALS (1956), ISLAND ZOO (1961).

Durrell, Lawrence (1912–1990): poet, travel writer and novelist. The people and locations around the Mediterranean, where he spent most of his life, provide the subject-matter and *themes* for much of his writing. Notable works include A PRIVATE COUNTRY (1943), PROSPERO'S CELL (1945), JUSTINE (1957), BITTER LEMONS (1957), COLLECTED POEMS (1960).

dystopias: very unpleasant fictional worlds (that is, the opposite of *utopias*), often the writer's projection into the future of ominous tendencies in contemporary society, e.g. *Huxley*'s BRAVE NEW WORLD, *Orwell*'s NINETEEN EIGHTY-FOUR, *Burgess*'s A CLOCKWORK ORANGE, *Atwood*'s THE HANDMAID'S TALE. *Science fiction* often depicts dystopian cultures.

e: a magazine for AS and A level candidates of English Literature (and English Language).

Eagleton, Terry (b.1943): literary critic. He is a controversial opposer of conventional orthodoxies, and is recognised as a foremost influence in *Marxist criticism*. Notable works include LITERARY THEORY: AN INTRODUCTION (1983).

Early National Period: sometimes used to cover literature written in America between approximately 1775 (the beginning of the Revolutionary War) and 1828 (the emergence of Jacksonian democracy).

Eden, Emily (1797–1869): travel writer and novelist. She writes about India from her experiences of living there for 14 years with her brother while he was Governor General. Influenced by *Austen*, her writing is *witty*, observant, and an excellent record of the attitudes and manners of fashionable society of the day. Notable works include PORTRAITS OF THE PEOPLE AND PRINCES OF INDIA (1844), UP THE COUNTRY (1866), LETTERS FROM INDIA (1872), THE SEMI-DETACHED HOUSE (1859), THE SEMI-ATTACHED COUPLE (1860).

Edgar, David (b.1948): playwright with a reputation for deftness in presenting socialist ideas. Notable works include DESTINY (1976), THE JAIL DIARY OF ALBIE SACHS (1978), adaptation (1980) of *Dickens'* NICHOLAS NICKLEBY for the Royal Shakespeare Company, PENTECOST (1994), THE PRISONER'S DILEMMA (2001).

edition: a printing of a *text* from which future impressions or re-printings or re-issues may be made. If there are substantial changes in a further printing, this printing is referred to as the 'second edition'; and so forth. The printing history of a text is normally detailed on one of the initial pages of the book.

Edwardian Period: used to refer to literature written in England between the death of Queen Victoria and the First World War (1901–14), during most of which time Edward VII was on the throne (1901–10). In American literature roughly the same timespan is referred to as the Naturalistic Period.

Ekwensi, Cyprian (b.1921): Nigerian novelist and *short-story* writer. He writes in an engaging, energetic and realistic way about city life in West Africa. Notable works include JAGUA NANA (1961).

elegiac: used of any *poem*, not necessarily a strict *elegy*, which has a sadly reflective *tone* and/or deals with the transience of things, e.g. *Gray*'s 'Elegy Written in a Country Churchyard'.

elegy: a *poem* of mourning for an individual, e.g. 'Adonais' (1821), *Shelley*'s lament for *Keats*. See *complaint, dirge, monody, threnody*.

Eliot, George – real name Mary Ann Evans (1819–80): novelist, critic and poet. Well educated, she was influenced by the Romantic poets, German literature and an interest in religion, towards which she had a liberal attitude. Moving in intellectual circles in London, she became assistant editor of the *Westminster Review*. She met George Henry Lewes and lived happily with him (despite the fact that he was already married) from 1853 until his death in 1878. In some senses a feminist, she is regarded by many as the foremost woman novelist of the 19th century, *Leavis* praising her 'luminous intelligence' and ranking her in THE GREAT TRADITION as central within the *canon* of great English novelists. Notable works include ADAM BEDE (1859), THE MILL ON THE FLOSS (1860), SILAS MARNER (1861), MIDDLEMARCH (1871–2), DANIEL DERONDA (1874–6).

Eliot, T.S. (1888–1965): poet, playwright, literary critic. Encouraged and influenced by *Pound*, Eliot began to write *poetry* which, in its use of cosmopolitan subject-matter, allusiveness, stark images and fragmentary *free verse*, led to his being regarded as a central figure in *modernism*, especially after the publication of THE WASTE LAND (1922). His critical writings show great admiration for the Elizabethan *dramatists* and *metaphysical* poets, and he was in the forefront of a mid-20th century revival of *verse drama*. In various ways he had the greatest impact of any twentieth century poet; but it is a *paradox* that his increasingly right-wing political and cultural views and his emphasis on *tradition* in his critical writings limited his influence over younger writers. Other notable works include THE LOVE SONG OF J. ALFRED PRUFROCK (1917), THE SACRED WOOD (1920), THE HOLLOW MEN (1925), THE WASTE LAND (1922), ASH WEDNESDAY (1930), MURDER IN THE CATHEDRAL (1935), FOUR QUARTETS (1935–42), COLLECTED POEMS (1909–62) (1963). See also *objective correlative*.

elision: the running together or eliding of two syllables to make the right number of syllables in a line e.g. 'o'er' instead of 'over', or 'e'er' in place of 'ever'. See *synaeresis, syncope*.

Elizabethan Age: used to refer to *literature* written in England during the reign of Elizabeth I (1558–1603).

Elizabethan drama: strictly speaking only referring to *drama* written during the *Elizabethan Age*, the term has also come to cover the whole of the great age of English drama from early in the Elizabethan era until the closing of the theatres in 1642 (again, strictly speaking drama written during the reign of James I should be referred to as *Jacobean* and that during Charles I's reign as *Caroline*).

Ellison, Ralph (1914–94): Black American novelist, essayist and *short-story* writer. Literary heir to *Richard Wright*, he writes of Afro-American culture and conditions. Notable works include INVISIBLE MAN (1952), a semi-autobiographical *novel*.

emblem: an *allegorical* picture or *symbol*. Scales may be emblematic of the scales of justice, and the spear on *Shakespeare*'s coat-of-arms is emblematic of his name. In THE PRELUDE *Wordsworth* writes of the prospect of a moonlit mountain range as 'the emblem of a mind/That feeds upon infinity'.

emblem book: a book of symbolic pictures explained by accompanying *verses*. Images from these books were frequent in 16th and 17th century *poetry* and *drama*, *Shakespeare* making much use of Geoffrey Whitney's A CHOICE OF EMBLEMES (1586); for instance, in Act I, Scene 7 of MACBETH, where Lady Macbeth tells her husband to 'Look like the innocent flower,/But be the serpent under it' (see illustration opposite, taken from Whitney). Quarle's EMBLEMES (1635) was also most popular.

Emecheta, Buchi (b.1944): Nigerian novelist, and writer of children's *literature* and television scripts. Her writing shows her feminist concern for women's rights, and mostly she sets her *novels* in West Africa. Notable works include the semi-autobiographical SECOND-CLASS CITIZEN (1974), THE BRIDE PRICE (1976), THE JOYS OF MOTHERHOOD (1979).

Emblem book (see page 48)

Emerson, Ralph Waldo (1803–82): American essayist and poet. A leading member of the transcendentalists, he was very interested in philosophy and religion, and attracted to a Wordsworthian reverence for nature which has become very important in American thought. He became committed to the abolition of slavery. Notable works include NATURE (1836), REPRESENTATIVE MEN (1850).

empathy is a term used in literature to describe an emotional (and sometimes physical) identification with a character which goes beyond *sympathy*. *Keats* claims that he becomes 'a part of all I see' and expresses his empathy in that 'if a sparrow comes before my window I take part in its existence and pick about the gravel.' In Act V, Scene 1 of *Shakespeare*'s MACBETH the Doctor may be said to empathise not only with the sleepwalking Lady Macbeth but with all humanity when he says 'God, God forgive us all!'.

Empson, William (1906–84): critic and poet. Taught and influenced by *Richards*, he was one of the founders of the Cambridge University English Literature degree. In his SEVEN TYPES OF AMBIGUITY (first published 1930; latest *edition* Penguin 1995) he advocated such ultra-close analysis of the *text* that *T.S. Eliot* called his *method* 'the lemon squeezer school of criticism'. Other notable works include COLLECTED POEMS (revised 1955). His *poetry* influenced younger poets such as those associated with *The Movement*, and the critic John Wain (1925–94) praised it for its 'passion, logic and formal beauty'.

encomium has come to mean any piece or writing of praise, and was very popular in the 17th and 18th centuries, e.g. *Dryden*'s 'A Song for Saint Cecilia's Day', *Gray*'s 'Hymn to Adversity'.

end-rhyme is rhyming at the end of lines, and hence the most common kind of rhyming. See *rhyme*.

end-stopping/end-stopped: where the end of a *verse* line is marked by a pause, usually indicated by punctuation. For an example see *enjambement*. End-stopped lines tend to emphasise the *rhythm* in verse which has a regular structure. See *versification*.

English Review is a magazine aimed at AS and A level English Literature candidates and published by Philip Allen Publishers.

English sonnet: another name for the *Shakespearean sonnet*.

English Stage Company: an influential theatre company operating at the Royal Court Theatre, London, during the mid-20th century, and responsible for innovative plays by *Osborne, kitchen-sink drama*, and other *avant-garde* work.

enjambement is the running-on of the sense of one line of *verse* into the next without *end-stopping*. Often used together with *caesura* in order to lend variety and a natural effect to the *rhythm* of verse. In the following example there is enjambement between lines 3 and 4, a caesura in line 4, and lines 1 and 2 are end-stopped:

> The thirtieth of November.
> Snow is starting to fall.
> A peculiar silence is spreading
> over the fields, the maple grove.

> (from *Rich*'s Toward the Solstice, 1978)

enlightenment: a western European literary, intellectual, philosophical and cultural climate which prevailed between roughly 1660 and 1770, and which advocated faith in clarity of thought and writing, and good sense in all affairs. The period is sometimes known as the Age of Reason as it was thought that human reason would solve all problems, stimulating scientific discoveries and all other kinds of progress. The thinking and writing of *Johnson* is sometimes seen as characterising the English spirit of that age.

Enright, D.J. (b.1920): poet and editor. Using understatement and irony, he tends to combine anger over inequality with compassion for the human condition. He often uses an Eastern location. Notable works include The Laughing Hyena (1953).

envoi, anglicised as **envoy**, is a message (literally 'send-off') at the end of a piece of literature. Originally a four-line *stanza* which concluded a certain *form* of French *poem*, it has been used in English literature in *poetry*, as in *Chaucer*'s The Clerk's Tale (one of the Canterbury Tales), and in *prose*, as in *A.N. Wilson*'s The Healing Art. Among others *Swinburne* and *Wilde* have employed the *device*.

epic: a long narrative *poem* recounting heroic achievements and epic events in a grand, elevated style of writing. Some epics spring from an oral *tradition*, e.g. *Homer*'s Iliad and Odyssey or the anonymous Old English Beowulf; others such as the Latin Aeneid by Virgil (70–19bc) or *Milton*'s Paradise Lost are literary. Although the word has become widened to embrace anything on a large scale (e.g. *epic* scale, *epic* imagery, *epic* film, *epic* voyage), students should be careful before using it in other than its strict literary sense. See also *mock-epic*.

epic or extended simile: a long *simile* which characteristically interrupts the narrative of an *epic poem*. Much used, for example, by *Milton* in PARADISE LOST. There is another good example in *Arnold*'s SOHRAB AND RUSTUM (1853).

epic theatre has much in common with *documentary theatre* in that it uses *devices* such as *song, plot* summaries, film and slide projection, and/or a *chorus* to present a *story* which often ranges over a wide period of time, geographic area and/or cast of *characters*, with frequent doubling up of parts; all of which encourages an *alienation effect* on the part of the audience. This type of theatre was developed by *Brecht* (1898–1956) between the 1920s and 1950s. See *brechtian, distance.*

epigram: a short *witty* statement in *prose* or *poetry*. The *form* became popular in the 17th and 18th centuries with such as *Jonson, Herrick, Donne, Dryden, Jonathan Swift* and *Pope,* and there was a revival of interest by later 19th and 20th century writers, e.g. the Americans *Emerson, Dickinson, Pound,* Ogden Nash (1902–71). *Wilde* used many epigrams in his plays, an epigram in prose sometimes being called an *apothegm.* See *aphorism, clerihew, maxim.*

epigraph: in a literary sense used to hint at the significance of what follows by means of a quotation or motto at the beginning of a book, chapter, section or *poem*, e.g. 'Mistah Kurtz – he dead' *T.S. Eliot* quoting from *Conrad*'s HEART OF DARKNESS at the beginning of THE HOLLOW MEN; 'Ours was the marsh country' *Graham Swift* quoting from *Dickens*' GREAT EXPECTATIONS at the beginning of WATERLAND; and *Fowles* quoting from various sources at the beginning of every chapter of THE FRENCH LIEUTENANT'S WOMAN.

epilogue: either:

- a passage which concludes and often comments upon the preceding work, e.g. the Doctor's speech which emphasises the moral of the anonymous Morality play Everyman. With a play it is often a plea for applause, e.g. Puck at the end of Shakespeare's A Midsummer Night's Dream. Sometimes an epilogue is a summary of what has gone before, or is an afterthought; or
- the name of the *character* who speaks the epilogue.

See *coda, prologue.*

epiphany in a literary sense has come to mean a sudden experience of revelation or understanding. *Joyce* used it in this sense in A PORTRAIT OF THE ARTIST AS A YOUNG MAN (1916). *Wordsworth* experiences many epiphanies in THE PRELUDE, calling such moments 'spots of time'. *Characters* frequently experience epiphanies in *Murdoch*'s novels, e.g. Jake Donaghue in UNDER THE NET.

episode is a term which may indicate:

- a single incident or relatively self-contained passage within a longer work
- a single section of a serialised work.

episodic describes the structure of a work which consists of a sequence of loosely connected events, usually happening to the same person. The term is often applied to *picaresque* novels.

epistolary novel: a kind of *novel* made popular in the 18th century in which the story is told through the letters or diary of the *protagonist*, e.g. *Richardson*'s PAMELA, *Walker*'s THE COLOR PURPLE.

epithalamium: a *poem* celebrating marriage, e.g. *Spenser*'s EPITHALAMIUM, written for his own marriage.

epithet: an adjective or adjectival phrase used to describe a particular characteristic. The term is variously used in connection with:

- a person, e.g. Long John Silver, Richard the Lionheart
- a thing, e.g. when Falstaff talks of 'grinning Honour' in *Shakespeare*'s HENRY IV PART 1
- eighteenth century poetic diction, where an epithet was attached to almost every noun, sometimes to ludicrous effect, e.g. 'fish' were describe as the 'finny tribe'
- Homeric epithets, often compound adjectives in the style of the Greek Homer, whereby a recurrent formula was used in description, e.g. 'fleet-foot Achilles', 'wine-dark sea'. This kind of epithet was often used in Anglo-Saxon *poetry*.

eponymous: when the main character gives his or her name to the title of a work, e.g. King Lear, Silas Marner, or Gatsby in *F. Scott Fitzgerald*'s THE GREAT GATSBY. Hamlet might be referred to as the 'eponymous hero' of *Shakespeare*'s HAMLET.

Equiano, Oloudah (1745–97), an Ibo who was captured and enslaved, worked for masters in Barbados, Virginia and England. He saved money, bought his freedom, and then worked with others for the abolition of slavery. Notable works include THE INTERESTING NARRATIVE OF THE LIFE OF OLOUDAH EQUIANO, OR GUSTAVUS VASSA, THE AFRICAN, WRITTEN BY HIMSELF (1789).

Erdich, Louise (b.1954): American novelist and poet of German and native American descent. Using her knowledge of native American Indian life, tribal issues and ancestry, she often locates her *novels* in North Dakota. Her *method* is sometimes related to *magic realism*. Notable works include LOVE MEDICINE (1984), JACKLIGHT (1984), THE BEET QUEEN (1986), TRACKS (1988), THE CROWN OF COLUMBUS (1991), THE BINGO PALACE (1994).

essay: a term nowadays used mainly to describe a discursive piece of writing, often by a student; but also referring to short *prose* pieces of an informal nature made popular in the 18th century by writers such as *Addison, Steele* and *Lamb*, and still featuring in such periodicals as THE OLDIE and THE SPECTATOR.

Etherege, George (1635–91): playwright of *Restoration comedy* in the *comedy of manners* style. Notable works include THE MAN OF MODE (1676).

euphuism: an elegant and elaborate *prose* style (not to be confused with 'euphemism'). See *Lyly*.

Eurocentric is a term used, sometimes pejoratively, when a course of literary study, programme or similar is centred upon European literature.

exegesis is a detailed critical analysis and explanation of difficulties in a literary *text* (the term was originally confined to examination of the *Bible*).

exemplum: a short *tale* illustrating a moral point. Exempla were frequent in sermons and medieval literature. Examples are to be found in much of *Chaucer*'s work.

existentialism is a philosophy which proposes that every individual must assume responsibility for the nature of her or his existence in a dangerous and meaningless universe. These ideas had their origins in the 19th century and rose to prominence in the mid-20th century through the writings of, among others, the Frenchmen Albert Camus (1913–1960) and Jean-Paul Sartre (1905–80). See *Absurd, Theatre and Literature of.*

exordium: in *rhetoric*, the introductory part of a speech or *essay.*

explication is the kind of *close reading* advocated by the *New Critics*. See *intrinsic attitude, leavisite.*

exposition: the *setting* of the scene in a play or story, sometimes dealing with essential events prior to the opening of the *narrative.* For instance, the information revealed in the opening scene of *Shakespeare*'s Hamlet. See *act.*

expressionism is a movement in literature and art, mainly German in origin, which rejects *realism* and objective portrayal, preferring to depict inner states of mind by distorted images. In art Edvard Munch's painting The Scream (1894) is probably the most famous expressionist image, and Vincent Van Gogh's turbulent landscapes are characteristic. Among other areas of *literature* expressionism had some impact upon American *dramatists* such as *O'Neill* in The Emperor Jones, *Wilder* in The Skin of our Teeth and *Miller* in Death of a Salesman; and *Tennessee Williams* uses expressionist techniques, for example in The Glass Menagerie. *Expressionism* also had an impact upon *Beat Movement* writers (such as *Ginsberg*) and the *Theatre of the Absurd.*

extenuatio is an alternative term for *meiosis.*

extrinsic attitude embraces the idea that an objective scrutiny of a *text* is not enough and that the historical *context* in which a text is produced decides meaning. Many of the newer literary theories assume an extrinsic attitude, e.g. *psychoanalytic criticism, feminist criticism.* This approach is also known as *historicism.*

eye-rhyme, sometimes called 'sight rhyme', is when words look as if they rhyme, but they do not (as in 'come/home'), e.g.

> …Until this morning and this snow.
> If anything might rouse him now…

> (from Owen's 'Futility')

Half-rhyme is created by *eye-rhyme*, but the reverse is not necessarily true, e.g. once/France is half-rhyme, but not eye-rhyme.

F

fable: a *short story* in *prose* or *verse* which concludes with a moral. Often it takes the *form* of a 'beast fable', where animals assume human characteristics. The Greek writer Aesop (?620–560BC) is the earliest well-known writer of this kind of fable, a modern example being *Orwell's* ANIMAL FARM. Other fables include *Chaucer's* THE NUN'S PRIEST'S TALE (from THE CANTERBURY TALES), *Kipling's* JUST SO STORIES, *Thurber's* FABLES OF OUR TIME (1940). See *allegory*.

fabliau: a short, satirical, earthy, bawdy *story* about ordinary folk, often portraying promiscuous women and cuckolded husbands. In *tone* and subject-matter the *genre* is the *antithesis* of *courtly love* tales. Fabliaux were popular in 14th century England, *Chaucer's* MILLER'S TALE and REEVE'S TALE (from THE CANTERBURY TALES) being *classics* of the type.

fabulation is a modern term which describes a *method* of *narrative* which deliberately defies a reader's traditional expectations of story-telling, experimenting with subject-matter, *form* and *style*, and combining all kinds of realistic and non-realistic elements in a self-consciously surprising – even shocking – way. See *anti-novel*.

faction is *literature* or other media which incorporate fact within *fiction*, or combine fact and fiction, e.g. *Mailer's* ARMIES OF THE NIGHT. See *New Journalism*.

fallible narrator: see *narrator*.

falling action is when the *action* of a play falls away from its *climax*.

falling rhythm: see *rising rhythm*.

fancy is another word for *imagination*, although *Coleridge* drew a fine distinction between the two terms. The word is sometimes used to denote the creative faculty which produces light-weight, humorous writing; whereas the *imagination* produces the more serious and passionate. It is worth reading *Keats'* 'Fancy' (1820).

fantastic is a term applied to literature where the reader is unsure whether events can be explained by natural causes/psychological explanations, or whether the supernatural is involved, e.g. *James'* THE TURN OF THE SCREW, or the Cathy's ghost in *Emily Brontë's* WUTHERING HEIGHTS.

fantasy, in a literary sense, refers to *short stories* or *novels* which create an alternative world imaginatively apart from the ordinary experience of the reader. It could describe *gothic* horror such as *Mary Shelley's* FRANKENSTEIN; or *science fiction* such as *Wells'* THE WAR OF THE WORLDS; or *utopias* and *dystopias* such as are found in *Jonathan Swift's* GULLIVER'S TRAVELS, *Huxley's* BRAVE NEW WORLD and *Orwell's* ANIMAL FARM. Fantasies are often also *allegories*.

Fanthorpe, U.A. (b.1921): poet. With objectivity and compassion her incisive *poetry* observes and explores the everyday. Prolific and popular, she is at times both disarmingly humorous and disturbingly direct. Notable works include SIDE EFFECTS (1978), SELECTED POEMS (1986), CONSEQUENCES (2000).

farce is a type of *drama* where comic situations are pushed to the point of hilarious absurdity. Unlike *satire*, farce is usually simple entertainment, and it may include any or all of: complicated plots (often involving mistaken identity), exaggerated *charac-ters*, bizarre situations and knock-about *action*. Many English *dramatists* have employed *farce*, for instance *Shakespeare* in THE COMEDY OF ERRORS (?1594), THE TAMING OF THE SHREW (1594) and THE MERRY WIVES OF WINDSOR (1602), *Jonson* in BARTHOLOMEW FAIR, *Wilde* in THE IMPORTANCE OF BEING ERNEST, and *Orton* and *Stoppard* in most of their plays. Farce is often an element in *Absurd Theatre*. See also *black comedy*.

Farquar, George (?1677–1707): playwright of *Restoration comedy* in the *comedy of manners* style. He is often more concerned with romantic love than is usual in the cynical world of Restoration comedies, and he broadened their scope by sometimes using locations in the provinces away from fashionable London. His plays are marked by a sense of reality, vitality and good *humour*. Notable works include THE RECRUITING OFFICER (1706), THE BEAUX' STRATAGEM (1707).

Farrell, J.G. (1935–79): novelist. Through meticulous research, a *witty* and ironic style, a symbolic approach and a wide range of *character*s, he explores his main *theme* of British Imperial decline, especially in his 'Empire trilogy'. Notable works include TROUBLES (1969), THE SEIGE OF KRISHNAPUR (1973), THE SINGAPORE GRIP (1978).

fatal flaw: see *Bradley, tragic flaw*.

Faulkner, William (1897–1962): American novelist, poet, *short-story* writer and journalist. In order to chart the changing situation of the Southern states he created a fictionised *setting* called Yoknapatawpha County (based on Mississippi, his home state); and this, together with his complex *style* which sometimes involves s*tream of consciousness* and multiple *narrator*s, at first led him to be regarded as a merely *regional* writer. In various of his writings he describes the decline of the Southern states with sombre lyricism. He is now generally recognised as one of America's greatest 20th century novelists. Notable works include THE SOUND AND THE FURY (1929), AS I LAY DYING (1930), LIGHT IN AUGUST (1932), ABSOLOM, ABSOLOM! (1936), COLLECTED STORIES (1950, a collection of *detective fiction*), THE FABLE (1954), THE REVIEW (1962).

Faulks, Sebastian (b.1953): novelist. He is noted for sensitive treatment of his subject matter. Notable works include BIRDSONG (1994), ON GREEN DOLPHIN STREET (2001).

feeling is a notion applauded by Romantic writers who elevate the benefits of feeling (that is, responding through the emotions) above those of the intellect. For instance, in TO MY SISTER (1798) *Wordsworth* emphasises the value of leaving behind books on a mild March day, going out into nature, and experiencing an 'hour of feeling'.

feet: see *metre*.

feminine ending: see *weak ending*.

feminine rhyme occurs when accented rhyming syllables are followed by identical unaccented syllables (survìval, revìval; clìpper, dìpper, fìnding, bìnding), as in this anonymous epitaph:

> Here I lie and my four daughters.
> Killed by drinking Cheltenham waters.

See *rhyme*.

feminist criticism sets out to redress what is regarded as the patriarchal, *phallo-centric* nature of society and literature, especially the *novel*. It covers both attitudes towards female writers and the treatment of women as role-models (or, more often, their marginalisation) in *literature*. One of its basic beliefs is the *post-structuralist* notion that the very language in which literature is written is based on a male-dominated society, and therefore that the subordination of women is reinforced by the repeated use of an inherited language. The roots of the feminism go back to the 18th century and *texts* such as A VINDICATION OF THE RIGHTS OF WOMAN (1792) by Mary Wollstonecraft (1759–1797), and may be traced via books such as *Woolf*'s A ROOM OF ONE'S OWN and *Rich*'s ON LIES, SECRETS AND SILENCE. See also *post-modernism*.

Ferlinghetti, Lawrence (b.1919): American poet. A leading figure in the 1950s *Beat Movement*, his *poetry* is characteristically light and satirical, sometimes experimental. Notable works include STARTING FROM SAN FRANCISCO (1961, revised 1967).

Fermor, Patrick Leigh (b.1915): travel writer of elegance, lyricism and vividness. Notable works include THE TRAVELLER'S TREE (1950), MANI (1958), ROUMELI (1966), A TIME OF GIFTS (1977).

fiction is a general word covering any imaginative work, but is usually applied to *novels* and *short stories* (in order to distinguish them from such as *biographies, travel literature* and so forth) rather than to *drama* and *poetry*. See also *faction*.

Fielding, Henry (1701–54): novelist and playwright. A lawyer by training, his early literary work was nearly all *drama*, often political *satire*. After the passing of a stage censorship law in 1737 he turned to journalism as a satirical outlet. He is best remembered now for his *novels* which, while still satirical in their attacks upon corruption and hypocrisy, show sharp observation and a generous compassion for the foibles of human beings, and have strong *narrative* lines. His flair for the broad comic sweep, a multiplicity of characters and his use of the *picaresque* make him an important writer in the development of the novel in England. Notable works include JOSEPH ANDREWS (1742), THE HISTORY OF TOM JONES, A FOUNDLING (1749).

figurative language (figures of speech): language with a meaning beyond the literal, usually involving *simile* and *metaphor*, and sometimes other *devices* such as *hyperbole*.

Findley, Timothy (b.1930): Canadian novelist, *short-story* and television script writer. He often explores the borderlines between *fiction*, history and truth. See *fabulation*. Notable works include THE WARS (1977), FAMOUS LAST WORDS (1981).

first person narrative/point of view: see *viewpoint, narrator.*

Fitzgerald, F. Scott (1896–1940): American novelist, *short-story* and screen writer. He wrote about and was a leading light of 'The Jazz Age', a phrase that he himself coined, and his writing gives a vivid picture of the social behaviour of his times. His fast-living lifestyle and neuroses, and those of his wife, are reflected in the *characters* and *action* of many of his *novels*, as is the deterioration caused by such a manner of living. Notable works include THIS SIDE OF PARADISE (1920), THE BEAUTIFUL AND THE DAMNED (1922), THE GREAT GATSBY (1925), TENDER IS THE NIGHT (1934), THE LAST TYCOON (1941).

Fitzgerald, Penelope (1916–2000): novelist and biographer. Her writing ranges over mystery, *romance, comedy*, history and social realism. Notable works include OFFSHORE (1979), THE GATE OF ANGELS (1990), THE MEANS OF ESCAPE (2000).

fixed form refers to any *form* in *poetry* which is bound by established rules which determine such things as *metre, rhyme* scheme, line length and so forth.

flashback, probably a term borrowed from films, is when during any kind of *literature* there is a scene or episode inserted which returns to an earlier time, e.g. in *Graham Swift's* WATERLAND. No doubt thanks to its use in the cinema, this technique has become increasingly common since the early 20th century. Sometimes called *analepsis*. See also *anachorism, in media res*.

flashforward: the corollary of *flashback*. Also known as *prolepsis*. See also *anachorism*.

flat characters, as defined by *E.M. Forster* in ASPECTS OF THE NOVEL, are *characters* who are two-dimensional and do not develop during the course of the *story*. He cites Mrs Micawber from *Dickens'* DAVID COPPERFIELD as an example. See *round characters*.

Fletcher, John (1579–1625): playwright. A skilled professional man of the theatre, he collaborated with many other playwrights including, almost certainly, *Shakespeare* on THE TWO NOBLE KINSMEN (?1613) and HENRY VIII (1613). Other notable works include THE FAITHFUL SHEPHERDESS (?1609), PHILASTER (1609), THE MAID'S TRAGEDY (?1611), the latter two in collaboration with *Beaumont*.

folio: largish page size formed by a printer's sheet that has been folded once only, thus creating four pages. The First Folio edition of *Shakespeare's* plays (1623) was printed in this size.

foot: see *metre*.

Ford, Ford Madox (1873–1939): novelist and editor. He had a powerful and positive influence upon his contemporaries, and as editor of THE ENGLISH REVIEW (a literary magazine founded in 1908) he did much to encourage previously unknown writers such as *Pound* and *Lawrence*. Notable works include THE GOOD SOLDIER (1915), PARADE'S END (1924–8).

Ford, John (?1586–?1640): playwright. His plays show interest in moral paradoxes and in the position of women in society. Notable works include TIS PITY SHE'S A WHORE (?1625), THE BROKEN HEART (?1629).

foregrounding is a technical term denoting language which draws attention to itself as consciously literary, hence pushing its 'literariness' into the foreground and demanding the attention of the reader. *Sterne's* TRISTRAM SHANDY is often cited as an example. Unless a student of literature is quite sure of its application the term is best avoided in *essays*.

foreshadowing occurs when a writer prepares the reader or audience in any way for later events in a *narrative* or *drama*.

form is the shape of a piece of *literature* as opposed to its *content*. Although for academic purposes each needs to be analysed in its own right, form and content are inseparable and depend upon one another, and the form is usually determined by the content. (The same is often true in other arts, hence the architectural notion that 'form follows *function*' – that is, the shape of a building should be determined by its purpose or content.) As a secondary meaning the word form is sometimes used to denote the kind or *genre* of work; but it is best avoided in this sense. See *mechanic form, organic form, structure*.

formalism: see *intrinsic attitude.*

format refers to the physical size and/or layout of a book.

Forster, E.M. (1879–1970): novelist, critic, essayist and biographer. He was influenced by the philosophers G.E. Moore (1873–1958) and Bertrand Russell (1872–1970) and had close contact with members of the *Bloomsbury Group.* He actively opposed censorship, and among other things his writing is noted for its gentle *satire,* humane liberal tolerance, and a sense that it is possible to rise above politics through love. Notable works include WHERE ANGELS FEAR TO TREAD (1905), A ROOM WITH A VIEW (1908), HOWARDS END (1910), THE CELESTIAL OMNIBUS (1911), A PASSAGE TO INDIA (1924), ASPECTS OF THE NOVEL (1927), ABINGER HARVEST (1936).

Fowles, John (b.1926): novelist and essayist. His *novels* often show an interest in experimenting with the conventional *narrative structures* of *fiction.* Notable works include THE MAGUS (1966, REVISED 1977), THE FRENCH LIEUTENANT'S WOMAN (1969).

Frame, Janet (b.1924): New Zealand novelist, *short-story* writer and poet. Influenced by the time she spent in institutions for the mentally ill, her writing can be disturbing: she often explores questions of the human identity and the borderline between reality and madness. She is also concerned with whether language can truly communicate her experience. Notable works include her autobiographical books TO THE ISLAND (1982), AN ANGEL AT MY TABLE (1984, made into a film in 1990), THE ENVOY FROM MIRROR CITY (1985).

Franklin, Benjamin (1706–1790): journalist, essayist and autobiographer. A key figure in the move towards American independence, his admired *prose* style was once described as 'terse, luminous, simple, pregnant with meaning, eminently persuasive'. Notable works include POOR RICHARD'S ALMANACK (1732–58), AUTOBIOGRAPHY (1793).

Franklin, Miles (1879–1945): Australian novelist, sometimes described as the first such. Renowned for her unconventional life and radical attitudes, among other things she explores feminism, Australian nationalism and the impact upon her as a writer of being brought up in the remote bush. Notable works include MY BRILLIANT CAREER (1901).

Frayn, Michael (b.1933): playwright, journalist, novelist, translator and adapter. Best known for his humorous stage comedies with a serious satirical edge. Notable works include THE RUSSIAN INTERPRETER (1966), A VERY PRIVATE LIFE (1968), ALPHABETICAL ORDER (1976), NOISES OFF (1982).

free indirect style/free indirect discourse: see *narrator/ narrative voice.*

free verse, sometimes referred to by the French term 'vers libre', is *verse* which does not conform to any fixed *metre,* pattern, *rhyme* or line length (although all these may partly be in evidence), relying upon the natural *rhythms* and *stresses* of the language. However, the use of *caesura* and *enjambement* are as significant as in more conventional verse. Most notably *Whitman* wrote LEAVES OF GRASS in free verse, and *Hopkins* used it in an innovative way. The *form* (or rather, lack of form) became increasingly popular with *modernist* poets during the 20th century, and *T.S. Eliot's* THE WASTE LAND is often cited as a free verse classic. Other notable exponents include *Pound, Lawrence, Ginsberg, Langston Hughes, William Carlos Williams* whose THIS IS JUST TO SAY, quoted in full under *minimalism,* is also a good example of a free verse *poem.*

Friel, Brian (b.1929): Irish playwright and *short-story* writer. Much of his sensitive, lyrical writing explores personal, family and Irish situations. He often locates his plays in and around Ballybeg, an imaginary village in Donegal. Notable works include Translations (1980), Dancing at Lughnasa (1990).

Frost, Robert (1874–1963) is a very popular American poet, localising a great deal of his writing in rural New England. He received much of his initial encouragement from England, notably through *Edward Thomas*. His *poem*s often concern the individual trying to come to terms with the world, and tend to employ a conversational *diction* and *tone* which is characteristic of New England speech patterns. Notable works include Mountain Interval (1916), New Hampshire (1923), Collected Poems (1930), In the Clearing (1962). His best known poem is probably 'The Road not Taken' (1916).

Fugard, Athol (b.1932): South African playwright, novelist and film scriptwriter. His father was of English descent, his mother an Afrikaner. He founded his 'poor theatre' in black townships, and his plays are often powerful yet compassionate explorations of what it was like to be a black South African living under apartheid. Notable works include The Coat (1966), Sizwe Bansi is Dead (1972), The Island (1973), A Lesson from Aloes (1980), 'Master Harold'… and the Boys (1983).

Fuller, Roy (1912–91): poet and novelist. Influenced by *Auden* and *Spender*, he is noted for his objective, refined, ironic view and his skilful poetic technique which combines traditional and innovative *form*s. Notable works include The Middle of a War (1942), Collected Poems: 1936–1961 (1962).

function is a term sometimes used to denote any event or *action* which moves along the *plot*. See function under Appendix 1.

G

Galsworthy, John (1867–1933): novelist, playwright and poet. In many of his works there is commentary on social injustice of one type or another, and his work had an impact upon contemporary attitudes, as when his play JUSTICE (1910) was influential in the abolition of solitary confinement in prisons. Other notable works include THE SILVER BOX (1906), STRIFE (1909), THE FORSYTE SAGA (1906–28), THE SKIN GAME (1920), COLLECTED POEMS (1934).

Gardham, Jane (b.1928): novelist, *short-story* and children's writer. Her *novel*s often have young protagonists, and are characterised by deft scene-setting, period detail, literary allusiveness and emotional scenes. Notable works include GOD ON THE ROCKS (1978), CRUSOE'S DAUGHTER (1988), TAMBOURINE (1988), FAITH FOX (1996).

Gardner, Helen (1908–86) was an extremely influential critic, specialising in *metaphysical literature*. Notable works include THE BUSINESS OF CRITICISM (1960) in which she underlined that the *function* of a critic is to 'shine a torch', not 'wield a sceptre' (in other words, to illuminate rather than attack).

Gaskell, Elizabeth (1810–65): novelist and biographer. A friend of *Charlotte Brontë* and encouraged by *Dickens*, her writing shows a marked development in *structure* during her writing career, becoming more disciplined. She carefully researched all background aspects of her *character*s, whether industrial workers or country folk, especially their speech. Among other things she has been noted for her *narrative* skill and her compassionate treatment of the less fortunate in society. Notable works include MARY BARTON (1848), CRANFORD (1851–53), RUTH (1853), NORTH AND SOUTH (1855), THE LIFE OF CHARLOTTE BRONTË (1857), WIVES AND DAUGHTERS (1866). See also *regional novel*.

Gatheru, Mugo (b.1925): Kenyan novelist. Among other things he deals with the social frictions between a traditional and a modern society. Notable works include CHILD OF TWO WORLDS (1964).

genre: a category into which types of literature may be placed, e.g. *metaphysical* poetry, *revenge tragedy, science fiction, short story.*

Georgian Period, in *literature*, is generally considered to cover writing in England during the reign of George V (1910–36). In historical terms the Period covers the consecutive reigns of the first four Georges (1714–1830).

Georgian poetry covers poets who wrote fairly traditional work, often rural in *setting* and delicate in touch, during the early part of the *Georgian Period*, e.g. *Blunden, Brooke, De la Mare, Graves, Housman, Lawrence, Masefield, Owen, Sassoon, Edward Thomas,* many of whom were featured in anthologies published between 1912 and 1922 called GEORGIAN POETRY. The Georgians were considered to be minor and conventional by *modernists* such as *T.S. Eliot.*

Ghosh, Amitav (b.1956): Indian novelist and travel writer. His sometimes complex writings show his experience of various cultures. Notable works include THE CIRCLE OF REASON (1986), THE SHADOW LINES (1988).

ghost story: a *genre* popular since Anglo-Saxon times, stories of spirits who return to haunt the living are usually, but not exclusively, *short stories* in *prose*. Notable writers of such stories include Washington Irving (1783–1859) (THE LEGEND OF SLEEPY HOLLOW, 1820), *Poe, Dickens, Stevenson, Kipling, Henry James, Wilde* (THE CANTERVILLE GHOST, 1891), *Wharton* (TALES OF MAN AND GHOSTS, 1910), *De la Mare. Mary Shelley* began writing FRANKENSTEIN in response to a ghost story competition organised by *Byron*. A ghost story has traditionally been thought most fit for telling on or about Christmas Eve, *Dickens'* A CHRISTMAS CAROL (1843) being the most famous of these. *Novel*-length ghost stories are rare, an exception being *Susan Hill's* THE WOMAN IN BLACK. See also *gothic novel.*

ghost-writer: a professional writer who does most or all of the writing for a celebrity who then usually takes the credit for her or his *'autobiography'*.

Gibbons, Stella (1902–89): novelist and *short-story* writer. Most of her output was sentimental social comedies, but COLD COMFORT FARM (1932) is a very successful *parody* of the kind of popular rural *fiction* written by *Webb*. See also *rural novel.*

Ginsberg, Allen (b.1926): American poet. Influenced, among others, by *William Carlos Williams*, especially in his precise, short lyrics and use of *free verse*. A relentless critic of middle-class American values, in the 1960s he protested against the Vietnam War and was a leading light in the 'flower power' movement, a phrase of his own coining. Notable works include HOWL AND OTHER POEMS (1956), KADDISH AND OTHER POEMS (1961).

Globe Theatre, the: the famous Bankside theatre, near to the *Rose Theatre* and the River Thames, for which *Shakespeare* wrote many of his plays. Built in 1599, it was rebuilt after a fire in 1613, and dismantled in 1644 after all the theatres were closed. It has now been reconstructed near to the old site; meaning that it is once again possible to see in Southwark, London, the plays of Shakespeare and his contemporaries performed in the theatrical circumstances for which they were written.

glossary: a list of explanations of difficult words in a *text.*

Glück, Louise (b.1943): American poet. Influenced by *Plath*, she often treats autobiographical experience with intensity yet objectiveness. Notable works include THE TRIUMPH OF ACHILLES (1985).

Godwin, William (1756–1836): novelist, philosopher and biographer. A radical, almost anarchic, thinker in the Age of Reason, admired by *Coleridge* and *Wordsworth*, he became an atheist and believed that humans were rational beings capable of continually improving themselves and thus in no need of institutions or laws. By the 1820s his radicalism had dimmed and he became anti-reform. Notable works include ENQUIRY CONCERNING POLITICAL JUSTICE (1793), CALEB WILLIAMS (1794).

Golding, William (1911–93): novelist, essayist, playwright and poet, his reputation rests on the former of these. His work is often centred upon the darker impulses at the core of human existence. Notable works include LORD OF THE FLIES (1954), THE SPIRE (1964), RITES OF PASSAGE (1980).

Goldsmith, Oliver (?1730–74): playwright, poet, novelist and essayist. Dismissed by some at the time and ever since as light-weight, his most inventive work has nonetheless endured. He is difficult to classify as he could write on a variety of subjects and in a diversity of *manner*s, and thus perhaps it is unsurprising that best known works are in different *genre*s: a *novel*, a *poem* and a play, respectively THE VICAR OF WAKEFIELD (1776), 'The Deserted Village' (1770), SHE STOOPS TO CONQUER (1773). Other notable works include THE GOOD NATUR'D MAN (1768).

Goodison, Lorna (b.1947): Jamaican poet and *short-story* writer. She combines the Jamaican oral tradition with conventional poetic *form*s, and uses powerful *imagery* (influenced by her painting) to depict *viewpoint*s of Jamaican women. Notable works include TAMARIND SEASON (1980), I AM BECOMING MY MOTHER (1986), HEARTEASE (1988), TO US ALL FLOWERS ARE ROSES (1990).

Gordimer, Nadine (b.1923): South African novelist and *short-story* writer. Much of her work reflects her interest in politics and her stand against apartheid and censorship and, more recently, the time leading up to the democratic elections in her country. Notable works include THE SOFT VOICE OF THE SERPENT (1953), FRIDAY'S FOOTPRINT (1960), A GUEST OF HONOUR (1970), THE CONSERVATIONIST (1974), BURGER'S DAUGHTER (1979), JULY'S PEOPLE (1981), MY SON'S STORY (1910), NONE TO ACCOMPANY ME (1994).

Gosse, Edmund (1849–1928): prolific biographer, essayist, translator and poet. He helped to establish the reputation of *Ibsen* in Britain. Notable works include the autobiographical FATHER AND SON (1907).

gothic novel/fiction/romance refers to *literature* which deals with the passionate, mysterious, horrific and/or the supernatural, often in a medieval *setting* and especially popular between the 1760s and 1820s. The word 'Gothic' is derived from the Germanic tribe, the Goths, but came to denote the flying buttresses and pointed windows, arches and vaulting of medieval architecture. *Walpole*'s THE CASTLE OF OTRANTO is generally considered the earliest in the *genre*, and is sub-titled A GOTHIC STORY on account of its medieval setting. Other notable examples include THE MYSTERIES OF UDOLPHO (1794) by Ann Radcliffe (1764–1823), *M.G. Lewis'* THE MONK, *Beckford's* VATHEK and *Mary Shelley's* FRANKENSTEIN. *Austen* pokes fun at the genre in NORTHANGER ABBEY (written 1798, published 1818), as does *Peacock* in NIGHTMARE ABBEY. Later *novel*s with Gothic elements include *Emily Brontë's* WUTHERING HEIGHTS, *Charlotte Brontë's* JANE EYRE, *Dickens'* GREAT EXPECTATIONS, the stories of *Poe, Faulkner, Dineson, Mervyn Peake* (1911–1968) and *Carter*. See also *ghost story*.

Gower, John (?1330–1408): poet who was much admired in the 15th century and sometimes regarded, along with *Chaucer, Langland, Lydgate*, as a founding father of English *poetry*. As with others, he was concerned with the corruption of the times. Notable works include CONFESSIO AMANTIS (1386–93) which contains many *courtly love* stories, one used by *Shakespeare* as a basis for PERICLES (?1607) where Gower appears in the *character* of the Chorus.

Granville-Barker, Harley (1877–1946): playwright and literary critic. He deals with political and social issues which at the time were rarely dealt with on stage, and some of his contemporaries regarded his work as too intellectual and untheatrical. On the other hand *Shaw*, in whose plays Granville-Barker acted, admired him. Notable works include THE VOISEY INHERITANCE (1905), WASTE (1907), THE MADRAS HOUSE (1910).

Graves, Robert (1895–1985): poet, novelist, literary critic and translator. Early *poems* predominately concern his experiences in the First World War. A dissident in many respects, he is noted for his *love poems* and use of plain language within traditional *verse* forms. He often drew upon classical culture and *myth* for inspiration. Notable works include GOODBYE TO ALL THAT (1929), I, CLAUDIUS (1934), THE GREEK MYTHS (1955).

graveyard school of poetry refers to certain 18th century poets who wrote reflectively about mortality and death, e.g. THE GRAVE (1743) by Robert Blair (1699–1746). For a time this vogue was moderately fashionable. See also *black comedy, sick verse*.

Gray, Thomas (1716–71): poet. Friends, among others, with *Smart* and *Walpole*, he represents part of a movement away from the *neo-classical* and towards the *picturesque* which was accelerated by his visit to the Lake District as recorded in his JOURNAL (1775). His *verse* is characteristically polished, precise and readable. Notable works include the *mock-heroic* 'Ode on the Death of a Favorite Cat, Drowned in a Tub of Gold Fishes' (1748), 'Elegy Written in a Country Churchyard' (1751), which owes something to the *graveyard school of poetry*, 'The Progress of Poetry' (1757), 'The Bard' (1757), POEMS (1868).

Great Chain of Being: this refers to the notion, popular from ancient times and still current during the *Renaissance*, that all life makes up a hierarchical chain from God at the top down to the lowest life form on earth at the bottom. This kind of ordering is expressed in such as Ulysses' speech on 'degree' in Act I, Scene 3 of *Shakespeare*'s TROILUS AND CRESSIDA (?1602) and Epistle 1 Section 8 of *Pope*'s ESSAY ON MAN (1732–4).

Great Tradition, The refers to the five novelists (*Austen, George Eliot, Henry James, Conrad, Lawrence*) upon which *Leavis* based his Cambridge University course. See *leavisite*.

Greene, Graham (1904–1991): novelist, playwright, *short-story* and travel writer, and essayist. His writings often show characters in run-down or out-of-the-way places in various parts of the world who are presented with a moral dilemma involving a sense of failure and/or guilt. Notable works include BRIGHTON ROCK (1938), THE POWER AND THE GLORY (1940), THE HEART OF THE MATTER (1948), THE THIRD MAN (1950), THE QUIET AMERICAN (1955), OUR MAN IN HAVANA (1958), TRAVELS WITH MY AUNT (1969), THE HONORARY CONSUL (1973), THE LAST WORD (1990).

Greene, Robert (?1558–92): playwright, prose-writer and pamphleteer, he was associated with the *University Wits* and led a dissipated life, dying in poverty. Notable works include FRIER BACON AND FRIER BONGAY (?1589), THE ART OF CONEY-CATCHING (1591), GREENE'S GROATSWORTH OF WIT (1592), containing his attack upon that 'upstart crow' *Shakespeare*, who later based THE WINTER'S TALE (?1611) on Greene's *prose* romance PANDOSTO (1588).

Griffiths, Trevor (b.1935): playwright and television *dramatist*. His early work often adopts a Marxist standpoint and contains elements of political debate between the characters. Notable works include COMEDIANS (1975), BILL BRAND (1976), THE PARTY (1983).

grotesque is a term which denotes the bizarre, macabre, exaggerated, *fantastic*, aberrant, unpleasant, sick and/or pornographic in any art *form*. Writers in English who have employed elements of the *grotesque* include *Webster, Tourneur, Jonathan Swift, Smollett, Byron, Poe, Dickens, Robert Browning, Beckett, Waugh.*

Gunn, Thom (b.1929): Anglo-American poet. Influenced by 16th and 17th century *poetry* and identified with *The Movement*, his early work is noted for its disciplined use of conventional *form*s and objective view of its subject matter. Over the years he has developed his technical and thematic range, and later *verse* has become more flexible. He was drawn into the Californian 'alternative culture' of the late 1960s. Notable works include FIGHTING TERMS (1954), JACK STRAW'S CASTLE (1875), COLLECTED POEMS (1994).

Gurney Ivor (1890–1937): poet who also composed and sometimes set his work to music. Influenced by *Hopkins, Whitman* and *Edward Thomas*, he writes of rural Gloucestershire and of trench life during the First World War, when he was wounded and gassed, and which he deals with objectively but with a remarkable lyricism. Committed to a mental institution from 1922 until his death, his *poetry* can be uneven, but does not often show signs of his instability. Notable works include SEVEN AND SOMME (1917), WARS EMBERS (1919), COLLECTED POEMS (1982, ed. P.J. Kavanagh).

Guterson, David (b.1956): American *short-story* writer and novelist. Influenced by the Pacific North-west, where he grew up, his writing sometimes presents moral questions for reflection. Notable works include SNOW FALLING ON CEDARS (1995), THE COUNTRY AHEAD OF US, THE COUNTRY BEHIND (1996).

haiku: a Japanese verse *form* comprising a single three-line *stanza* of seventeen sylla-bles, the lines containing five, seven and five syllables respectively. Designed in its brevity to capture the essence of the poet's mood towards an idea, object, season or scene, a haiku can lose its concision in translation as it is difficult to replicate fully the poet's intention. The form interested the *Imagists,* e.g. in *Pound*'s 'In a Station of the Metro from Personae' (1909). Among others *Frost* and *Yeats* were also influenced by the haiku.

half-rhyme, sometimes called 'near', 'imperfect' or partial *rhyme,* or pararhyme, occurs when two words rhyme, but not perfectly. Its effect can be gentler and more subtle in pattern than a full rhyme. For example:

> Move him into the sun –
> Gently its touch awoke him once,
> At home, whispering of fields unsown,
> Always it woke him, even in France…

> (from Owen's 'Futility')

Here 'sun/unsown' and 'once/France' are half-rhymes. See *consonance.*

hamartia is an error of judgement which leads to the downfall of a tragic hero. In his POETICS *Aristotle* says that hamartia is not a moral failing: for instance, Oedipus kills his father on impulse and marries his mother through ignorance. It is close to, but not quite the same as, a tragic flaw (see *Bradley A.C.*).

Harbage, Alfred (1901–76): American scholar and literary critic, he specialised in Shakespearean research. Notable works include SHAKESPEARE'S AUDIENCE (1941).

hard ending: see *masculine ending.*

Hardy, Thomas (1840–1920): novelist, poet, *short-story* writer and *dramatist.* Broadly speaking he devoted the first part of his creative life to writing the *novel*s for which he is best known, the second part to *poetry* which he regarded, as do many critics, as his most important contribution to literature. He placed his novels into three cate-gories:

- novels of character and environment, e.g. THE MAYOR OF CASTERBRIDGE (1886)
- *romances and fantasies,* e.g. THE TRUMPET MAJOR (1880)
- *novels of ingenuity* e.g. A LAODICEAN (1881).

His predominant *theme* tends to be the struggle of men and women in the face of an ironic fate. He locates many of his novels in a region he calls Wessex which, roughly speaking, extends from the counties of Oxfordshire and Hampshire westward down to Cornwall (see also *regional novel*). His poetry may in some senses be seen as early *modernist* in its challenging of contemporary Victorian *convention.* He claimed that he wrote 'for poetic *texture* rather than poetic veneer', and his strong *imagery* stemmed from his passion and consideration of the natural world. Other notable works include FAR FROM THE MADDING CROWD (1874), THE RETURN OF THE NATIVE (1878),

THE WOODLANDERS (1887), TESS OF THE D'URBERVILLES (1891), LIFE'S LITTLE IRONIES (1894), JUDE THE OBSCURE (1895), WESSEX POEMS (1898), THE DYNASTS (1904–1908), SATIRES OF CIRCUMSTANCE (1914).

Hare, David (b.1947): playwright, television and cinema scriptwriter. Many of his plays concern such matters as the greed and corruption which he sees as having characterised British society in the second half of the 20th century. Notable works include BRASSNECK (1973, with *Brenton*), KNUCKLE (1974), TEETH 'N' SMILES (1975), FANSHEN (1975), PLENTY (1978), LICKING HITLER (1978), MAP OF THE WORLD (1982), PRAVDA (1985, with *Brenton*), RACING DEMON (1990), SKYLIGHT (1995).

Harlem Rennaissance is a term applied to the emergence of the first definable generation of black American writers in the 1920s and 1930s. They began to promote black consciousness and established a body of published black writings, mindful, among other things, of their African heritage. Leading writers include *Du Bois, Langston Hughes, Hurston.*

Harrison, Tony (b.1937): poet, translator and playwright. His *poetry* sometimes reflects his wide travels and is usually politically committed, and often uses tightly-controlled elements of colloquial speech and skilful rhyming. Notable works include THE LOINERS (1970), THE SCHOOL OF ELOQUENCE AND OTHER POEMS, a translation of Molière's THE MISANTHROPE (1973), V (1985), A COLD COMING: GULF WAR POEMS (1992), THE GAZE OF THE GORGON (1992).

Harte, Bret (1836–1902): American *short-story, verse* writer, novelist and playwright, he is mainly noted for his neatly structured short *tal*es. A friend of *Twain*, his notable works include THE LUCK OF ROARING CAMP AND OTHER SKETCHES (1870), MRS SKAGG'S HUSBANDS (1873).

Hartley, L.P. (1895–1972): novelist, *short-story* writer, literary critic and essayist. Influenced by *Henry James* and Sigmund Freud (1856–1939), frequent *theme*s in his writings, which show a strong moral concern, are of childhood memories and the search for personal identity. Notable works include EUSTACE AND HILDA (1947), THE GO-BETWEEN (1953).

Harwood, Gwen (1920–95): Australian poet who often conveys the anguish of life, yet has a fundamentally positive outlook. Her *lyric* poetry is markedly controlled. Notable works include POEMS (1963), LION'S BRIDE (1981), BONE SCAN (1990).

Harwood, Ronald (b.1934): South African playwright and novelist who is capable of transmitting ideas with convincing *realism*. Notable works include THE DRESSER (1980).

Hawthorne, Nathaniel (1804–64): American novelist, *short-story* and children's writer. Associated with the transcendentalists, his writing is often allegorical, exploring guilt, sin, redemptive dreams and other aspects of the American conscious and subconscious, and shows some fascination with the effects of Puritanism on the morality of New Englanders. Notable works include TWICE-TOLD TALES (1837–42), THE SCARLET LETTER (1850), THE HOUSE OF THE SEVEN GABLES (1851), TANGLEWOOD TALES (1852–3).

Hazlitt, William (1778–1830): essayist, literary critic and theatre critic. His *prose* is highly thought of in his writings on contemporary authors, politics and Elizabethan playwrights. He is a fine critic of the early Romantics. Notable works include AN ESSAY ON THE PRINCIPLES OF HUMAN ACTION (1805), LECTURES ON ENGLISH POETS (1818), THE SPIRIT OF THE AGE (1825), THE PLAIN SPEAKER (1826).

Head, Bessie (1937–86): South African novelist. She writes about experiences of exile together with the problems created by racism, town and rural values, male domination and tribal partisanship. Notable works include WHEN THE RAIN CLOUDS GATHER (1968).

headless line: an *iambic* verse line whose first syllable is missing, thus creating an initial *foot* containing a single stressed syllable.

> I'm / a méans, / a stáge, / aców / in hálf
>
> (from *Plath*'s 'Metaphors' 1965)

Heaney, Seamus (b.1939): Irish poet and critic. In his *poetry* he draws on his childhood experiences of life on an Irish farm and on many other aspects of Irish life. As the situation in Northern Ireland deteriorated during the 1970s his writing becomes more political. He is usually economic with words, and he has a facility for striking *metaphors*. Notable works include DEATH OF A NATURALIST (1966), NORTH (1975), THE GOVERNMENT OF THE TONGUE AND OTHER CRITICAL WRITINGS (1988), COLLECTED POEMS 1966–96 (1999), BEOWULF (1999, translation), ELECTRIC LIGHT (2001).

Heller, Joseph (1923–99): American novelist, *short-story* writer and playwright. His best-known *novel* CATCH-22 (1961) is a zany *satire* on the folly and turmoil of war which drew on his air force experiences in the Second World War. Other notable works include GOOD AS GOLD (1979).

Hemingway, Ernest (1899–1961): American novelist and *short-story* writer. Influenced by such writers as *Pound* and *Ford Madox Ford*, his prose *style* became famous for its laconic, 'tough guy', terseness, which matched his often very masculine subject-matter such as big game hunting and bull fighting. His work reflected mid-20th century disillusion and enjoyed a popular and critical acclaim which has since waned. Notable works include IN OUR TIME (1925), A FAREWELL TO ARMS (1929), FOR WHOM THE BELL TOLLS (1940), THE OLD MAN AND THE SEA (1952).

hendecasyllable: a *verse* line of eleven syllables, e.g.

> To be, or not to be: that is the question
>
> (from Act III of *Shakespeare*'s Hamlet)

See also *metre*.

hendiadys is a figure of speech whereby two nouns are brought together to express one idea, e.g. 'life and soul', 'doom and gloom'.

Henri, Adrian (b.1932): one of the *Liverpool Poets* of the 1960s and 1970s. Influenced by pop, rock and jazz music, and by the methods of poets such as *Burroughs*, his *poetry*, often impressionistic or surreal, is very varied in style and theme. Notable works include COLLECTED POEMS (1986), NOT FADING AWAY: POEMS 1989–1994 (1994).

Henry, O. (1862–1910): American *short-story* writer, he is a master of surprise, often introducing ironic twists at the end of his tales. Notable works include CABBAGES AND KINGS (1904), THE TRIMMED LAMP (1907).

Henryson, Robert (?1424–?1508): Scottish poet. Almost nothing is known of his life. Sometimes classified with *Dunbar* in a group known as Scottish Chaucerians, he wrote pastorals and allegories, his *tone* often strictly moral yet compassionate. Notable works include THE TESTAMENT OF CRESSEID (?) written as a sequel to *Chaucer*'s TROILUS AND CRISEYDE, ROBENE AND MAKYNE (?), MORALL FABILLIS OF ESOPE (?).

Henslowe, Philip (?1557–1616): theatre manager. In 1587 he built the *Rose Theatre* on *Bankside*, and was also involved in the Hope and Fortune theatres. He successfully ran *The Admiral's Men* and other acting companies. Many playwrights wrote for him, but not *Shakespeare* (despite what the film SHAKESPEARE IN LOVE would have us believe!). His diaries are an invaluable source of information about the Elizabethan theatrical life.

heptameter: see *foot*.

heptastich: a seven-line *stanza* used by many English poets, e.g. *Chaucer, Spenser, Shelley, Robert Browning, Longfellow, Auden*.

heptasyllable: a *verse* line of seven syllables, e.g.

> Through the forest have I gone
>> (from Act II scene 2 of *Shakespeare*'s A MIDSUMMER NIGHT'S DREAM)

See also *metre*.

Herbert, George (1593–1633): *metaphysical* poet whose works were often brief but distinguished by their careful construction, ingenious *conceit*s and deep religious faith. Notable works include THE TEMPLE: SACRED POEMS AND PRIVATE EJACULATIONS (1633). See also *concrete poetry*.

hermeneutics, originally applied to interpreting the *Bible*, now refers in general to the study of the *interpretation* of *text*s. See *code*.

hero/heroine: the leading *character* or *protagonist* in a story. Although, strictly speaking, in literary criticism it does not matter if s/he is good or bad (therefore Macbeth may be described as the hero), in this kind of case it has become the practice to refer to the *anti-hero*.

heroic couplets: pairs of rhyming *iambic pentameters*. *Chaucer* first made extensive use of them (they are sometimes known as 'riding *rhyme*', possibly because Chaucer's pilgrims tell their stories in this *metre* as they ride towards the shrine of St Thomas à Becket in THE CANTERBURY TALES). Many poets have employed them through the centuries. *Dryden* used them with skill (e.g. in MAC FLECKNOE), helping to make them popular in the *Neo-classical Period*. *Pope* excelled in their use, and *Crabbe* frequently employed them, e.g.

> Old Peter Grimes made fishing his employ
> His wife he cabined with him and his boy,
>> (the opening of 'The Borough')

See also *metre*.

heroic drama/tragedy: a term applied to a kind of *drama* popular during the *Restoration Period* and influenced by French classical drama. In the preface to his heroic tragedy THE CONQUEST OF GRANADA (1672) *Dryden* states that 'an heroic play ought to be an imitation, in little, of an heroic poem; and consequently… love and valour ought to be the subject of it.' This play, together with his ALL FOR LOVE and *Otway*'s VENICE PRESERVED, are the best of this type, but many were overblown *bombast*, satirised by *Fielding* in TOM THUMB (1731) and *Sheridan* in THE CRITIC (1779). See *Restoration tragedy*.

heroic poetry: another term for *epic* poetry.

heroic quatrain: a set of four *iambic pentameters* rhyming abab, e.g. in *Gray*'s 'Elegy Written in a Country Churchyard'.

Herrick, Robert (1591–1674): poet. Associated with *Jonson* and in some respects a *Cavalier* poet, *Swinburne* called him 'the greatest song-writer ever born of English race'. His versatility enabled him to write in a variety of *form*s, among them *epigram*, *song*, hymn, *elegy*, epitaph, *love poetry* (sometimes sensuously erotic) and, above all, *lyric* poems at which he was a master craftsman. Notable works include HESPERIDES (1648), NOBLE NUMBERS (1660). See also *carpe diem*.

hexameter: see *metre*.

hexastich: a six-line *stanza*.

high comedy is a term sometimes applied to *witty*, sophisticated *comedy* such as *Shakespeare*'s MUCH ADO ABOUT NOTHING, *Congreve*'s THE WAY OF THE WORLD, *Wilde*'s A WOMAN OF NO IMPORTANCE. The term can also be applied to *novel*s, e.g. *Austen*'s PRIDE AND PREJUDICE, or *poem*s, e.g. *Pope*'s 'The Rape of the Lock'. See *low comedy*, *comedy*.

Highsmith, Patricia (1921–95): American novelist and *short-story* writer. One of the most highly acclaimed *crime novel* writers of our time, best known for her Tom Ripley *novel*s, an interesting feature of which is the *narrative voice*: although writing in third person *narrative*, Highsmith leads the reader into seeing the world through the eyes of her amoral, psychopathic anti-hero. Notable works include STRANGERS ON A TRAIN (1950), THE TALENTED MR RIPLEY (1955), DEEP WATER (1957), THE STORYTELLER (1965), RIPLEY'S GAME (1974), EDITH'S DIARY (1977), PEOPLE WHO KNOCK ON THE DOOR (1983), THE SNAIL WATCHER AND OTHER STORIES (1983), THE BLACK HOUSE (1981).

Hill, Geoffrey (b.1932): poet and critic. Initially influenced by, among others, *Blake* and *Housman*, religious and historical *theme*s and *setting*s predominate in his richly textured *verse*. Notable works include FOR THE UNFALLEN (1959), KING LOG (1968), MERCIAN HYMNS (1971), TENEBRAE (1979), THE MYSTERY OF THE CHARITY OF CHARLES PEGUY (1983), ENEMY'S COUNTRY: WORDS, CONTEXTURES AND OTHER CRITICISMS OF LANGUAGE (1991), COLLECTED POEMS (1994).

Hill, Susan (b 1942): novelist, *short-story* and children's writer, playwright and auto-biographer. She can generate considerable atmosphere in her writing, which often shows acute psychological insight into loneliness. Notable works include GENTLEMEN AND LADIES (1968), I'M THE KING OF THE CASTLE (1970), THE BIRD OF NIGHT (1972), THE WOMAN IN BLACK (1983).

historical novel: a kind of *faction* in which historical events are used as the basis for a fictional story. Much *gothic fiction* was set in the Middle Ages, and then *Walter Scott* wrote the first of many of his historical novels with WAVERLEY (1814), since when the *genre* has remained popular. Notable among such works are *Thackeray*'s VANITY FAIR, *Dickens*' A TALE OF TWO CITIES (1859), *George Eliot*'s ROMOLA (1863), *Graves'* I, CLAUDIUS, GONE WITH THE WIND (1936) by Margaret Mitchell (1900–49), THE KING MUST DIE (1958) by Mary Renault (1905–83), *Farrell*'s THE SIEGE OF KRISHNAPUR, *Golding*'s RITES OF PASSAGE.

historicism/new historicism: the critical view that all literature must be studied with regard to the historical context within which it was produced, an approach which reacts against that of the *New Critics*, and conflicts with some aspects of *structuralism* and *deconstruction*. See *extrinsic approach*.

history play: broadly speaking, any play set in a historical period, although the term is often used to refer to the *chronicle play*s written by *Shakespeare* and his contemporaries.

Hoffman, Eva (b.1945): Polish-Canadian writer, journalist and editor. As a Jewish displaced person her concerns include coming to grips with a different culture and language. Notable works include LOST IN TRANSLATION: A LIFE IN A NEW LANGUAGE (1989), EXIT INTO HISTORY (1993), SHTETL (1997).

Holtby, Winifred (1898–1935): novelist, journalist, literary critic and *short-story* writer. Interested in pacifism, feminism and racial tolerance, she is at her best depicting the doings of local communities within the *setting* of her native East Yorkshire. Her friend *Brittain* wrote much about her in TESTAMENT OF YOUTH. Notable works include ANDERBY WOLD (1923), THE LAND OF GREEN GINGER (1927), SOUTH RIDING(1936). See also *regional novel*.

Homer: the name given to the supposed ancient Greek author(s) of two *epics*, THE ILIAD and THE ODYSSEY. Nothing is known about him/them (or her – research by the 19th century *Samuel Butler* led him to believe that the author was female). These *poem*s were central to the culture of ancient Greece, and their impact and influence has survived through all ages to the present day.

Hopkins, Gerard Manley (1844–89): poet. His early *poetry* is noted for its sensuous detail, and all his output is marked by sensitivity to aural and rhythmical effects. He coined the terms *inscape, instress* and *sprung rhythm* which are important in understanding his *verse*. He converted to Roman Catholicism and then became a Jesuit, never managing to reconcile service to God with writing *poetry*. Notable works include 'The Wreck of the Deutschland' (1875), POEMS (published 1918, containing among others 'The Windhover', 'Spring', 'Pied Beauty', 'Binsey Poplars').

Horation ode: an *ode* written in the *style* of the Roman poet Horace (65–8BC).

Hospital, Janette Turner (b.1942): Australian/Canadian novelist and *short-story* and *detective fiction* writer. In some respects a *post-modernist*, she locates her stories in various places around the world, and her subjects often include dislocated wanderers. Notable works include TIGER IN THE TIGER PIT (1983), DISLOCATIONS (1986).

Housman, A.E. (1859–1936): poet and literary critic. His love of an idealised English countryside mellowed by a dark nostalgia made his work very popular around the time of the First World War. Notable works include A SHROPSHIRE LAD (1896), LAST POEMS (1922).

Hove, Chenjerai (b.1956): Zimbabwean poet and novelist. His writing explores the Zimbabwean situation during the war of liberation, and pre- and post-independence. Notable works include BONES (1988).

hovering stress/accent occurs in *poetry* when it is unclear whether or not a syllable should be stressed.

Howard, Henry: see *Surrey*.

Howells, William Dean (1837–1920): American novelist, critic, editor, *dramatist,* travel and *prose* writer. A friend of *Henry James,* he wrote many *romances,* but later work moves towards *realism* and a concern for social issues. Notable works include A MODERN INSTANCE (1882), THE RISE OF SILAS LAPHAM (1885), INDIAN SUMMER (1886), A HAZARD OF NEW FORTUNES (1890).

hubris: a weakness in a Greek tragic hero which means he fails to take notice of the warnings of the Gods and disobeys their laws. This leads to his downfall and *nemesis,* e.g. Oedipus in *Sophocles'* OEDIPUS THE KING, Creon in his ANTIGONE, Pentheus in *Euripedes'* THE BACCHAE (5th century B.C.). See also *tragedy, tragic flaw.*

Hughes, Langston (1902–67): Black American novelist, *short-story* writer, poet, journalist and playwright. An important figure in the *Harlem Renaissance,* he often uses jazz rhythms to explore black consciousness and became known as the Negro Poet Laureate. He can be a shrewd observer of black/white relationships. Notable works include NOT WITHOUT LAUGHTER (1930), THE WAYS OF WHITE FOLKS (1933), SHAKESPEARE IN HARLEM (1942), BLACK NATIVITY (1961).

Hughes, Richard (1900–76): novelist, playwright and poet. His themes include the extreme severity of nature, and the ways in which apparent innocence is disturbed, and sometimes destroyed, by violent events. Notable works include A HIGH WIND IN JAMAICA (1929, published in America as THE INNOCENT VOYAGE), A FOX IN THE ATTIC (1961).

Hughes, Ted (1930–98): poet, children's writer, critic, translator and editor. His *poetry* often concerns nature and harsh, disturbing, violent and highly imaginative aspects of the animal world, but emphasises the necessity of struggling to endure in the face of adversity. Some of his work may be classed as *topographical poetry,* drawing on his native Pennines and adopted Devon. His *style* has been regarded as influenced by *Hopkins* and *Lawrence.* He was *poet laureate* from 1984–98. Notable works include THE HAWK IN THE RAIN (1957), LUPERCAL (1960), WODWO (1967), CROW (1970), CAVE BIRDS (1978), NEW SELECTED POEMS 1957–1994 (1995).

Hulme, Keri (b.1947): New Zealand novelist, *short-story* writer and poet who is of mixed English, Maori and Scots ancestry and who draws on a wide range of approaches and techniques in her writing. Notable works include THE BONE PEOPLE (1984), THE WINDEATER/TEKAIHAU (1985).

humanism/humanist: these terms, in a literary sense, are most often used to apply to the moral and philosophical ideas (that is, 'humanities' as opposed to 'sciences') of *Renaissance* writers and thinkers such as Erasmus (1456–1536), *More, Sidney, Spenser* and, later, *Milton.* Classical and Christian ideas were blended, placing at the centre of thinking the achievements, dignity and positive aspects of human beings in this world, rather than their innate corruption and the spiritual afterlife.

The attitude may be typified by the Prince's speech beginning 'What a piece of work is man. How noble in reason, how excellent in faculty...' in Act II, Scene 2 of *Shakespeare*'s HAMLET. Later on these terms came to refer to the ideas of those such as *Johnson* and *Arnold* who advocated a liberal philosophy of mankind, adopting in general the views of *Renaissance* humanists. During the 20th century the terms began to denote a non-religious, even anti-religious, moral philosophy of the kind which *Marxists* consider feebly liberal and bourgeois.

humour, in a literary sense, has since the 18th century tended to indicate that which gives rise to laughter, as distinct from *wit*, which has a more intellectual appeal.

humours: a theory current from ancient times until the 17th century held that people's physiology was composed of four liquids, or 'humours', which determined their character. These were black bile, blood, choler and phlegm; excess of any one of these led respectively to a temperament which was melancholic, sanguine, choleric, or phlegmatic. When Duke Ferdinand in *Shakespeare*'s As YOU LIKE IT is described as 'humorous' it means not that he is funny, but that his humours are out of balance, and thus that he is dangerously 'ill-humoured'. Robert Burton (1577–1640) describes the qualities of the different humours in his ANATOMY OF MELANCHOLY (1621). See also *comedy of humours*.

Hunt, Leigh (1784–1859): poet, journalist, critic, essayist and autobiographer. Among his friends he counted *Byron, Lamb* and *Keats*. In THE EXAMINER, his radical weekly *journal*, he printed works by *Shelley, Keats*, other Romantics, and also *Tennyson*, all of whom owed Hunt much for his support. Notable works include BOOK OF GEMS (1838), POETICAL WORKS (1844), TABLE TALK (1851).

Hurston, Zora Neale (c.1891–1960): Black American novelist, *short-story* writer and essayist. Associated with *Langston Hughes* she writes, among other things, about the black experience and that of black women in particular. Notable works include THEIR EYES WERE WATCHING GOD (1937), SPUNK (1984), THE COMPLETE STORIES (1995).

Huxley, Aldous (1894–1963): novelist, *short-story* writer, journalist and poet. Several of his *novels* challenge the accepted notions of his time through sharp, sometimes bleak, *satire* on the state of contemporary humanity, and BRAVE NEW WORLD (1932), his best known work, portrays a *dystopia* which can be read as a stark warning. Religious mysticism and the use and abuse of drugs are other interests which feature in his fictional and non-fictional writings. Other notable works include CHROME YELLOW (1921), POINT COUNTER (1928), EYELESS IN GAZA (1936), THE DEVILS OF LOUDUN (1952), ISLAND (1962).

hypallage: another term for *transferred epithet*.

hyperbaton: a technical term for the reversal of usual word order for poetic effect, e.g. In Surrey's sonnet 'Complaint by Night of the Lover not Beloved' he writes 'Calm is the sea' rather than 'The sea is calm', breaking the *metre* and throwing a *trochaic stress* on 'Càlm' in order to emphasise the calmness of the sea in contrast to the disturbance of his mind. See also *anastrophe, inversion*.

hyperbole: a literary word for 'exaggeration'. Common in everyday speech ('I've told you a million times') and literature, e.g.

Will all great Neptune's ocean wash this blood
Clean from my hand? No, this my hand will rather
The multitudinous sea incarnadine
Making the green one red.

(from Act II, Scene 2 of Shakespeare's M<small>ACBETH</small>)

The opposite of hyperbole is *litotes.*

iamb: a single *iambic* foot. See *metre*.

iambic: see *metre*, also *hexameter, tetrameter, trimeter.*

iambic pentameter: the most common rhythmical pattern in English, and the *metre* in which *Shakespeare* and his contemporaries wrote the vast majority of their plays. Playwrights found the *iambic* rhythm sufficiently akin to the *rhythm*s of English speech to sound natural yet at the same time providing musicality; and the five *foot* line carried a dignity and weight suitable for dramatic purpose. The development and refinement of its use can be traced from plays such as GORBODUC by *Norton* and *Sackville*, through *Marlowe* (who is credited by some commentators as perfecting the *form, Jonson* calling the iambic pentameter 'Marlowe's mighty line') to Shakespeare.

Ibsen, Henrik (1828–1906): Norwegian playwright who is generally regarded as the founder of modern *prose* drama. His work has been much translated into English and among other things, his *realism*, exploration of the unconscious mind, concern for human rights and the tragedies of ordinary people, and innovative staging have made him a very important influence upon the English-speaking theatre. Notable works include PEER GYNT (1867), AN ENEMY OF THE PEOPLE (1882), THE WILD DUCK (1885), THE DOLL'S HOUSE (1889), GHOSTS (1889), HEDDER GABLER (1890), THE MASTER BUILDER (1894), JOHN GABRIEL BORKMAN (1896).

identical rhyme: the use of the same word as a *rhyme* in order to create emphasis, e.g.

> All close they met again, before the dusk
> Had taken from the stars its pleasant veil
> All close they met, all eves, before the dusk
> Had taken from the stars its pleasant veil…

> (from *Keat*'s 'Isabella')

idyll: a poem with usually a peaceful, happy *pastoral* setting (hence the adjective 'idyllic'). *Tennyson*'s THE IDYLLS OF THE KING are stories of *Arthurian* romance.

imagery is, strictly speaking, a picture in the mind which arises through the use of words. However, the literary term is extended to cover language which gives rise to any of the five senses – hearing, touch, taste and smell, as well as sight. Imagery may be evoked by a direct description, or by *figurative language*. If asked to discuss imagery in an examination a candidate should be careful not merely to consider the images in themselves, but to view them in the *context* of the writer's purpose within the *text* as a whole.

imagination: the mental faculty which creates objects, *character*s, *scene*s and all things not actually visible and present. *Coleridge*, who used the word Romantic to mean 'imaginative', considered that imagination was the key element in the creative process, and one which underlies and harmonises literary and all other artistic creation.

Imagists: a group of early 20th century poets whose leading light was *Pound*. They aimed to use *free verse* in order exactly to depict subjects drawn from all areas of life.

Imbuga, Francis (b.?1945): Kenyan playwright and novelist. His plays are interesting for their portrayal of leadership figures, and he has said that he is glad to have seen theatre 'bring hope and courage to those who had participated in it', and to see theatre 'take up issues of social misbehaviour, political oppression, religious bigotry, [and] betrayal at all levels.' Notable works include THE BURNING OF RAGS (1980), BETRAYAL IN THE CITY (1987), AMINATE: A PLAY (1988).

imitation carries four broad senses:

- a re-creation of the *style, tone* or subject-matter of another writer, such as *Pope's* IMITATIONS OF HORACE (1733–8) or *Lowell's* IMITATIONS (1961)
- the notion that all art should imitate the standards of excellence achieved by previous 'masters'
- the notion that all art should imitate nature and human actions as exactly as possible (in his POETICS *Aristotle* calls this 'mimesis', that is, imitation)
- *plagiarism* of the literary work of others.

imperfect rhyme: see *half-rhyme.*

impersonal narrator: see *narrator.*

impersonality is the general belief that a writer's personality should in no way intrude into her/his work. The point is well expounded in *T.S. Eliot's essay* TRADITION AND THE INDIVIDUAL TALENT (1919).

implication is when words imply a meaning beyond their literal meaning.

implicit metaphor: a *metaphor* where the *tenor* is implied, e.g. in *Shakespeare's* 'Sonnet 18' where 'the eye of heaven' is understood to be the sun, but not explicitly stated.

implied author: the sense of the author's voice and presence which every reader has when reading a work.

implied reader: the 'ideal' of a reader for whom a writer constructs her or his *text* in anticipation of a specific reader response which is objective and free of the reader's own assumptions and prejudices. On the other hand there is the '*actual reader*', who inevitably brings to a text her or his own subjective experience, knowledge and prejudices.

impressionism is a term from art which describes paintings where the artist has used the effects of light to create a personal subjective view of the subject. The application of the term to literature is vague, but writing such as the *poetry* of *Wilde* and the *prose* of *Woolf* has been described as impressionist.

in media res means, in Latin, starting a *text* in the middle of the story and later going back to cover the early stages. This device was often used in *epic* poetry. See also *anachorism, analepsis, flashback, flashforward, prolepsis.*

incident: a single occurrence in the *action* of a play or the *plot* of a *story*, possibly the entire matter of a *short story.*

incremental repetition occurs when a line or *stanza* in a *ballad* is repeated as a *refrain* but slightly altered in order to advance the action or comment upon it. Popular in English and Scottish ballads.

index may refer to:

- a page-referenced alphabetical list of main items in a *text*, normally located at the end
- a list of texts or passages which were formerly forbidden reading for members of the Roman Catholic Church
- a category of *sign* in *semiotics*.

induction: another term for a *prologue*. See *Shakespeare*'s THE TAMING OF THE SHREW (?1594).

influence is the conscious or unconscious impact which previous or current cultures, and specifically writers, have upon the writer in question.

initiating action denotes the event or events which create tension and act as a trigger to the *plot*.

inscape and instress: respectively the unique spiritual shape of something which makes it beautiful to the beholder, and the internal tensions which create that image. Both of these difficult terms were invented by *Hopkins*.

inspiration: the notion that a helping spirit, either external or from within a person, gives to a writer the impetus to write. See *spontaneity*.

instress: see *inscape*.

intention: see *authorial intention*.

intentional fallacy: a term introduced by the *New Critics* to describe the mistaken belief, in their view, that what a writer explicitly or implicitly intended to convey when s/he wrote a *text* is important. They considered that the text itself, viewed objectively, is the only proper interest of the reader. See *authorial intention, death of the author*.

interior monologue is taken by some critics as meaning the same as *stream of consciousness*; but others see the term as an aspect of stream of consciousness whereby the *author* attempts to recreate with all its randomness the process of thought precisely as it occurs in a person's mind.

interlude: a short entertainment, often humorous and sometimes moral (see *Morality plays*) staged between the courses of a meal or the *acts* of a play, and popular in Tudor times, e.g. Thomas Heywood's THE PLAY OF THE WETHER (?1527). See *Medwall*.

internal evidence is the evidence within a *text* such as *diction, imagery*, spelling, *style*, topical references and so forth which help to date a work.

internal rhyme is rhyming within lines, e.g.

> I sift the snow on the mountains below,
>   And their great pines groan aghast;
> And all the night 'tis my pillow white,
>   While I sleep in the arms of the blast.

(from *Shelley*'s 'The Cloud', 1820)

See *rhyme*.

interpolation occurs when a section not by the writer has been inserted into the *text*. There are many claimed examples in *Elizabethan drama*, e.g. the comic *scenes* in

Marlowe's Doctor Faustus, the Hecate scene in *Shakespeare*'s Macbeth, a *song* in *Webster*'s The Duchess of Malfi.

interpretation is a term which covers the explaining, and different methods of explaining, literary *texts*. Traditional attitudes consider that it is possible to interpret texts in such as way that the puzzle of meaning is solved and the meaning arrived at. The *New Critics* reacted against this, *Macleish* declaring that a *poem* simply 'is', and that it does not 'mean'. Recent *literary theory* such as *structuralism, post-structuralism* and *deconstruction* hold that all interpretations are impossible – yet, paradoxically, these very theories are themselves interpretations. See *code, hermeneutics sign.*

intertextuality: the idea that *texts* do not exist in a literary vacuum, but that writers and readers are aware of the relationship between texts and that making comparisons between them can be illuminating. For instance, *Marvell* wrote 'The Definition of Love' (1681) in the light of *Donne*'s earlier 'A Valediction of Forbidding Mourning'; and *Day Lewis* wrote 'Song' (1935) as a *parody* of *Marlowe*'s 'A Passionate Shepherd to his Love', written almost four hundred years earlier, and possibly with 'The Nymph's Reply to the Shepherd' (1600) by Walter Raleigh (1552–1618) in mind (who himself was probably replying to Marlowe's *poem*). See *allusion.*

intrinsic attitude towards a *text,* sometimes called *formalism,* concentrates upon an objective scrutiny of *form, structure* and language; that is, upon the words on the page, regarding the text as standing alone and ignoring external and historical influences. Such an approach may be regarded as a relatively traditional way of viewing literature, and is fundamental to *I.A. Richard*'s method of *practical criticism.* See *close reading, leavisite.* By contrast, see *extrinsic attitude.*

intrusive narrator: see *narrator.*

invention, a term derived from *rhetoric*, refers to the *originality* of a work which may not rely on *imitation* or established *convention*. Inevitably innovative writers through the ages such as *Donne, Whitman, Joyce* and *Woolf* have created conventions which others have imitated.

inversion is a reversal of normal word order for impact, e.g. *Donne* quite often uses inversion in his *poetry* to draw attention to the words, as in

> She's all states, and all princes, I,
> Nothing else is.

> [from 'The Sun Rising', 1633)

See also *anastrophe, hyperbaton.*

invocation: an appeal to a god or muse for *inspiration,* usually by a poet, at the beginning of a work, e.g. *Milton*'s appeal to the Holy Spirit at the beginning of Paradise Lost. See also *apostrophe.*

involvement is a term used to indicate the emotional involvement in the subject matter of a piece of literature by either the writer or the reader. This may occur because the *character*s and circumstances of the *story* are close to those of the reader's or writer's own life. See *alienation, distance.*

Irish Revival, The: see *Celtic Renaissance/Revival/Twilight.*

irony is a term used to describe words which are charged with a layer of meaning different from the literal one, the subtler interpretation of which the hearer may or may not be aware. The least subtle *form* of irony is blatant sarcasm. Among many great writers who have made much use of irony in their writings are *Austen, Chaucer, Dryden, Fielding, Hardy, Henry James, Jonson, Milton, Pope, Shakespeare, Jonathan Swift, Waugh*, e.g.

> It is a truth universally acknowledged that a single man in possession of a good fortune must be in want of a wife.

> (from *Austen*'s PRIDE AND PREJUDICE)

The irony here is based on the assumption from a feminine *viewpoint* that such a man must wish to marry, the reader understanding that this 'truth' is by no means true. The 'truth' is that unmarried women want rich husbands, and the irony of *Austen*'s way of putting it would not have been lost on the readership of her time.

See *dramatic irony*.

irregular ode: an *ode* in which the number and length of lines and the *rhyme* scheme are different in each *stanza*, e.g. *Coleridge*'s 'Dejection: an Ode', *Wordsworth*'s 'Ode: Intimations of Immortality' (1807). Sometimes called a Cowleyan Ode, Abraham Cowley (1618–87) being credited with devising the *form*.

Isherwood, Christopher (1904–86): novelist, playwright, *short-story* and screenplay writer. Friends with *Spender* and *Auden*, with whom he collaborated (see Auden for these), he is candid in his writings about his homosexuality. Notable works include MR NORRIS CHANGES TRAINS (1935) and GOODBYE TO BERLIN (1939), two semi-autobiographical works based upon his experiences of the disintegrating fabric of society in Berlin in the early 1930s. The latter was adapted by John Van Druten into a play called I AM A CAMERA (1951), and into the musical CABARET (1968).

Ishiguro, Kazuo (b.1954): novelist, *short-story* and television writer. A student of *Bradbury*'s creative writing course at the University of East Anglia, his early work is influenced by Japanese culture although he left Japan at the age of six and did not revisit until briefly in 1989. His novels sometimes concern the self-deceptions of the central figure. Notable works include A PALE VIEW OF HILLS (1982), AN ARTIST OF THE FLOATING WORLD (1986), THE REMAINS OF THE DAY (1989), WHEN WE WERE ORPHANS (2000).

Italian sonnet: see *sonnet*.

Jacobean Age: generally considered to cover *literature* written in England during the reign of James I (1603–25).

Jacobean drama covers plays written during the reign of James I; however, the period 1558–1642 is sometimes covered by the overall term *Elizabethan drama*.

Jacobson, Dan (b.1929): South African novelist and *short-story* writer. Much of his writing explores aspects of being a South African or living in South Africa. Notable works include BEGGAR MY NEIGHBOUR (1964), HER STORY (1987).

James, C.L.R. (1901–89): Trinidadian novelist, political essayist and literary critic. His work has been regarded as documentary and socialist realist, and as part of the anti-colonial feeling which became evident during the 1930s and 1940s. Notable works include TRIUMPH (1929) and MINTY ALLEY (1936), which had a considerable influence upon Caribbean fiction.

James, Henry (1843–1916): American novelist, *short-story* and travel writer, critic, essayist and playwright. He was influenced by his friendship with *Howells*, and later by his growing knowledge of continental European *literature*. In 1876 he settled in England, and in his early *novels* such as THE PORTRAIT OF A LADY (1881) he often observes and studies experiences of Americans amongst Europeans, subtly comparing the New World values of the former with the older civilisation of the latter. For WASHINGTON SQUARE (1880) and THE BOSTONIANS (1886) he reverted to an American *setting*, and for works such as THE ASPERN PAPERS (1888) he adopted what he called his 'international *theme*'. Other notable works include WHAT MAISIE KNEW (1897), THE TURN OF THE SCREW (1898), THE WINGS OF THE DOVE (1902), THE AMBASSADORS (1903), THE GOLDEN BOWL (1904).

James, P.D. (b.1920): crime writer. Her *style* is often harsh and realistic, and her experience of forensic science aids the use of close factual detail in her stories. Notable works include COVER HER FACE (1962, which introduces the poetry-writing police detective Adam Dalgleish who features in many of her stories – see *police procedural*), DEATH OF AN EXPERT WITNESS (1977), INNOCENT BLOOD (1980, not a crime *novel*), CHILDREN OF MEN (1991), DEATH IN HOLY ORDERS (2001).

jazz poetry is *poetry* which is recited to the accompaniment of jazz. *Langston Hughes* in the 1930s was one of the first poets to collaborate with musicians, and the poets of the American *Beat Movement* experimented with the *form*. In Britain Christopher Logue (b.1926) was a leading figure.

Jellicoe, Ann (b.1927): playwright. Early writing included youthful, energetic pieces for the *English Stage Company*, since when she has become very active in community *drama* in the west of England. Notable works include THE SPORT OF MY MAD MOTHER (1958), THE KNACK (1961), SHELLEY: OR THE IDEALIST (1965).

Jennings, Elizabeth (b.1926): poet and *prose* writer associated with *The Movement*. Noted for the clarity and discipline of her *verse*, and her metaphysical interests, her subjects range from childhood, love and friendship to religion and art. At one time in her life she was afflicted with mental illness. Notable works include A SONG FOR A BIRTH OR A DEATH AND OTHER POEMS (1961), COLLECTED POEMS (1986).

Jhabvala, Ruth Prawer (b.1927): Anglo-Indian novelist, adapter, screenplay and *short-story* writer. Born in Germany of Polish parents and educated in England, she has lived for long periods in India and America, and is fascinated by the interface between East and West. Notable works include THE HOUSEHOLDER (1960), SHAKESPEARE WALLAH (1963, screenplay), HEAT AND DUST (1975).

Johnson, Age of: a term which used to be used to define literature written during the 18th century and roughly contemporary with the life of *Johnson*. Nowadays the terms *Augustan* and *Age of Sensibility* tend more often to be used to cover two halves of the same period.

Johnson, Samuel (1709–84): critic, lexicographer, scholar, essayist, translator, poet, biographer, editor and playwright. His prolific output was in his early years stimulated by lack of money. During his time he was influenced by, influenced or was friends with most of the important literary and artistic figures of his age. He was a brilliant conversationalist in an age when this was valued. Much of his writing radiates good sense and his literary *criticism*, whilst superseded by subsequent thinking, is still well worth reading. *Boswell*'s biography, which did as much to flesh out Johnson as a colourful, eccentric, larger-than-life personality as to praise his writings, has helped to raise him to almost legendary status as England's greatest all-round man of letters. Notable works include THE VANITY OF HUMAN WISHES (1749), A DICTIONARY OF THE ENGLISH LANGUAGE (1755), RASSELAS (1759), A JOURNEY TO THE WESTERN ISLES OF SCOTLAND (1775, an account of a tour accompanied by Boswell, who wrote his version under a different title), THE LIVES OF THE POETS (1781).

Johnsonian is a term given to writing in the *manner* and *style* of Johnson.

Jones, David (1895–1974): poet and graphic artist. IN PARENTHESIS (1937), considered a work of genius by *T.S. Eliot*, combines his First World War experiences with Welsh legend and *Malory*'s MORTE D'ARTHUR and, as sometimes with his other *poetry*, moves in *form* between *prose* and *free verse*. Other notable works include THE ANATHEMATA (1952), THE SLEEPING LORD (1974).

Jonson, Ben (1572–1637): playwright and poet. Friends with among others *Bacon*, *Beaumont*, *Chapman*, *Donne*, *Fletcher* and *Shakespeare*, he became foremost in a literary club which met at the Mermaid Tavern in London. His positive personality led to frequent clashes with his fellow actors and playwrights, and with the authorities. In 1597 he began work for *Henslowe*. His *comedy of humours* EVERY MAN IN HIS HUMOUR (1598), in which Shakespeare acted, was popular and helped to make him famous. He devised several *masques* in collaboration with the architect Inigo Jones (1573–1652). He excelled in creating satirical portraits of the grasping and self-interested. In 1616 he published a folio of his works which helped to establish *drama* as a respected literary *form*, and became unrivalled as the leading literary figure of his day, greatly influencing various younger poets who became known as 'the Tribe of Ben'. During the 18th and 19th centuries his reputation diminished as *Shakespeare*'s increased, but his standing has since in some measure been restored, mainly on the basis of the great comedies VOLPONE (?1605), THE ALCHEMIST (1619) and BARTHOLOMEW FAIR (1614). Unofficially he was the first *poet laureate*.

journal:

- any kind of magazine, newspaper or *periodical*
- a *diary*.

journalese: style of compressed writing employed by journalists which generates clichés and was famously parodied by *Waugh* in Scoop.

Joyce, James (1882–1941): Irish novelist, *short-story* writer and poet. Best known for his influence on *modernism*, especially in the development of his *stream of consciousness* technique, 'Joycean' has come to describe a style of *prose*. He often uses Dublin as a setting. Notable works include Dubliners (1914), A Portrait of the Artist as a Young Man (1916), Ulysses (1922), Finnegan's Wake (1939).

K

kafkaesque: a term sometimes applied to the characteristic *tone* and the nightmarish insecurity of *characters* as in the works of the Czech writer Franz Kafka (1883–1924).

Kavanagh, Patrick (1904–67): Irish poet. Influenced in part by *T.S. Eliot*, he in turn has influenced such poets as *R.S. Thomas* and *Heaney* in his determination that *regional* writing need not be narrow and parochial (see *local colour/colourists*). His realistic view of rural life is partly a reaction to *Yeats'* lyrical treatment. Notable works include THE GREAT HUNGER (1942), COME DANCE WITH KITTY STOBLING (1960).

Keats, John (1795–1821): poet. Trained as an apothecary-surgeon, he abandoned medicine to write poetry and became a leading figure in Romanticism, highly regarded by his contemporaries such as Shelley, although attacked and hurt as a 'Cockney poet' by right-wing reviewers. His status as a foremost English poet has remained high. His versatility covers sonnets, odes, narrative poems, children's poetry and other forms and types. His work is noted among other things for wit, sensitivity, use of the senses, medievalism, creation of interior landscapes, escapism. The latter is debatable, but it is true that he was not so directly political or social in his comments as were some of his contemporary Romantics such as Blake, Shelley, Byron. He thought deeply about literary concepts including his notion of negative capability. His letters to Fanny Brawne and others are highly readable, T.S. Eliot considering them significant documents. His early death from tuberculosis has tended to add to his Romantic mystique. Notable works include 'Endymion' (1818), 'To Autumn' (1819), 'Hyperion' (1819), 'The Eve of St Agnes' (1819), 'La Belle Dame Sans Merci' (1819), 'Lamia' (1819), 'Isabella' (1820), 'Ode to a Nightingale' (1820), 'Ode on a Grecian Urn' (1820), 'Ode to Psyche' (1820).

Keene, Molly (1904–96): Anglo-Irish playwright and novelist. A successful writer of *drawing-room comedy*. Her *novels* document with sharp observation and caustic humour the social behaviour of her background, a departed upper-class world of hunting, fishing, servants, large country houses and sport, both in the field and of a sexual nature. Her writing career was interrupted by the death of her husband in the 1950s, but she was persuaded to resume and more recent notable works include GOOD BEHAVIOUR (1981), TIME AFTER TIME (1983), LOVING AND GIVING (1988).

Keiller, Garrison (b.1932): American *short-story* writer and novelist. His *tales* are often gently humorous, notable works including LAKE WOBEGON DAYS (1985).

Kempinski, Tom (b.1938) is a playwright in whose writings an interest in psychoanalytical theory is apparent. Notable works include DUET FOR ONE (1980), WHEN THE PAST IS STILL TO COME (1992).

Keneally, Thomas (b.1935): Australian novelist, playwright and travel writer. Many of his books have Australian themes or subject-matter, and sometimes show an interest in moral failure. Notable works include SCHINDLER'S ARK (1982, re-titled SCHINDLER'S LIST after the success of the film version of that name), THE PLAYMAKER (1987, adapted for the stage by *Wertenbaker* as OUR COUNTRY'S GOOD).

kenning: in Old Norse and Old English literature, a word compound which creates a standard metaphor, e.g. helmet-bearer ('helm-berend' in Old English) for warrior, sea-wood ('sae-wudu') for ship, whale-road ('hron-rad') for sea.

Kermode, Frank (b.1919): influential scholar, literary critic and editor whose main focus is the *Renaissance*. His liberal-minded curiosity led him to reject any dogmatic approach to literary studies. He has done much to advance thinking in, among other things, the fields of *hermeneutics, reader-response theory, structuralism*. Notable works include ROMANTIC IMAGE (1957), THE SENSE OF ENDING (1967).

Kerouac, Jack (1922–69): American novelist. A leading light of the *Beat* generation, he developed his characteristically free-wheeling *style* of *prose*. Notable works include ON THE ROAD (1957), LONESOME TRAVELLER (1960).

Kesey, Ken (b.1935): American novelist and essayist, his 1960s reputation endures as a West Coast cult figure and social rebel with a wild lifestyle. Notable works include ONE FLEW OVER THE CUCKOO'S NEST (1962) in which he utilised his experiences as a ward attendant in a Californian hospital.

Kincaid, Jamaica (b.1949): Antiguan novelist and *short-story* writer. Her writing sometimes uses a Caribbean *setting*, and often concerns the adjustments to the modern world of those with an Antiguan cultural background. Notable works include AT THE BOTTOM OF THE RIVER (1983), ANNIE JOHN (1985), LUCY (1990).

King's Men, The: founded in 1594 as the Lord Chamberlain's Men, they were the Elizabethan theatre company of which *Shakespeare* was a member and shareholder.

Kingsley, Mary (1862–1900): travel writer. Her tough-minded writing on such matters as missionaries' inappropriate attempts to change the ways of African people had some political impact. Notable works include TRAVELS IN WEST AFRICA (1897), WEST AFRICAN STUDIES (1899), THE CONGO SCANDEL (1900).

Kingston, Maxine Hong (b.1940): Chinese-American *prose* writer. Among other things she is noted for her *poetic diction* and generally experimental *style*. She uses Chinese folklore, blending it into American *settings*. Notable works include THE WOMAN WARRIOR, MEMOIRS OF A CHILDHOOD AMONG GHOSTS (1976), CHINA MEN (1980).

Kipling, Rudyard (1865–1936): poet, *short-story* and children's writer, novelist, autobiogapher and journalist. As the latter in India he acquired knowledge of the Anglo-Indian life which inspired many of his carefully crafted *poems* and *stories*, gaining for him a reputation as the 'Poet of Empire'. Back in England he made friends with *James* and others in the literary world. His early stories of the Raj were noted for sceptical *realism*, but later he was accused of jingoism, and with the onset of *modernism* he began to go out of fashion. KIM (1901), a *picaresque* novel set in India, is generally considered to be his masterpiece. Other notable works include PLAIN TALES FROM THE HILLS (1888), LIFE'S HANDICAPS (1891), BARRACK-ROOM BALLADS AND OTHER VERSES (1892), MANY INVENTIONS (1893), STALKY AND CO. (1899), JUST SO STORIES (1902), PUCK OF POOK'S HILL (1906).

kitchen-sink drama: a term applied to plays of the 1950s and 1960s which centred upon the domestic problems of ordinary people, the kitchen sink being taken as a metaphorical focus. They were in part a reaction against the drawing-room *dramas* of playwrights such as *Rattigan*. *Osborne's* LOOK BACK IN ANGER is credited with beginning the fashion for such plays, radio and the rise of television *drama* giving them impetus. See *Angry Young Men*.

Kopit, Arthur (b.1939): American playwright. Influenced by *Brecht* and *Pirandello*, his social concerns are often expressed through *satire*. Notable works include OH DAD, POOR DAD, MAMA'S HUNG YOU IN THE CLOSET AND I'M FEELIN' SO SAD (1961, a parody of the *Theatre of the Absurd* and the *avant-garde* theatre of the 1960s), INDIANS (1968), WINGS (1978).

Kureshi, Hanif (b.1952): novelist and screenwriter. He is able to combine sensitivity and honesty with *humour* when dealing with immigrant issues, sexuality, and the poverty and violence of life in London in the 1970s and 1980s. Notable works include MY BEAUTIFUL LAUNDRETTE (1986), SAMMY AND ROSIE GET LAID (1988), THE BUDDHA OF SUBURBIA (1990), LONDON KILLS ME (1991), GABRIEL'S GIFT (2001).

Kyd, Thomas (1558–94): Elizabethan playwright about whom little is known for certain. Associated with *Marlowe*, his notable works probably include THE SPANISH TRAGEDY (?1589), a classic *revenge tragedy*, and he may have written a lost play HAMLET, an *urtext* of which *Shakespeare* made use.

La Guma, Alex (1925–85): South African novelist. Many years of his life were spent under house arrest as a result of his strong political views against apartheid and this is conveyed through his writings, which depict a *realistic* and dark picture of the slums of South Africa. Notable works include A WALK IN THE NIGHT (1962), AND A THREEFOLD CORD (1964), THE STONE COUNTRY (1967), IN THE FOG OF THE SEASON'S END (1972), TIME OF THE BUTCHERBIRD (1979).

Laing, Kojo (b.1946): Ghanaian novelist and poet who is an accomplished African *modernist*. Influenced by *magic realism*, his writing often takes a positive approach to African matters. Notable works include SEARCH SWEET COUNTRY (1986), WOMAN OF THE AEROPLANES (1988), MAJOR GENTL AND THE ACHIMOTA WARS (1992), GODHORSE (1989).

Lake Poets or Lake School, a term used, sometimes mockingly by *Byron* and others, to describe the group of poets and writers who lived in and were influenced by the Lake District around the turn of the 19th century, including *Coleridge, Southey, Wordsworth* and *De Quincey.*

Lamb, Charles (1775–1834): essayist, poet, letter and children's book writer and literary critic who was friends with *Coleridge, Southey, Leigh Hunt* and *Wordsworth* and had an influence upon all of them. Notable works include TALES FROM SHAKESPEAR (1807), which he wrote in collaboration with his sister, Mary (1764–1847), THE ESSAYS OF ELIA (1820–3).

lament: a *poem* expressing deep sorrow for any kind of loss. See also *complaint, dirge, elegy, monody, threnody.*

Lamming, George (b.1927): Barbadian novelist, poet, essayist and editor. His writings contain perceptive explorations of themes such as Caribbean identity and experience, colonialism and West Indian views of Britain. Notable works include IN THE CASTLES OF MY SKIN (1953), THE EMIGRANTS (1954), OF AGE AND INNOCENCE (1958), WATER WITH BERRIES (1971), NATIVES OF MY PERSON (1972), the latter having been regarded as his masterpiece.

lampoon: a satirical and often vulgar attack. A piece of writing which *caricatures* or ridicules its target, e.g. *Dryden*'s attack on Thomas Shadwell (1642–92) in ABSALOM AND ACHITOPHEL, *Pope*'s attack on Hervey in EPISTLE TO ARBUTHNOT (1735). See also *burlesque.*

Langland, William (?1330–86): notable works include PIERS PLOWMAN, a religious *allegory* which shows concern with the ordinary person and with contemporary corruption of the Church. It is considered to be one of the first major *poems* in English.

Language, the English: some understanding of the development of the language is necessary in order to appreciate its use in *literature.* Brought to the British Isles by Germanic tribes in 449AD, the language we call Anglo-Saxon developed and was enriched by a series of infusions such as the arrival of Christianity (and hence many additional Latin words), by the Viking invasions of the 8th and 9th centuries, and the

Norman invasion of 1066 (bringing French). During the later Middle Ages the language settled down into what we call Middle English (the language of *Chaucer*). Recognisably modern English emerged during the Renaissance, after which the vocabulary was further expanded by the development of the British Empire, drawing on words from other languages world wide and giving English a far larger vocabulary than any other language. This has been consolidated in modern times by the powerful influence of the United States as an English-speaking country and by the development of computer and other technical languages based upon English.

Larkin, Philip (1922–85): poet, novelist and essayist. *Yeats* and *Hardy* influenced his early *poetry*. A foremost member of *The Movement*, he disliked *modernism* and his pessimistic yet *witty* verse has been regarded as perfectly defining the situation of a certain kind of solitary individual within his age. Notable works include A GIRL IN WINTER (1947), THE LESS DECEIVED (1955), THE WHITSUN WEDDINGS (1964), HIGH WINDOWS (1974).

Laurence, Margaret (1926–87): Canadian novelist and *short-story* writer. Some of her writing concerns the lives of women in the *context* of Canadian small town life. Notable works include THIS SIDE JORDAN (1960), THE STONE ANGEL (1964), A JEST OF GOD (1966, published in the UK as NOW I LAY ME DOWN), A BIRD IN THE HOUSE (1970), THE DIVINERS (1974, a *novel* which interweaves the past and present).

Lawrence, D.H. (1885–1930): British novelist, *short-story* and travel writer, poet, critic and playwright. Much of his work explores his cultural surroundings (see also *regional novel*), reflected through political, sexual and social relations, and he incorporates many autobiographical elements into his *fiction*. Extending the boundaries of *narrative prose*, he is stylistically innovative, moving from the ordinary to the highly imaginative in his quest to explore the psychology of the individual. Controversial in his lifetime, his critical standing has varied since from those who see him as crucial in the 20th century *canon* to feminist critics who consider him to be *phallocentric*. Notable works include SONS AND LOVERS (1913), LOVE POEMS (1913), THE RAINBOW (1915), WOMEN IN LOVE (1920), LADY CHATTERLEY'S LOVER (1960), ENGLAND, MY ENGLAND (1922), STUDIES IN CLASSIC AMERICAN LITERATURE (1923).

Lawson, Henry (1867–1922): Australian poet and *short-story* writer who drew upon his sometimes harsh experiences in the New South Wales outback, he is known especially for his vigorous and colloquial bush *poems*. His *short stories* came to characterise much of late 19th century Australian experience. Notable works include STORIES IN PROSE AND VERSE (1894), JOE WILSON AND HIS MATES (1901).

lay: a short medieval *narrative poem*, e.g. *Chaucer*'s THE FRANKLIN'S TALE (?1387), *Walter Scott*'s LAY OF THE LAST MINSTREL (1805), LAYS OF ANCIENT ROME (1842) by Thomas Macauley (1899–59).

Layton, Irving (b.1912): Canadian poet and essayist who is strongly outspoken on a wide range of social and political issues. Notable works include HERE AND NOW (1945), THE BULL CALF AND OTHER POEMS (1956), COLLECTED POEMS (1971), COLLECTED SOCIAL AND POLITICAL WRITINGS (1977), A WILD PECULIAR JOY: SELECTED POEMS 1945–82 (1982).

Leavis, F.R. (1895–1978): see *leavisite*.

leavisite: a traditional approach to English *literature* derived from the thinking and writing of the Cambridge critic and his wife Queenie (1906–81), two early graduates of the new Cambridge University English degree. They held that:

- there is an accepted *canon* of great English literature – *Leavis* identifies *Austen, George Eliot, James* and *Conrad* in THE GREAT TRADITION (1948) as the great writers
- a *text* has an intrinsic artistic worth for all time, its *context* being irrelevant
- a text can and should be studied objectively, an individual reader's individual response being irrelevant. The word 'I' therefore has no place in a critical essay
- yet, perhaps paradoxically, a reader should respond with a natural sensibility to a text so that what is read will have a civilising effect upon her/him
- *close reading* of the text is essential.

These views dominated English teaching at all levels until two-thirds of the way through the 20th century, and are still influential. See *theories of criticism*.

Le Carré, John (b.1931): novelist. The complex plots and grim detail of his highly regarded *spy stories* overturn the glamorous James Bond image, transcending the limitations of the *genre* and giving *realistic* insights into the international tensions of the Cold War between East and West before the fall of communism. Notable works include CALL FOR THE DEAD (1961), THE SPY WHO CAME IN FROM THE COLD (1963), THE LOOKING GLASS WAR (1965), TINKER TAILOR SOLDIER SPY (1974), THE HONOURABLE SCHOOLBOY (1986), THE NIGHT MANAGER (1993), THE CONSTANT GARDENER (2001).

Lee, Harper (b.1926): American novelist whose only *novel*, TO KILL A MOCKINGBIRD (1960), tells the story of racism in Alabama through the eyes of a six-year-old white girl.

Lee, Laurie (1912–97): autobiographer and poet, through both of which mediums he shows his love of the countryside of his Gloucestershire youth and elsewhere. Notable works include MY MANY COATED MAN (1955), CIDER WITH ROSIE (1959), AS I WALKED OUT ONE MIDSUMMER MORNING (1969).

leitmotif, a term derived from opera, is often used interchangeably with *theme* and *motif*, although unlike the latter leitmotif refers to recurrence within a single work. Some critics confine the meaning to either:

- a recurrent image, e.g. blindness in *Shakespeare's* KING LEAR
- a recurrent pattern of words or repeated phrase, such as frequently happens in works by, for instance, *Faulkner, Joyce* and *Woolf.*

Lessing, Doris (b.1919): novelist, poet, *short-story* and travel writer. Her radical, feminist politics are expressed through her experimental *narrative form* and *style*, and she frequently delves into the psychological, drawing on her personal experiences to voice her views on society and in particular social prejudices. Notable works include THE GRASS IS SINGING (1950), THIS WAS THE OLD CHIEF'S COUNTRY (1951), THE GOLDEN NOTEBOOK (1962), THE SUMMER BEFORE THE DARK (1973), MEMOIRS OF A SURVIVOR (1974), THE FIFTH CHILD (1988), LOVE, AGAIN (1996).

level stress occurs when *stress* falls evenly on two concurrent syllables, as in 'domehead' or 'home run'. In *verse* a *spondee* sometimes results.

Lewis, Alun (1915–44): Welsh poet. His writings are formed from personal experiences of growing up in a poor mining village in the 1930s Depression and his time spent as a soldier. He explores feelings of isolation and expresses an understanding for the struggles of Welsh communities. Notable works include RAIDERS' DAWN (1942), THE LAST INSPECTION (1942), HA! HA! AMONG THE TRUMPETS (1945), IN THE GREEN TREE (1948).

Lewis, M.G. (1775–1818): novelist, poet and playwright. Inspired by German *Romanticism*, his best known work is his *gothic* novel THE MONK (1796), hence his nickname 'Monk' Lewis. Some influence on *Walter Scott*'s poetry has been noted.

Lewis, Sinclair (1885–1951): American novelist. His prolific output covers a range of subjects such as his desire for political and social change, race relations, American-Indian struggles, small town American life and fear of fascism in the USA. His *novels* changed complacent attitudes towards the American way of life. Notable works include MAIN STREET (1920), BABBITT (1922), ARROWSMITH (1925), ELMER GANTRY (1927), ANN VICKERS (1933), IT CAN'T HAPPEN HERE (1935), THE GOD-SEEKER (1949).

lexicon: strictly speaking a dictionary of some kind, the word has come to be applied to the characteristic stock of words or *diction* used by a particular writer.

liberal humanism: a traditional approach to *literature* which suggests that great literature explores a fixed and constant human nature; that, broadly speaking, is the *leavisite* approach. It rejects various theoretical and/or political ways of reading the *text*.

light comedy is a term used to denote undemanding light-hearted plays. Most (but not all) of *Coward*'s comedies have been so described.

light ending is another term for *weak ending*.

light stress is when, in *verse*, a *stress* is required on a syllable not normally stressed in everyday speech.

limited point of view: see *narrator/narrative voice*.

line: a unit in *poetry*, the length of which (except in *free verse*) is determined by the *metre*, e.g. *pentameter* has five feet in a *line*.

linguistics: the scientific study of most aspects of language including etymology, morphology, phonetics, *semantics* and syntax.

linked sonnet: see *sonnet*.

literary/critical theory: the various new approaches to literature which evolved during the latter part of the 20th century as a reaction to the notion that there is one objective view of literature and culture – see *leavisite*. Among these theories are:

- *structuralism*
- *post-structuralism* and *deconstruction*
- *post-modernism*
- *feminist criticism*
- *historicism/new historicism*
- *cultural materialism*
- *Marxist criticism*
- *colonial/post-colonial criticism*

literati: a term, often used pejoratively, for those who know a great deal about *literature.*

literature is a vague general term used to describe anything written in any *genre* which reaches a certain undefined standard of artistic merit.

litotes: a figure of speech, often involving a negative, whereby an understatement is used to emphasise an opposite quality (e.g. 'not good' implying 'rather bad'). Often used both in all kinds of *literature* and everyday speech, and sometimes a part of *irony.* The opposite of *hyperbole.* See *negation.*

Lively, Penelope (b.1933): novelist; children's, *short-story,* screenplay and non-fiction writer, and playwright. She is often concerned with the haunting impact of the past upon the present, drawing her *characters* with *humour* and sensitivity. Notable works include THE GHOST OF THOMAS KEMPE (1973), THE ROAD TO LICHFIELD (1977), MOON TIGER (1987).

Liverpool Poets: the name given to *Henri, MacGough* and *Patten* who, influenced by the 1960s Liverpool pop culture including the Beatles music, set out to popularise *poetry* and revive live performances. Much of their *imagery* was taken from the Liverpool urban landscape, and their *humorous,* colloquial, cheerfully subversive *poems* were remarkably successful. Two anthologies of their work, THE LIVERPOOL SCENE (1967) and THE MERSEY SOUND (1967), sold very well indeed. NEW VOLUME (1983) contains a *selection* of their *poetry* written during the 1970s and early 1980s.

Livings, Henry (b.1929): playwright. His plays are entertainingly anarchic and anti-authoritarian, eccentric in *style,* and sometimes feature a working class *anti-hero.* Notable works include NIL CARBORUNDUM (1962), EH? (1964), KELLY'S EYE (1964).

local colour/colourists are terms used of the depiction in *fiction* of the details of a region or place, often rural (e.g. customs, dress, flora and fauna), and of writers so preoccupied (e.g. *Hardy*'s Wessex or *Twain*'s Mississippi region). Sometimes unfairly used in the pejorative sense of writings which are confined in their interest and lack universal appeal or applicability. Some critics consider that local colour merely refers to decorative detail, and that the term '*regionalism*' should be applied when such detail is intrinsic and essential to a work.

Lochhead, Liz (b.1947): Scottish poet, *dramatist* and translator. Her technically skilful *verse,* which she often performs (see *performance poets*) uses Glasgow dialect to *dramatic* effect. Notable works include MEMO FOR SPRING (1972), BLOOD AND ICE (1982), DREAMING FRANKENSTEIN, AND COLLECTED POEMS (1984).

Lodge, David (b.1935): novelist, literary critic and essayist. His literary sympathies embrace both *traditional* approaches and modern *literary theory,* and he is best known for his *campus novels.* Notable works include THE LANGUAGE OF FICTION (1966), CHANGING PLACES (1975 – a campus novel), HOW FAR CAN YOU GO? (1980), WORKING WITH STRUCTURALISM (1981), WRITE ON: OCCASIONAL ESSAYS (1986), NICE WORK (1988), THE ART OF FICTION (1992), THINKS...(2001).

longeur: a boring passage of writing.

Longfellow, Henry Wadsworth (1807–82): American poet and translator. He sought to establish through his *poetry* an American mythology to match what he found in his reading of European *literature*, and in his day he rivalled *Tennyson* in popularity with English-speaking readers. Notable works include VOICES OF THE NIGHT (1831), EVANGELINE (1847), THE SONG OF HIAWATHA (1855), THE COURTSHIP OF MILES STANDISH (1858), TALES OF THE WAYSIDE INN (1863), CHRISTUS (1872).

love poetry deals with the emotions and virtues of love rather than the physical side (which is defined as 'erotic *poetry*'). In *Renaissance* times an ability to write a reasonable *poem* to one's mistress was considered to be an important accomplishment for a courtier: Ophelia describes Hamlet as a poet, and in *Shakespeare*'s As YOU LIKE IT, Orlando goes around the forest hanging on the trees love poems to Rosalind. Among many poets who have written love poems, often *sonnets* and sometimes whole sequences are *Chaucer, Wyatt, Surrey, Marlowe, Spenser,* Shakespeare, *Donne, Herrick, Burns, Keats, Byron, Tennyson, Dickinson, Elizabeth Barrett Browning, Dante Gabriel Rossetti, Christina Rossetti, Housman, Yeats, Hardy, Edward Thomas, Brooke, Auden, Betjeman, Cope, Duffy.*

Lovelace, Richard (1618–58): *Cavalier* poet whose reputation rests upon a few stylish *lyric* poems. Notable works include 'To Althea from Prison' (?1642), LUCASTA: EPODES, ODES, SONNETS, SONGS, ETC. (?1649).

low comedy is a term sometimes applied to unsophisticated *drama* which aims to make the audience laugh by very simple means such as rude jokes or slapstick. There are examples throughout all periods from ancient Greek drama to the present day.

Lowell, Robert (1917–77): American poet, *prose* writer and translator. His work often concerns his New England background, but not exclusively so, much falling under the label of *confessional poetry*. Notable works include LORD WEARY'S CASTLE (1946), POEMS, 1938–1949 (1950), LIFE STUDIES (1959), FOR THE UNION DEAD (1964), NEAR THE OCEAN (1967), THE DOLPHIN (1973).

Luthuli, Albert (?1898–1967): a South African anti-apartheid political activist, he is known for his *autobiography* LET MY PEOPLE GO (1962).

Lydgate, John (?1370–1449): prolific poet influenced by *Chaucer*, his contemporaries rated him on a par with Chaucer and *Gower*. Lydgate remained popular until the 17th century, but his *metre, style, verse* form, liking for *cliché* and the length of his works has left him largely unread since. Notable works include THE TROY BOOK (1412–21).

Lyly, John (1554–1606): playwright and writer of *prose* romances. His EUPHUES: OR, THE ANATOMY OF WIT (?1598), written in elegant and elaborate prose, set a fashion for a style of prose writing which became known as *euphuism* (not to be confused with 'euphemism'). Other notable works include CAMPASPE (?1584) and ENDIMION: THE MAN IN THE MOON (?1591).

lyric: the term is a broad one covering such relatively short poetic *forms* as the *elegy, ode* and *sonnet*. The word comes from the Greek for a *song* to be accompanied by the lyre, the subject-matter being personal and often concerning love expressed through a *persona*. The *genre* has been popular through the ages in many cultures, and was increasingly used in *Renaissance* England, first by *Wyatt* and *Surrey*, then by *Sidney, Shakespeare, Spenser, Jonson* and the *Elizabethans*, and then with more disturbing undertones by *Donne, Herbert, Marvell* and other *metaphysical* poets. The genre has remained popular through the ages (with such as *Coleridge* and *Wordsworth* during the *Romantic* period, and *Tennyson* during the 19th century) and many 20th century poets can be classed as lyric poets.

Macaulay, Rose (1881–1958): novelist, essayist and travel writer whose *historical novels* are sharply perceptive, sometimes satirical, yet compassionate in their view of human nature. Notable works include THE WORLD OF MY WILDERNESS (1950), THE TOWERS OF TREBIZOND (1956).

Macbeth, George (1932–92): poet and novelist. In the 1950s he was a major figure in a kind of writers' critical club called The Group (later to become the Writers' Workshop), participated in *performance poetry* in the 1960s, and produced *poetry* and arts programmes for the BBC. His work is always inventive, his *themes* often gruesome and morbid. Notable works include THE BROKEN PLACES (1963), THE COLOUR OF BLOOD (1967), COLLECTED POEMS 1958–1970 (1971), THE SAMURAI (1976), THE SEVEN WITCHES (1978), ANATOMY OF A DIVORCE (1988), TRESPASSING: POEMS FROM IRELAND (1991).

MacCaig, Norman (1910–96): Scottish poet. Considered to be one of Scotland's foremost poets, over the years he moved from *traditional* to freer *verse forms*. Interested in the nature of perception, Edinburgh and the mountains of the West Highlands have inspired much of his writing (see *topographical poetry*). Notable works include FAR CRY (1940), THE INWARD EYE (1946), RIDING LIGHTS (1955), RINGS ON A TREE (1968), THE EQUAL SKIES (1980), VOICE-OVER (1988), COLLECTED POEMS (1985, revised 1990).

MacEwan, Ian (b.1948): novelist, *short-story*, television and screenplay writer. His subject matter is characteristically disturbing and sometimes shocking, and it is conveyed with great clarity of *style*. Notable works include FIRST LOVE, LAST RITES (1975), THE CEMENT GARDEN (1978), THE PLOUGHMAN'S LUNCH (1983), THE CHILD IN TIME (1987) BLACK DOGS (1992), ENDURING LOVE (1997), AMSTERDAM (1998).

McGonagall, William (?1830–1902) Scottish poet. Most of his work is *doggerel*, characterised by lines of wildly irregular length and awkward *rhymes*. Audiences flocked to his readings to laugh at him (not least because he took himself seriously as 'Poet and Tragedian'). He is often deemed to be the worst poet of all time, but he has his supporters. Notable works include POETIC GEMS (1890), his best known *poem* probably being 'The Tay Bridge Disaster'.

McGough, Roger (b.1937): poet and playwright, and one of the three *Liverpool Poets*. Among other things his writing is distinguished by sharp *wit*, *humour*, clever word-play and *puns*. He wrote lyrics for the music group 'The Scaffold'. Notable works include SELECTED POEMS 1967–1987 (1989).

McGrath, John (b.1935): playwright and director. Interested in working-class theatre, his plays often have an emphasis on local communities. Notable works include EVENTS WHILE GUARDING THE BOFORS GUN (1966), THE CHEVIOT, THE STAG AND THE BLACK, BLACK OIL (1974), LITTLE RED HEN (1977), A GOOD NIGHT OUT (1981).

MacInnes, Colin (1914–73): novelist, journalist and essayist. Describing himself as an 'anarchist sympathiser', he writes vividly about the lives of young blacks in Notting

Hill at the time when London is beginning to become a multi-racial society. Notable works include ABSOLUTE BEGINNERS (1959).

MacLaverty, B. (b.1942): Irish novelist and *short-story* writer. His books are often about loneliness, and he writes in a clear, unfussy, economic *prose* style. In CAL (1983) he conveys the human impact of the violence in Northern Ireland in a matter-of-fact yet tender way. Other notable works include SECRET AND OTHER STORIES (1977), LAMB (1980), WALKING THE DOG AND OTHER SHORT STORIES (1994).

Macleish, Archibald (1892–1982): American poet and playwright. Influenced by *Pound* and *T.S. Eliot*, his early work explores perceptions of intellectual and traditional ideas. Later he became interested in American political and social perceptions of itself and others, and its reactions to world events and social developments such as the Second World War and communism. He led an active public and academic life. Notable works include THE POT OF EARTH (1925), NOBODADDY (1926), ACT FIVE (1948), J.B. (1958), POETRY AND EXPERIENCE (1960), A CONTINUING JOURNEY (1968), RIDERS ON THE EARTH (1978).

Macleod, Alistair (b.1936): Canadian *short-story* writer and novelist. His works are often located in rural Nova Scotia, his treatment of the sometimes doomed struggles of men and women, young and old, are haunting and compassionate. Notable works include THE LOST SALT GIFT OF BLOOD (1976), AS BIRDS BRING FORTH THE SUN AND OTHER STORIES (1986), NO GREAT MISCHIEF (2000).

MacNeice, Louis (1907–63): poet. Associated with *Spender, Day-Lewis* and *Auden*, he collaborated with the latter on LETTERS FROM ICELAND (1937). He became an excellent writer of feature programmes and radio plays for the BBC. His *poetry* displays delicacy of touch and deft use of such *devices* as *assonance, internal rhyme, half-rhyme*, ballad-like repetitions, and he wrote some distinctive *love poetry*. Notable works include BLIND FIREWORKS (1929), THE DARK TOWER (1947), SOLSTICES (1961), THE BURNING PERCH (1963), COLLECTED POEMS (1966).

magic realism is a term used to denote *fiction* which combines *realism* and the outlandish and the *fantastic*, thus reminding the reader that all *narratives* are inventions. Although the roots of *magic realism* go as far back as the *gothic novel*, the term is most frequently applied to *novels* of the 1970s and 1980s, e.g. *Rushdie*'s MIDNIGHT'S CHILDREN, in which the hero receives telepathic messages. Other writers employing magic realism include *Angela Carter, Fowles, Winterson;* and non-English experimenters include the German Günter Grass (b.1927), especially in THE TIN DRUM (1959) and the Columbian novelist Gabriel García Márquez (b.1928) in ONE HUNDRED YEARS OF SOLITUDE (1967).

Mahapatra, J (b.1928): Indian poet and *prose* writer. Drawing on the *imagery* of his Indian surroundings and writing in both English and Oriya, his *poetry* is both loving and critical. Notable works include CLOSE THE SKY, TEN BY TEN (1971), FALSE START (1980), LIFE SIGN (1983), SELECTED POEMS (1987).

Mailer, Norman (b.1923): American novelist, journalist, essayist and literary critic. His writings have ranged widely in subject-matter and *style* and he has always been controversial, adopting staunchly personal stances in his criticism of society. During the 1960s he became disillusioned with left-wing politics and became a leading member of the *New Journalism* movement which, broadly speaking, merged fact and *fiction* (see *faction*). His novels sometimes explore the subconscious. Notable works include THE NAKED AND THE DEAD (1948), ARMIES OF THE NIGHT (1968), OF A FIRE ON THE MOON (1971), THE EXECUTIONER'S SONG (1979), since when his work has been less well received, although THE GOSPEL ACCORDING TO THE SUN (1997) is an interesting supposed *autobiography* of Christ.

Mais, Roger (1905–55): Jamaican novelist, poet, playwright and journalist. His work is based on interests in the black working class and their dreadful conditions in slums and prisons during British colonial rule. His writing often displays strong biblical *rhythms* and *allusions*. Notable works include THE HILLS WERE JOYFUL TOGETHER (1953), BROTHER MAN (1954).

Malamud, Bernard (1914–86): American novelist and *short-story* writer who characteristically explores Jewish experience. Notable works include THE FIXER (1967).

Malan, Rian (b.1954): South African journalist. Notable works include the semi-autobiographical MY TRAITOR'S HEART (1990) which he subtitles A SOUTH AFRICAN EXPLORES THE MADNESS IN COUNTRY, IN HIS TRIBE [that is, the Afrikaaners] AND HIMSELF and in which with a reporter's eye he remorselessly examines the paradox of being a white liberal Afrikaaner in the land of apartheid.

malapropism: a misuse of long words, called after *Sheridan*'s character Mrs Malaprop (from the French 'mal à propos' = 'not to the purpose') who repeated misapplied long words in an attempt to sound impressive, e.g. '...she should have a supercilious [instead of 'superficial'] knowledge... that she might reprehend [comprehend]... I don't think that there is a superstitious [superfluous] article in it...'. This kind of comic mistake, and the type of *character* who makes it, have a long English tradition, from Dogberry in *Shakespeare*'s MUCH ADO ABOUT NOTHING to Alf Garnett in the 1960/70s television situation comedy TILL DEATH DO US PART.

Malory, Thomas (?1408–?71): little is known of him but his famous *prose* version of Arthurian legends, LE MORTE D'ARTHUR (?1470), was probably written in Newgate Prison, and was one of the first *texts* to be printed in English by *Caxton*.

Malouf, David (b.1934): Australian novelist, poet and opera librettist. He has moved between Australia and Europe, and the range of subject matter and interests in his writings draw upon this. Notable works include MY BICYCLE AND OTHER POEMS (1970), AN IMAGINARY LIFE (1978), WILD LEMONS (1981), REMEMBERING BABYLON (1993).

Mamet, David (b.1947): American playwright and essayist. A prolific writer of plays and screenplays, he is a leading light in contemporary American theatre, much of his *drama* displaying discontent with contemporary American ways of life. Influenced by and intensely interested in *Chekhov*, he tends to focus upon *character* rather than *plot*, and his *style* has been compared with that of *Pinter*. Notable works include SEXUAL PERVERSITY IN CHICAGO (1974), AMERICAN BUFFALO (1977), GLENGARRY GLEN ROSS (1983), HOUSE OF GAMES (1987), OLEANA (1992), THE CRYPTOGRAM (1994).

manner is a term used to describe the characteristic *form* and *style* of a writer or piece of writing.

mannerism: a distinctive, repetitious (and sometimes irritating) feature of a writer's *style*. The word is used when describing art and architecture, most particularly of certain recurrent Italian features of the 16th century.

Mansfield, Katherine (1888–1923): Anglo-New Zealand *short-story* writer who is considered to be a fine writer in the *genre*. Her intelligent, well-shaped stories often draw on her New Zealand childhood, a focus partly developed by the trauma of her brother's death in the First World War. Associated with the *Bloomsbury Group* and influenced by *Chekhov*, through her writing there comes a sense of the fragility of life, and this came to be underlined by her own failing health. Notable works include PRELUDE (1918), THE GARDEN PARTY (1922), THE DOVE'S NEST (1923), SOMETHING CHILDISH (1924).

marginalia: annotation written in the margins of books and manuscripts, ranging from those added by great writers in books which they own to the notes of students who are preparing for an examination.

Marlowe, Christopher (1564–93): playwright and poet. His colourful reputation is variously that of athiest, blasphemer, government spy, homosexual and free-thinker, and he clearly enjoyed dramatising unconventional *characters* who defy secular, political, moral and/or religious authority such as TAMBURLAINE (1590), EDWARD II (?1592) and DOCTOR FAUSTUS (?1592), in which he uses the *Morality play* tradition but subverts it by having Faustus condemned to hell at the end. Educated at Cambridge University, he is influenced by his study of classical writers such as Virgil and Ovid, but his plays move on from the traditional *form* of *Senecan tragedy* to something much more lively, partly through his development of *blank verse* (called 'Marlowe's mighty line' by *Jonson*) which he made much more flexible than previous users such as *Norton* and *Sackville* in GORODUC. A friend of *Kyd*, he is generally regarded as the greatest contributor to *Elizabethan drama* before *Shakespeare*, whose early history plays such as the three parts of HENRY VI (?1593) were influenced by him. Other notable works include JEW OF MALTA (?1592), HERO AND LEANDER (1598), 'The Passionate Shepherd to his Love' (1599).

Marston, John (1576–1634): playwright and poet. His capabilities ranged from *comedy* through biting *satire* to *revenge tragedy*. In the 1590s he rivalled and disputed with *Jonson*, but later collaborated with him and *Chapman* on EASTWARD HOE (1605). Other notable works include ANTONIO AND MELINDA (?1599), ANTONIO'S REVENGE (?1600), THE DUTCH COURTEZAN (?1602), THE MALCONTENT (1604), whose main *character* is cast in the same melancholic, disaffected mould as Hamlet.

martian poetry is the name given to a kind of *verse* popular in the late 1970s and 1980s which observes human affairs as if seen through the *eyes* of a *persona* from space. The name derives from A MARTIAN SENDS A POSTCARD HOME (1979) by Craig Raine (b.1944).

Marvell, Andrew (1621–78): poet and essayist. Influenced by *Donne* and his *conceits*, he was friends with *Milton* and *Lovelace* (who, unlike Marvell, was a Royalist). Nowadays he is best known as a *metaphysical* lyric and *pastoral* poet, but he was not known as a poet in his day. He was discovered by *Lamb* (in the 19th century he became known as 'the green poet'), reappraised by *T.S. Eliot,* and is now admired for his arrestingly direct treatment of common poetic subject-matter, e.g. the *carpe diem*

'To His Coy Mistress' (?1653). In his time he was known as the *author* of *ironic* and *witty* political and religious *satires*, a good example of which is 'Last Instructions to a Painter' (1667), and he was Member of Parliament for Hull for almost 20 years. Other notable works include 'An Horatian Ode upon Cromwell's Return from Ireland' (1650), 'The First Anniversary' (1665), MISCELLANEOUS POEMS (1681), POEMS ON AFFAIRS OF STATE (1689–97).

Marxist criticism is rooted in the cultural theories of Karl Marx (1818–83) and Friedrich Engels (1820–95). One of its basic beliefs is that all *literature* is culture-bound, and that the economic, political and other *contexts* within which a *text* is produced is vital to its understanding and *interpretation*. Much Marxist criticism is devoted to assessing a text's level of *realism*, and exposing the unconscious *sub-text*. The development of *structuralism* and *post-structuralism* has done much to stimulate Marxist criticism, the foremost theorist of which in Britain is *Eagleton*. See also *deconstruction, post-modernism*.

masculine ending, or 'hard ending', occurs when a line of *verse* ends on a stressed syllable, as with most *iambic* verse. Trochaic verse (see *metre*) also often drops the final unstressed syllable in the line. For instance:

- 'Alas! so all things now do hold their peace' (*iambic*, from *Wyatt*'s 'A Complaint by Night')
- 'Lord, what fools these mortals be!' (*trochaic*, from *Shakespeare*'s A MIDSUMMER NIGHT'S DREAM).

See *weak ending*.

masculine rhyme is monosyllabic rhyming on the final stressed syllable of consecutive lines (as in bark/lark), e.g.

Sweet Auburn! loveliest village of the plain
Where health and plenty cheer'd the labouring swain
(from *Goldsmith*'s 'The Deserted Village')

It is the most common type of rhyming in English *poetry*.

Masefield, John (1875–1967): poet, playwright, journalist and children's *story* writer. His earlier *verse* is distinctive for *realism* of *character* and *setting* (often the sea), later work for lyrical rural evocations. His prolific output made *poetry* popular, and he was *poet laureate* from 1930–67. Notable works include SALT-WATER BALLADS (1902, containing perhaps his best known *poem* 'I Must Go Down to the Sea Again'), BALLADS AND POEMS (1910), COLLECTED POEMS (1923), SARD HARKER (1924), THE MIDNIGHT FOLK (1927), THE BOX OF DELIGHTS (1933), DEAD NED (1938), LIVE AND KICKING NED (1939).

masque: a late 16th/early 17th century courtly entertainment involving such features as *poetry, song*, mime and dancing within a dramatic framework. The *plots* tended to be loosely constructed around a central *allegory* or mythological subject. Often elaborate costumes and masks were worn by the actors, and there were spectacular stage effects. At the end the courtly audience joined in a dance with the actors. *Jonson* and the architect Inigo Jones (1573–1652) collaborated on masques, *Milton* wrote COMUS for performance in Ludlow Castle in 1634, and *Shakespeare* incorporated elements of masque into Love's Labour's Lost (?1593) and The Tempest. See *antimasque*.

Massinger, Philip (1583–1640): playwright who worked for *the King*'s *Men* from 1613 until his death. Capable of sharp *satire*, he collaborated with *Dekker, Fletcher* and Nathan Field (1587–?1620). Notable works of which he was sole *author* include A New Way to Pay Old Debts (?1622), The Roman Actor (1626), The City Madam (1632).

Masters, Olga (1919–86): Australian novelist, journalist and *short-story* writer. Narrow-mindedness and private pain often feature in her writing. Notable works include The Home Girls (1982), Amy's Children (1987).

Matura, Mustapha (b.1939): Trinidadian playwright who emigrated to Britain in 1961. Humorous and satirical, his plays often focus upon the impact on the individual of the demise of indigenous Caribbean cultures. Notable works include As Time Goes By (1972), Play Mas (1974), Nice Rum and Cola and Welcome Home Jacko (1980), Independence and Meetings (1982), The Playboy of the West Indies (1984, based on *Synge*'s The Playboy of the Western World).

Maugham, Somerset (1874–1965): novelist, *short-story* writer and playwright. Much of his writing has been popular, but his short stories are most admired. Critics have remarked upon his *narrative* skill and shrewd observation, and several of his *novels* may be classed as *roman à clef*. He considered himself to be a leading 'second-rater'. Notable works include Liza of Lambeth (1897), Lady Frederick (1907), Of Human Bondage (1915), The Moon and Sixpence (1919), Cakes and Ale (1930), The Summing Up (1938), Creatures of Circumstances (1947).

maxim: a short, neatly expressed statement or *proverb* about human behaviour. In some languages (e.g. French) there are books of maxims, but examples in English are scattered through various kinds of literature, e.g. in the writings of, among others, *Bacon, Blake, Coleridge, Johnson, Pope, Shaw*. They are common in English drama, for instance:

> The great are like the base, nay, they are the same,
> When they seek shameful ways to avoid shame
>
> (*Webster*, The Duchess of Malfi)
>
> Experience is the name everyone gives to their mistakes
>
> (*Wilde*, Lady Windermere's Fan)

Mayhew, Henry (1812–87): journalist, playwright, novelist and *short-story* writer, he is best remembered for his investigations into the plight of the London poor which did much to affect the public conscience and stimulate reform. His London Labour And The London Poor (a series of articles published between 1849 and 1864) is very useful background material for the study of contemporary *authors* such as *Dickens*. Other notable works include The Criminal Prisons of London and Scenes of Prison Life (1862).

meaning is what a writer intends to say. See *significance*.

measure is another word for *metre*.

mechanic form is where a writer determines the *form* of a work according to a predetermined set of rules, as opposed to *organic form* where the form is allowed to arise naturally from the subject-matter and *theme*. It has been observed that the classical French *dramatists* of the 17th century constructed their plays according to mechanic form, and looked down upon *Shakespeare's* preference for organic form, which they considered careless and shapeless. See also *unities, dramatic*.

medievalism, in a literary sense, is an emphasis on the *style*, subject-matter, ways of thinking and/or any other aspect of the Middles Ages (approximately 800–1450AD). In particular *Romanticism* and the associated revival of interest in the *gothic* saw a resurgence of medievalism, above all in much of *Keats'* poetry. Others who have shown an interest in the medieval include *Spenser, Coleridge, Walter Scott, Tennyson*.

Medwall, Henry (c.1462–1502): playwright. Only two works survive: NATURE (printed in 1530), a *Morality play;* and FULGENS AND LUCRECE (printed ?1515), first performed in about 1497 and thought to be the earliest known secular play (that is, a *drama* not on a scriptural or explicitly moral subject) in English.

meiosis is a deliberate understatement such as 'rather good', and is often a part of *irony*. See also *litotes*.

melodrama was originally a play with a musical accompaniment which often reinforced the emotional aspect of the *drama;* hence it came to refer to plays in which *characters* are two dimensional or *flat* – typically *villains, heroes* or *heroines* – and the *action* bold, sentimental and far-fetched, sensational thrill and stage effects being more important than credibility. The *genre* reached a height of popularity during the *Victorian Age* with plays such as MARIA MARTEN; OR, MURDER IN THE RED BARN (?1830), SWEENEY TODD, THE BARBER OF FLEET STREET (1842) by George Dibdin Pitt (1799–1855), THE TICKET-OF-LEAVE MAN (1853) by Tom Taylor (1807–80), LADY AUDLEY'S SECRET (1863) by Miss Braddon (1835–1915). Victorian melodramas are occasionally staged today, often for amusement in the *context* of a modern audience which will receive them very differently from their original audiences. The popularity of melodrama has continued through the cinema (cowboy and horror films) and television (various soap operas).

melodramatic is a term used to denote any *drama* which has the characteristics of *melodrama*, and is usually applied with a derogatory sense implying that the drama is of a poor standard.

Melville, Herman (1819–91): American novelist, poet and *short-story* writer who developed a friendship with *Hawthorne*. His experiences at sea led him to write his early sea tales, which proved popular. The greatness of MOBY DICK (1851) was recognised by the discerning, but the book was not widely esteemed at the time. During the 20th century Melville's reputation grew, and recently MOBY DICK has been described as 'the closest approach the United States has had to a national *epic*.' His *metaphysical* themes and psychological insights were ahead of his time. Other notable works include TYPEE (1846), MARDI (1849), BILLY BUDD (1924).

memoir: an account by a writer of events and people encountered during a certain period in her or his life, rather than a focusing upon the writer's own developing self, and which therefore does not set out to be a comprehensive *autobiography*, e.g. *Graves'* GOODBYE TO ALL THAT or *Sassoon's* MEMOIRS OF A FOX-HUNTING MAN, both memoirs of their experiences in the First World War. See also *diary*.

memoir-novel: a kind of *novel* which by convention is written as if a true *memoir*, yet is *fiction*, e.g. *Defoe*'s ROBINSON CRUSOE, *Smollett*'s RODERICK RANDOM, *Ishiguro*'s THE REMAINS OF THE DAY, Kate Atkinson's BEHIND THE SCENES AT THE MUSEUM (1995).

Meredith, George (1828–1909): novelist, poet, critic and journalist who is associated with the *Pre-Raphaelites*. His *novels* are intelligent and wittily comic, acute in their portrayal of *character*, especially female, and show a mastery of *narrative* skill. His standing was high until the mid-20th century, but his writing is not very accessible to today's readers. Notable works include THE ORDEAL OF RICHARD FEVEREL (1859), MODERN LOVE (1862), THE EGOIST (1879), THE TRAGIC COMEDIANS (1880), POEMS AND LYRICS OF THE JOY OF EARTH (1883), DIANA OF THE CROSSWAYS (1885), ON COMEDY AND THE USE OF THE COMIC SPIRIT (1897).

merismus: a rhetorical device whereby a subject is divided into sub-categories, e.g. in *Shakespeare*'s MACBETH Malcolm refers to

> the king-becoming graces,
> As justice, verity, temperance, stableness,
> Bounty, perseverance, mercy, lowliness,
> Devotion, patience, courage, fortitude   (Act IV, Scene 3)

metacriticism is critical writing about literary *criticism*, e.g. a book which explores *structuralism*.

metadrama/metatheatre: a play or aspect of a play which deals with the nature of *drama*, e.g. it could be said that various aspects of *Shakespeare*'s HAMLET are metadrama.

metafiction/metanovel: *novels* about novels or novel-writing in which the *author* departs from *realism* and deliberately highlights an awareness that writer and reader are together creating the *fiction*. Examples include *Sterne*'s TRISTRAM SHANDY, *Lessing*'s THE GOLDEN NOTEBOOK (1962) and *Fowles*' THE FRENCH LIEUTENANT'S WOMAN, with its alternative endings. See *anti-novel, narrative*.

metaphor, like a *simile*, is a comparison between two things not usually compared in order to illuminate or provoke thought in the reader through the striking nature of the comparison. However, whereas a simile says that something is 'like' something else, a metaphor describes something in terms of something else, e.g. 'The road snaked its way up the mountain-side'. In *Theroux*'s THE GREAT RAILWAY BAZAAR he talks of hearing 'the smashing of paper parcels being stuffed into corners', arresting the reader by giving to paper a quality not usually associated with it. Metaphors help the reader to see objects and ideas in a fresh light, for instance:

> In the lower sky
> Television aerials, Chinese characters
>   from *Dunn*'s ON THE ROOFS OF TERRY STREET.

See *implicit metaphor, tenor and vehicle*.

metaphysical is a term now mainly used to define a group of 17th century poets including *Donne* (who is usually credited with setting the trend), *Herbert* and *Marvell* whose *poetry* contains common elements, such as:

- striking *imagery* and comparisons, often drawn from the new scientific and geographic discoveries of the day

- an inter-linking of the physical and the philosophical
- complex thought and *themes*
- witty *conceits*
- *paradoxes*
- colloquially direct language (as opposed the formal fluency of much *Elizabethan* lyric *love poetry*)
- economical, tightly-packed expression
- a strong sense of mortality
- flexibility of *rhythm* and *metre.*

The term is more widely applied to matters of philosophy (in Greek it means 'after physics': in his academy *Plato* playfully used the term for the philosophy classes which he ran after his physics classes).

method refers to the way in which a writer goes about communicating his *content* to the reader.

metonymy means, literally, 'change of name', and is a figure of speech whereby the name of something is substituted by a feature associated with it, e.g. 'The Crown [for 'King' or 'Queen'] has decreed…'; 'When one sees Marlowe [for 'the plays written by Marlowe'] on stage…'; 'The Stage [for 'acting on the stage'] is a great profession.' Similar to *synecdoche.*

metre is, in *poetry*, the regular use of a dominant unit of *rhythm*, known as a *'foot'*. The following terms are used to describe the number of 'feet' in a *verse* line:

- monometer – a single foot (very rare), e.g.
  I'm made
  A shade
  And laid
  I'th'grave
  There have
  My cave
  (Herrick's 'Upon His Departure Hence', 1648)

- dimeter – two feet (rare), e.g.
  Their's not to / reason why
  Their's but to / do and die
  (Tennyson's 'The Charge of the Light Brigade')

- trimeter – three feet, e.g.
  I look / into / my glass
  And view / my wast/ing skin
  (Hardy's 'I Look into my Glass', 1898)

- tetrameter – four feet, e.g.
  The Assy/rian came down / like a wolf / on the fold
  (Byron's 'The Destruction of Sennacherib', 1815)

- pentameter – five feet, e.g.
  He nev/er lift/ed up / anoth/er stone
  (Wordsworth's 'Michael', 1800)

- hexameter – six feet (sometimes known as an *Alexandrine*), e.g.
  I will / arise / and go / now, and go / to Inn/isfree
  And a small / cabin / build there, / a hive / for the hon/ey-bee
  (*Yeats'* 'The Lake Isle of Innesfree', 1892)

- heptameter – seven feet, e.g.
  I went / into / a pub/lic-'ouse / to get / a pint / o' beer
  (*Kipling*'s 'Tommy', 1890)

- octameter – eight feet, e.g.
  There beneath the Roman ruin where the purple flowers grow
  Came that 'Ave Atque Vale' of the poet's hopeless woe
  (*Tennyson*'s 'Frater Ave Atque Vale', 1880)

The most common metrical feet in English *poetry* are:

- iambic (an unstressed syllable followed by a stressed, which tends to give a relatively stately rhythm). This is the most common of all, and is employed in the majority of English poetry and dramatic *verse*, such as *Wordsworth*'s poetry and *Shakespeare*'s plays, e.g.
  He név/er líft/ed úp / anóth/er stóne
  (from *Wordsworth*'s 'Michael', 1800)

- trochaic (a stressed syllable followed by an unstressed, which tends to give a relatively bouncy rhythm), as in *Longfellow*'s HIAWATHA (that is, the reverse of an *iamb*). Whole *poems* written in *trochees* are rare in English, one of the best known being Longfellow's HIAWATHA where the insistent trochees create the aural effect of the Red Indian drumbeat. Another example is in *Shakespeare*'s A MIDSUMMER NIGHT'S DREAM where Puck's trochees emphasise his bouncy, mischievous *character*, e.g.
  Thróugh the / fórest/ háve I / góne
  Bút Ath/énian / fóund I / nóne…

  This example shows how the final unstressed syllable of trochaic lines is often omitted.

- anapaestic (two unstressed syllables followed by a stressed), e.g.
  The Assý/rian came dówn / like a wólf / on the fóld

- dactylic (one stressed syllable followed by two unstressed), e.g.
  Théirs not to / máke reply
  Théirs not to / réason why
  Théirs but to / dó and die

- spondaic (two stressed syllables), which can only be an occasional *foot*, e.g. in the fourth foot of:
  And às / she dìed / so mùst / wè dìe / oursèlves
  (*Robert Browning's* 'The Bishop Orders His Tomb At Saint Praxed's Church', 1845)

Whole poems cannot be written in spondees as it is impossible, of course, to stress every single syllable in a poem!

- pyrrhic (two unstressed syllables) which, again, can only be an occasional *foot*, e.g.

To a / grèen thòught / in a / grèen shàde

(from Marvell's 'The Garden', 1681)

In this example the first and third feet are pyrrhics, the second and third are spondees. See *stress*.

Michaels, Anne (b.1958): Canadian poet and novelist. She has been praised for her language which is rich yet clear, and for the density of her *imagery*. Notable works include THE WEIGHT OF ORANGES (1986), MINER'S POND (1991), FUGITIVE PIECES (1996).

Middle English Period: generally considered to cover *literature* written in England between approximately 1066 (the Norman Conquest) and 1500.

Middleton, Thomas (1580–1627): playwright who collaborated with many of his contemporaries including, probably, *Shakespeare*. His versatility extended to the writing of *pageants* and *masques* for special occasions. Notable works include his tragedies WOMEN BEWARE WOMEN (?1620) and THE CHANGELING (1622), written in collaboration with *Rowley*. Some critics ascribe THE REVENGER'S TRAGEDY to him rather than *Tourneur*.

miles gloriosus: Latin name for a boasting, swaggering self-glorifying soldier who was a stereotype in Greek and Roman comedy. He remained a popular stage figure, and elements of him are to be found in *Udall's* RALPH ROISTER DOISTER and *Shakespeare's* FALSTAFF AND PISTOL.

Miller, Arthur (b.1915): American playwright and essayist. Influenced by *Ibsen*, he is interested in family conflict, which is sometimes precipitated by the false values of contemporary society and often unfolds like a Greek drama, his *characters* usually experiencing an *anagnorisis*. Plays such as THE PRICE (1968) have done much to broaden the notion of *tragedy*. Regarded as one of America's leading *dramatists*, his other notable works include ALL MY SONS ((1947), DEATH OF A SALESMAN (1949), THE CRUCIBLE (1953), A VIEW FROM THE BRIDGE (1956), THEATRE ESSAYS (1971), PLAYING FOR TIME (1981), BROKEN GLASS (1994).

Milton, John (1608–74): poet, *dramatist*, pamphleteer and translator. Regarded as one of the finest poets and *prose* writers of any age, he is particularly admired for his use of *blank verse*. In his middle years he was distracted from writing *poetry* by his strongly held political views concerning civil and religious liberties, becoming a staunch supporter of the parliamentarians and later the Commonwealth against the monarchy. During this time he wrote some of the finest prose *polemics* in the English language. After the onset of blindness his friend *Marvell* assisted him. Following the Restoration, and consequent harassment and the public burning of his works, a quieter life gave him time to return to *literature*, whereupon he completed his masterpiece PARADISE LOST (1667), which *Dryden* described as one of the 'most noble and sublime *poems* that this age or nation has produced'. His reputation gained steadily after his death and, notwithstanding the attacks of critics such as *Johnson, T.S. Eliot* and *Leavis*, he is established as pre-eminent amongst English poets. The Romantics in particular applauded his radical politics and his creation of a great

English *epic* in PARADISE LOST. Other notable works include 'Ode Upon the Morning of Christ's Nativity' (1629), 'L'allegro' (1645), 'Il Penseroso' (1645), COMUS (1637), 'Lycidas' (1637), AREOPAGITICA (1644), PARADISE REGAINED (1671), SAMSON AGONISTES (1671).

miltonic sonnet: see *sonnet*.

mimesis: see *imitation*.

minimalism/minimalist: general term used to describe things presented in their barest possible essentials, as in some of *Beckett*'s plays, *Carver*'s short stories, or in this *poem* by *William Carlos Williams:*

> I have eaten
> the plums
> that were in
> the icebox
>
> and which
> you were probably
> saving
> for breakfast
>
> Forgive me
> they were delicious
> so sweet
> and so cold

('This is Just to Say', 1934)

Miracle plays: see *Mystery plays*.

Mistry, Rohinton (b.1952): Indian novelist and *short-story* writer. One of his major concerns is the problem of personal identity within society and history. Notable works include TALES FROM FIROZSHA BAAG (1987), SUCH A LONG JOURNEY (1991).

Mitchell, Adrian (b.1932): poet, novelist and playwright. Since the 1960s his writing has been mainly entertaining, *witty* and left-wing, and he tends to use a *free verse* form which is characteristic of *underground literature*. Notable works include MARAT/SADE (1966, an adaptation), OUT LOUD (1969), FOR BEAUTY DOUGLAS: COLLECTED POEMS AND SONGS (1981), ALL SHOOK UP: POEMS 1997–2000 (2001).

mock-epic: a *poem* of *epic* form which treats the ordinary or trivial in the grand, elevated language of the epic, e.g. *Dryden*'s MAC FLECKNOE, or *Pope*'s THE RAPE OF THE LOCK which uses a *mock-heroic* style in order to ridicule the behaviour of the galants and belles of Queen Anne's days. See *burlesque*.

mock-heroic is a term applied when a trivial subject is dealt with in an apparently heroic *manner* or lofty *style*, creating the effect of mocking the subject. It was especially popular in *Augustan* and 18th century literature. It is a feature of the *mock-epic* and other poetic and literary *forms*, e.g. *Gray*'s poem 'Ode on the Death of a Favourite Cat, Drowned in a Tub of Gold Fishes', or *Fielding*'s play TOM THUMB (1730), or the description of the battle in the churchyard in his *novel* TOM JONES. See *burlesque*.

mode: the *style, manner* or *method* employed by a writer in communicating her or his subject-matter to the reader. The term is similar in meaning to *form*, but is sometimes confused with *genre*. For instance, one might read something from the *science fiction* genre, written in a comic mode.

Modern Period: generally considered to cover *literature* written in England since 1914 (the outbreak of the First World War).

modernism/modernist: terms used to describe a European and American movement in all the arts with roots in the 19th century and lasting through much of the 20th century. As with *Romanticism*, the movement:

- was about breaking away from old rules, conventions and traditions
- experimented with *form* and *style*
- had no definite start or ending, but most critics suggest that it was at its height in the 1920s.

Among other things *modernism* embraced the *avant-garde, free verse, formalism, existentialism, expressionism, surrealism, symbolism, naturalism, Theatre of the Absurd,* and points the way towards *structuralism.* Important modernist works in English include *Joyce's* ULYSSES, *T.S. Eliot's* THE WASTE LAND, *Woolf's* JACOB'S ROOM (1922), *Pound's* CANTOS, the *poetry* of *Yeats;* and among other important modernist thinkers are Friedrich Nietzsche (1844–1900), Karl Marx (1818–83), Sigmund Freud (1856–1939). See *postmodernism.*

moment: a less formal word for *epiphany*, used by *Percy Shelley* in his DEFENCE OF POETRY (1821). See also *spots of time.*

monodrama is a play with only one *character*, e.g. *Beckett's* KRAPP'S LAST TAPE. *Tennyson* described his dramatic *monologue* 'Maud' thus. The term could also be applied to a 'one man show' (or, more correctly, one person show) such as Howard Burnham's (b.1946) LEWIS CARROLL (1984), or *Ackroyd's* THE MYSTERY OF CHARLES DICKENS.

monody: a mourning *ode*, originally said or sung by an individual, e.g. *Arnold's* THYRSIS, A MONODY (1866) in memory of the poet *Clough*, and in his introduction to 'Lycidas' *Milton* describes his *poem* as a monody. See *complaint, dirge, elegy, threnody.*

monologue is a term which may refer to:

- a *monodrama*
- a *poem* in the *form* of a dramatic *monologue* where the poet speaks through a *persona*, e.g. 'My Last Duchess' and several other poems by *Robert Browning. Tennyson, Hardy, Kipling, Yeats, T.S. Eliot, Pound, Frost* and others all exploit this form. See *stream of consciousness*
- a *soliloquy*.

monometer: see *metre.*

mood is the *atmosphere* which prevails in a work, or part of a work – often early on when the *tone* establishes an expectation in the reader or audience as to the future course of events. For instance, in the opening 40 lines or so of *Shakespeare's* HAMLET the mood is established by such factors as the unease of the sentinels (manifested by the tenseness of their dialogue), the time of night, the cold, their apprehension about the Ghost, and by its actual reappearance. See *ambience, tone.*

moral: in literary terms, a lesson which may be learnt from a piece of writing. For instance, it may be said that the *moral* of *Coleridge*'s 'The Rime of the Ancient Mariner' is that, in *Blake*'s words, 'every thing that lives is holy'.

Morality plays flourished during the mid-15th and first half of the 16th centuries, typically involving an *allegorical* struggle between *characters* representing vices and virtues over the soul of a figure called variously Man, Everyman, Mankind or similar, who stands as one person representing all humanity. After much temptation the virtues always win. In many ways the plays show the struggle between good and evil which is characteristic of most drama. Two of the best plays in this *genre* are MANKYNDE (?1475) and EVERYMAN (?1500). Performances were sometimes given by travelling troupes who may be regarded as the first professional actors, and who set up stages in town squares, inn yards or in the great halls of gentry or noblemen. THE CASTLE OF PERSEVERANCE (?1425) was an exception, requiring an elaborate circular earthwork within which the play was performed. Elizabethan playwrights use the *tradition*, e.g. *Shakespeare*'s Falstaff is a kind of Vice who tempts in his HENRY IV plays; and *Marlowe* subverts the tradition by having the vices (in the shape of Mephistopholes) win the soul of his main *character* in DOCTOR FAUSTUS. See also *Medwall*.

More, Sir Thomas (?1477–1535): writer, critic, patron of the arts. A friend of Erasmus (1466–1536), Holbein (1497–1543) and many others of cultural importance, he is a key figure in humanist *Renaissance* thinking. He held high office under Henry VIII, became Lord Chancellor, refused to support the King's break from the Church in Rome, was condemned as a traitor and beheaded. Notable works include UTOPIA (1516 in Latin, English translation 1551). *Shakespeare* probably contributed to the play SIR THOMAS MORE (?1594), and *Bolt*'s A MAN FOR ALL SEASONS is a notable treatment of the latter part of his life.

Morgan, Sally (b.1951): Australian novelist, biographer, playwright and artist. Her work is greatly influenced by her Aboriginal heritage which she did not know she had until her mother told her when she was 15. Notable works include MY PLACE (1987), THE STORY OF JACK MCPHEE (1989), SISTER GIRL (1992).

Morris, Mervyn (b.1937): Jamaican poet and editor. His concerns are both for the social fabric and the private and personal. He has experimented with conventional *verse forms*, and some of his short *poems* are strikingly powerful. Notable works include THE POND (1973), ON HOLY WEEK (1976), SHADOWBOXING (1979), THE FABER BOOK OF CONTEMPORARY CARIBBEAN SHORT STORIES (1990), EXAMINATION CENTRE (1992).

Morrison, Toni (b.1931): Black American novelist. She blends folktale, history and *myth* in powerful, *realistic* and consciously political stories of black people living in a white society, and of the position of black women within society as a whole. Notable works include THE BLUEST EYE (1970), SULA (1974), SONG OF SOLOMON (1977), BELOVED (1987).

Mortimer, John (b.1923): novelist, playwright, television and radio scriptwriter, adapter, *short-story* writer, editor and barrister. Capable of both cool and warm *humour*, he created Horace Rumpole, an eccentric barrister, and amongst his adaptations is a television screenplay of *Waugh*'s BRIDESHEAD REVISITED. He has been active against censorship. Notable works include WHAT SHALL WE TELL CAROLINE? (1958),

COME AS YOU ARE (1970), A VOYAGE ROUND MY FATHER (1970), RUMPOLE OF THE BAILEY (1978), PARADISE POSTPONED (1985).

motif: a recurring element in *literature,* such as a *character, device,* emotion or occurrence. It may be an aspect of a theme (with which the term is sometimes regarded as interchangeable). For instance:

- the malcontent is a recurrent motif in *Jacobean drama*
- *carpe diem* is a recurrent device in much literature
- jealousy is a motif in *Shakespeare's* OTHELLO
- the course of true love not running smooth is a frequent occurrence in *comedy.*

See *leitmotif, theme.*

Motion, Andrew (b.1952): poet, novelist and biographer. His lyrical *poetry* shows the influence of *Edward Thomas* and *Larkin,* with whom he worked at Hull University. He was appointed *poet laureate* in 1999 after the death of *Hughes.* Notable works include THE PLEASURE OF STEAMERS (1978), SECRET NARRATIVES (1983), DANGEROUS PLAY (1984), LOVE IN A LIFE (1991). He has also written biographies of Larkin and *Keats.*

Movement, The: a term used in the 1950s to describe a loose-knit group of writers including *Kingsley Amis, Davie, Enright, Gunn, Jennings* and *Larkin.* Their work was typically *witty, ironic,* sardonic and intellectual, and they aimed at a high degree of skilled craftsmanship in their writing. The key publication containing their work is NEW LINES (1956) edited by Robert Conquest (b.1917).

Mphalele, Es'Kia (b.1919): South African novelist, essayist, *short-story* writer and literary critic. He writes with sharp narrative skill about such matters as oppression, dispossession and poverty, exile, and corruption in African politics. Notable works include the autobiographical DOWN SECOND AVENUE (1959), THE AFRICAN IMAGE (1962, revised 1974), THE WANDERERS (1971).

Muir, Edwin (1887–1959): Scottish poet, novelist, translator, critic and autobiographer. Mainly traditional in *form* and *manner,* his approach to his subject matter is usually radical, allegorical and/or philosophical. His experiences of travel and of undergoing psychoanalysis combine to produce *poems* which tell of dream journeys with an underlying feeling of menace. He and his wife collaborated on significant translations of the Czech writer Franz Kafka (1883–1924) (see *kafkaesque*). Other notable works include FIRST POEMS (1925), CHORUS OF THE NEWLY DEAD (1926), THE LABYRINTH (1949), THE HORSES (1952).

Muldoon, Paul (b.1951): Irish poet, playwright and librettist. His *poetry* is refreshingly honest, imaginative and innovative. His elegant handling of *form, metre* and *rhyme* are supported by verbal ingenuity and *wit.* He is also capable of lyrical simplicity and emotional directness. He experiments with *narrative,* and displays a tension born of his Ulster background. Notable works include NEW WEATHER (1973), MULES (1977), WHY BROWNIE LEFT (1980), QUOOF (1983), MEETING THE BRITISH (1987), MADOC: A MYSTERY (1990), THE ANNALS OF CHILE (1995), HAY (1998), COLLECTED POEMS 1968–1998 (2001).

Mungoshi, Charles (b.1947): Zimbabwean novelist, *short-story* writer, poet and publisher. He is generally regarded as the most eminent Zimbabwean author writing in

English and Shona, and his stories often evoke his country's landscape. There are aspects of political protest in his writing, especially in the *collection* of *stories* COMING OF THE DRY SEASON (1972), which was banned before Independence. Notable works include WAITING FOR THE RAIN (1975), THE SETTING SUN AND THE ROLLING WORLD (1980).

Munro, Alice (b.1931): Canadian novelist and *short-story* writer, she is widely regarded as highly accomplished in the latter *genre*, often using provincial Ontario for her fictionalised *settings*. She combines the everyday and the extraordinary as two sides of the same coin. Notable works include LIVES OF GIRLS AND WOMEN (1971), WHO DO YOU THINK YOU ARE? (1978, published in the UK as BEGGAR MAID), PROGRESS OF LOVE (1980).

Murdoch, Iris (1919–99): novelist and philosopher. Her prolific output often contains philosophical *symbolism* and debate within the *novel* form. Her *characters* often undergo an *epiphany*. Notable works include UNDER THE NET (1954), THE SANDCASTLE (1957), THE BELL (1958), A SEVERED HEAD (1961), THE ITALIAN GIRL (1964), THE SEA, THE SEA (1978).

Murphy, Dervla (b.1931): Irish travel writer who writes with compassion about those whom she encounters in her travels from Ireland to India and Africa. Notable works include FULL TILT: IRELAND TO INDIA BY BICYCLE (1965), TIBETAN FREEHOLD (1966), ETHIOPIA WITH A MULE (1968), THE IKIMWI ROAD: FROM KENYA TO ZIMBABWE (1993).

Murray, Les (b.1939): Australian poet. Always keen that *poetry* should reach a wider audience and not just intellectuals, he writes authoritatively as he draws upon Australian culture, folklore and landscape. Notable works include THE ILEX TREE (1965, a collaborative work), THE WEATHERBOARD CATHEDRAL (1969), THE BOYS WHO STOLE THE FUNERAL (1980), DOG FOX FIELD (1990).

Mystery plays are dramatisations of Old and New Testament stories from the Creation through to the Last Judgment. Their origins may be traced to 10th century Easter plays in Latin. Over the years the plays moved out of the churches into the churchyards, were developed in English, and were taken over by guilds of workers who often performed a play suitable to their craft (e.g. in one cycle NOAH'S FLOOD was performed by those who brought fresh water to the town, and in another THE CRUCIFIXION by the butchers). Cycles of plays developed in, among other places, Chester, York, Coventry and Wakefield. They were usually performed on Corpus Christi Day, and staging was either on fixed scaffolds in the town square, or on *pageant* carts which travelled round the streets performing each play at appointed stations before moving on. Performances died out during the 16th century. It is an attractive idea that a 22-year-old Warwickshire man called *William Shakespeare* might have been present at one of the last recorded performances in Coventry in 1586.

myth: originally meaning anything passed on by word of mouth, the term has assumed complex meanings and *connotations*. Among them are:

- a *story* from a religion which one no longer believes in, e.g. *Keats, Victorian* poets and others make considerable use of classical mythology in their *poems*
- a tale of supernatural beings

- a system or way of thinking devised by a writer, e.g. *Blake* developed his own mythology, a mixture of inherited myths, biblical stories and his own imagination; as did *Yeats*, who made considerable use of Celtic legend
- an imagined territory (sometimes of the mind as much as literal) within which a *narrative* occurs, e.g. *Faulkner*'s Yoknapatwapha County; or the psychological world created by *Melville* in MOBY DICK
- a commonly held fallacy, usually one with a grain of truth, or at least a psychological truth, around which elaborate *fictions* have been woven
- as used by *structuralist* critics, myth denotes the system of *signs* by which society expresses itself.

myth critics adopt a view that all *literature* is developed from *myths*. The leading exponent of this attitude was the Canadian critic Northrop Frye (1912–91).

N

Nabokov, Vladimir (1899–1977): American novelist, *short-story* writer, translator and poet. Much critical interest in his work has focused upon the influence of his Russian background upon his American writings, and he has been regarded as a *post-modernist*. Notable works include THE EYE (1930), THE GIFT (1938), LOLITA (1955), PALE FIRE (1962), LOOK AT THE HARLEQUINS! (1974).

Naipaul V.S. (b.1932): Trinidadian novelist, travel and *short-story* writer of Indian descent. His *themes* include 20th century insecurity and the bad effects of colonialism; his *style* is often *witty* and sardonic. Notable works include THE MYSTIC MASSEUR (1957), MIGUEL STREET (1959), THE HOUSE OF MR BISWAS (1961), THE MIMIC MEN (1967), IN A FREE STATE (1971), A BEND IN THE RIVER (1979), AMONG THE BELIEVERS (1981), FINDING THE CENTRE (1984), THE ENIGMA OF ARRIVAL (1987), HALF A LIFE (2001).

naïve narrator: see *narrator*.

Narayan, R.K. (1906–2001): Indian novelist and *short-story* writer. An uncomplicated *diction* and clear *narrative* prose *style* both link him with the Indian story-telling *tradition* and make him appealing to Western readers. Notable works include SWAMI AND FRIENDS (1935), THE BACHELOR OF ARTS (1937), THE ENGLISH TEACHER (1945), WAITING FOR MAHATMA (1955), THE PAINTER OF SIGNS (1976).

narrative is a piece of *prose* or *poetry* which tells a *story*. In *drama* the narrative evolves through the *action*.

narrative verse is a *poem* which tells a *story*. There are three main types: *ballad, epic* and *romance*. *Verse* rather than *prose* was the common method of telling a *story* before the 18th century. Examples are *Chaucer*'s CANTERBURY TALES, *Spenser*'s THE FAERIE QUEENE, *Milton*'s PARADISE LOST, *Wordsworth*'s THE PRELUDE, *Keats*' THE EVE OF ST AGNES, *Owen*'s STRANGE MEETING, *Auden*'s LETTER TO LORD BYRON (1940) *Larkin*'s WHITSUN WEDDINGS.

narrator/narrative voice: these terms refer to the *voice* from whose *viewpoint* or *standpoint* a *story* is told. Critics have identified various categories of:

- first person narrator, who adopts a persona in order to tell the story her/himself. Such a narrator may also be 'unreliable' (see below)
- second person narrator: this is a less used *form* where the *author* addresses 'you' as if you, the reader, are a part of the action
- third person narrator, or omniscient narrator, where the story is told from a god-like bird's eye view, seeing all
- unreliable (or 'fallible') narrator, where the author makes clear by various means that the narrator's opinions do not coincide with the author's. *Henry James* often used this *technique*. Stevens, the central *character* in *Ishiguro*'s THE REMAINS OF THE DAY, is an unreliable narrator because he suppresses and evades the truth about himself and others
- limited (or 'restricted') point of view narrator, where the author shows the world from the limited perspective of only one or a few characters, e.g.

Talbot and Colley in *Golding*'s RITES OF PASSAGE, the former being particularly 'unreliable'

- intrusive narrator. *Dickens* sometimes intervenes in the action to ensure that he hammers home a point to his reader
- impersonal narrator, where the author attempts to report events as objectively as possible, sometimes not even accessing characters' feelings, e.g. in some of *Hemingway*'s stories
- self-conscious narrator where the writer reminds us that what we are reading is *fiction*, and thus dispels the reader's illusion, e.g. Tristram in *Sterne*'s TRISTRAM SHANDY, or Nellie Dean in *Emily Brontë* 's WUTHERING HEIGHTS
- naïve narrator, such as Gulliver in *Jonathan Swift*'s GULLIVER'S TRAVELS, who is naïvely impressed by what he sees in the countries which he visits, and through whose naïvety the reader is expected to see the truth of things (thus giving rise to *irony*).

Of the above, first and third person narrator are by far the most common. A third person narrator is not always as impartial as at first sight appears, and a reader must be alert to notice such *devices* as an intrusive adverb by which an author seeks to guide a reader into an opinion. For instance, ' "I remember being so proud," he said pathetically' (from *Lessing*'s THE HABIT OF LOVING, 1957). The insertion of 'pathetically' gives an authorial bias which the reader cannot ignore. Sometimes an author moves between both modes of narration, moving inside and outside a character's head in a mixture of third and first person narrative known as *free indirect style* or *free indirect discourse*. For instance, 'Tom sat opposite him... It crossed Tom's mind to steal the green ring... It would be easy...' (from *Highsmith*'s THE TALENTED MR RIPLEY). Here the narrative moves from objective fact, to reported thought, to being inside a character's head. See *persona, showing and telling, voice*.

naturalism, in a literary sense, is the use of realistic *settings* and *characters* to convey philosophical truths. A development of *realism* and influenced by Charles Darwin's biological ideas, theories of naturalism were developed during the 19th century in Germany and France by writers such as Emile Zola, and affected novelists such as *Hardy*. Sometimes naturalism is used in connection with the writings of those who see nature and natural beauty as fundamental, e.g. *Wordsworth*.

naturalistic drama, a development of *naturalism*, is a term used of *drama* which in its *setting* and all surface appearances tries to imitate real life. Naturalism should not be confused with *realism*, which refers to the psychological reality of what is being presented. Thus a *drawing-room comedy* may be perfectly naturalistic, taking place in a setting which exactly replicates a house interior and with the language of the *characters* being true to life; but there may be little psychological realism in their thinking and behaviour.

near rhyme: see *half-rhyme*.

negation is a way of expressing a situation by denying something else. For instance, Macbeth says 'light thickens' in order to indicate gathering darkness; and in 'Hyperion' *Keats* writes 'No stir of air was there' to indicate stillness. See *litotes*.

negative capability is a phrase coined by *Keats* to indicate a state wherein a writer appreciates and accepts the beauty of things without endlessly striving to understand everything down to the last detail, suppressing his own intellect and entering into an imaginative appreciation of most aspects of the surrounding world. He defined it as a literary quality 'which *Shakespeare* possessed so enormously – I mean "Negative Capability"; that is, when man is capable of being in uncertainties, mysteries, doubts, without any irritable reaching after fact and reason … with a great poet the sense of beauty over comes every other consideration'. This appreciation of imaginative response before reason is a central aspect of *Romanticism*.

nemesis: punishment or retribution served on a tragic *hero* or *heroine*. The Greeks had a goddess Nemesis who was thought to hand out such punishment to those who ignored the gods' warnings, thus displaying *hubris*.

Neo-classical Period: covers *literature* written in England between 1660 (the *Restoration* of the monarchy) and approximately 1780.

neo-classicism is a label applied to the *style* of certain *literature* and other arts (such as architecture) created during the *Neo-classical Period*, and is often contrasted with *Romanticism*. Essentially, the neo-classicists valued reason, intellect and a balanced outlook, distrusting the emotions (today we might say that they regarded the functions of the cognitive left-hand side of the brain above those of the affective right-hand side). They looked back to the rational, intellectual world of ancient Greece and Rome as models of common sense and balance. Notable neo-classical writers include *Dryden, Jonathan Swift, Pope, Fielding, Goldsmith*.

neologism: a newly-coined word (from the Greek 'new word'). Neologisms may be of various types, for instance

- a completely new word (e.g. 'hassle', 'hippie')
- a word derived from an existing prefix or root (e.g.'stereophonic', 'camcorder')
- an established word with a new meaning (e.g. 'gay', 'wicked')
- an acronym (e.g. 'quango' from 'quasi-autonomous non-governmental organisation').

A language which opens its arms to new words is a healthy, vibrant language, and today's slang becomes tomorrow's accepted usage. *Shakespeare* seems to have invented, or at least brought into currency, numerous words; for example, the first recorded use of words such as 'accommodation', 'assassination', 'obscene' are in his plays.

New Critics advocated *objective criticism*, affirming that the *text* alone matters, and that biographical, sociological and other contextual information surrounding a text is irrelevant. Influenced by *Richards* and in turn influencing *F.R. Leavis*, the movement was primarily American, and UNDERSTANDING POETRY (1938) by Cleanth Brooks (1906–94) and Robert Penn Warren (1905–89) made New Criticism the standard teaching approach in America for several decades. See *close reading, intrinsic attitude, leavisite*.

new historicism: see *historicism*.

New Journalism refers to a kind of writing which, very generally speaking, sought to explore contemporary *reality* by blurring the boundaries between fact and *fiction*, journalism with literary *technique*. Dissatisfied with pure journalism as a means of expressing the enormity of contemporary events such as the Vietnam War, the movement emerged in America during the 1960s with the publication of such books as IN COLD BLOOD (1965) by Truman Capote (1924–84) and *Wolfe's* THE KANDY-KOLORED FLAKE STREAMLINE BABY. Other notable New Journalism might include *Mailer's* ARMIES OF THE NIGHT, *Wolfe's* THE ELECTRIC KOOL-AID ACID TEST, and DISPATCHES (1974) by Michael Herr (b. 1940). *Wolfe* described the aims of the movement in NEW JOURNALISM (1973). See *faction*.

Newgate fiction: an early *form* of *crime fiction* popular in the 1830s, e.g PAUL CLIFFORD (1830) by Edward Bulwer-Lytton (1803–73). The Newgate Calendar or Malefactors Bloody Register gave a record of scandalous crimes committed between 1700–74 and from 1826 onwards which provided excellent original material on which to base novels, some of which we might now describe as *faction*. Dickens' depiction of the criminal world in OLIVER TWIST was something of a reaction against *Newgate fiction*.

newspeak: jargon language which deliberately sets out to obscure the plain truth. Invented by *George Orwell* in his *novel* NINETEEN EIGHTY-FOUR.

Ngugi wa Thiong'o (b.1938): Kenyan novelist, *short-story* writer, playwright and essayist. He writes in English and his native Gîkûyû, and among his *themes* of social and political injustice is the cultural and political necessity that Africans should write in their local language. Notable works include WEEP NOT, CHILD (1964, the first novel in English by an East African writer), A GRAIN OF WHEAT (1967), WRITERS IN POLITICS (1975), PETALS OF BLOOD (1977), DEVIL ON THE CROSS (1980).

Nicholson, Norman (1914–87): poet, playwright and critic. Influenced by *T.S. Eliot* and *Wordsworth*, much of his *poetry* is *topographical* and draws on the people, industry and general *setting* of his native town of Millom, Cumbria, and the adjacent Lake District countryside. He writes with imaginative vision about man in his natural environment. Notable works Include THE POT GERANIUM (1950), LOCAL HABITATION (1972), THE LAKES (1977), SEA TO THE WEST (1981), COLLECTED POEMS (1994).

Nissim, Ezekiel (b.1929), poet, playwright and editor, has been regarded as the 'Grand Old Man' of Anglo-Indian literature. Notable works include THE UNFINISHED MAN (1960), THE EXACT NAME (1965), THREE PLAYS (1969), HYMNS IN DARKNESS (1977).

Nobel Prize for Literature: a valuable prize awarded every year since 1901 to the writer who, in the opinion of the awarding committee, has 'produced in the field of literature the most outstanding work of an idealistic tendency'. Former winners include *Yeats* (1920), *T.S. Eliot* (1948), *Faulkner* (1949), *Hemingway* (1954), *Steinbeck* (1962), *Beckett* (1969), *Patrick White* (1973), *Bellow* (1976), *Golding* (1984), *Soyinka* (1986), *Walcott* (1992), *Morrison* (1993).

noble savage: the concept that in a primeval time man was more worthy and honourable than modern man, who has been corrupted by modern civilisation. This man is embodied in *Behn's* OROONOKO. The notion of the noble savage, close to nature, was attractive to writers during the *Romantic Period*. See also *primitivism*.

nom de plume: another term for *pseudonym*.

non-fiction novel: see *faction, New Journalism*.

Norton, Thomas (1533–84): playwright and poet, best known for co-authorship with *Sackville* of GORBODUC (1561), sometimes considered to be the first proper

English stage tragedy. The play is written in *blank verse*, but the lines are overly regular and heavily *end-stopped* and the result is mechanical and plodding.

nouveau roman: an experimental *avant-garde* type of *novel* which emerged in France during the mid-20th century. Established *devices* such as *plot, characterisation, action,* and *narrative* were rejected in favour of a disconnected observation of things. See *anti-novel*.

novel: a novel can be described as a continuous piece of *prose*, longer than a *short story* or *novella* and anything from 60,000–200,000 words. It characteristically consists of *characters* within a *plot* which tells a *story*, covering any subject from any angle, and may range from the amusing to the tragic, the easily accessible *thriller* to the most intensely learned work, from Alistair Maclean (1922–88) to *Rushdie* or *Joyce*. *Boccaccio*'s DECAMERON, although essentially a cycle of *short stories*, is sometimes regarded as the forerunner of the novel. As regards the first 'true novel' in English, some say *Bunyan*'s PILGRIM'S PROGRESS, others *Defoe*'s ROBINSON CRUSOE or MOLL FLANDERS (an early example of a *picaresque novel*) or *Richardson*'s PAMELA (an early example of the *epistolary novel*). After the 18th century rise of the novel, the 19th century saw its heyday with novelists such as *Austen*, the *Brontë* sisters, *George Eliot* and *Thackeray* producing novels for a vast and avid market of readers. *Scott* explored the possibilities of the *historical novel*. The novels of *Dickens* and others were first published in instalment *form* in periodicals, making them easily available to a wide public. *Trollope* developed the *saga novel*. By the late 19th century the *genre* was further stretched with *Hardy*'s *regional novels*. In the 20th century *Joyce* and *Woolf* pioneered *stream of consciousness, Fowles* and others played with *narrative structure, Winterson* and others used *magic realism*. Despite increasing competition from media such as television the novel has remained a popular form as more *styles* emerge and the genre is continually re-invented. See *anti-novel, campus novel, crime novel, detective fiction, fabulation, gothic fiction, metafiction, modernism, narrator/narrative voice, nouveau roman, novel of adventure, novel of ideas, novel of sensation, police procedural, novel of the soil, novelette, novella, propaganda, roman à clef, roman-fleuve, science fiction, sentimental novel*.

novel of adventure: ROBINSON CRUSOE by *Daniel Defoe* is an example of this *genre*, which includes much *desert island fiction* and *romance* literature. Among exponents of this type are John Buchan (1875–1940), Anthony Hope (1863–1933), *Arthur Conan Doyle*, Alistair Maclean, Neville Shute (1899–1960).

novel of ideas: a type of *fiction* in which *dialogue* and erudite debate are foremost rather than storyline and *character* development. One notable exponent is *Huxley* in *novels* such as CHROME YELLOW and POINT COUNTER POINT.

novel of sensation: a *form* of *novel* popular from about the 1860s in which events are sensational and *melodramatic*, often involving crime and undisclosed secrets. Notable examples include *Collins*' THE WOMAN IN WHITE and Mary Braddon's LADY AUDLEY'S SECRET. Such novels may be regarded as forerunners of the *thriller* and *detective fiction*. See also *crime novel, gothic fiction, Newgate fiction*.

novel of sensibility: see *sentimental novel*.

novel of the soil: a *novel* where a major *theme* is man's relationship with the natural forces of the earth, e.g. Steinbeck's THE GRAPES OF WRATH, *Lawrence*'s THE RAINBOW. See also *rural novel*.

novelette: a *fiction* shorter than a *novel* and longer than a *short story*. It can be used as a demeaning term for such as trivial romances. See *novella*.

novella has a similar meaning to *novelette*, but without its pejorative connotations. Sometimes the *plot* is restricted to the development of a single event. Examples are *Conrad*'s TYPHOON (1903), *Lawrence*'s THE VIRGIN AND THE GYPSY (1930), *Hemingway*'s THE OLD MAN AND THE SEA.

Nowlan, Alden (1933–93): Canadian poet. Influenced, among others, by *William Carlos Williams,* his *poetry* focuses on such matters as family relationships and the damaging effects of puritanism. Notable works include THE ROSE AND THE PURITANS (1958), THE THINGS WHICH ARE (1962), SMOKED GLASS (1977).

Nowra, Louis (b.1950): Australian playwright. His theatrical, non-naturalistic plays often explore individuals isolated in their own, obsessional, worlds. Notable works include, ALBERT NAMES EDWARD (1975), VISIONS (1978), SUMMER OF ALIENS (1992), RADIANCE (1993).

objective correlative refers to the notion that in all art, and especially *poetry*, every emotion should be defined objectively in relation to a set of facts. The term was made popular by *T.S. Eliot* in his *essay* HAMLET AND HIS PROBLEMS (1919), in which he stated that Hamlet's emotions are excessive given his situation, and thus unrealistic; but that Macbeth's and Lady Macbeth's are appropriate to their situation. Eliot's idea was viewed quite favourably in the first part of the 20th century, but is nowadays considered too scientifically prescriptive.

objective criticism, popular among the *New Critics,* advances the critical view that a piece of *literature*, once created, exists as an object in its own right, free of the writer and the reader. Its value is intrinsic, and its *context* is irrelevant. Since the advent of *literary theory* this approach has fallen out of favour. See *close reading, intrinsic attitude, leavisite, Richards.*

objectivism is achieved, it is supposed, when in a fictional work a writer presents events and *characters*' feelings in a detached and non-committal fashion. *James' novels* and *Larkin*'s *poetry* have been, to some extent, so described. Subjectivism occurs in works such as *autobiography,* or in *conversation* or *lyric* poems such as *Coleridge*'s 'Frost at Midnight' or *Wordsworth*'s 'Tintern Abbey', in which the 'I' *persona* is associated with the poet. In truth, few works are either wholly objective or subjective, but combine the two. See *narrator/ narrative voice.*

objectivity: the idea that it is possible to find an objective 'truth' about the meaning of a work of *literature*. This concept was important to the *leavisite* school, but since the advent of *literary theory* it is out of fashion. See *subjectivity.*

obligatory scene: a scene which a playwright is obliged to include because the development of the *drama* leads an audience to look forward to it. For instance, in *Shakespeare*'s MACBETH it would be difficult to imagine the play without an eventual confrontation between Macbeth and MacDuff.

oblique rhyme: another term for *half-rhyme.*

obscurity is when a reader is challenged to understand a writer because of such features as difficult language, strange sentence constructions, complex verse *forms*, use of foreign words or multiple *allusion*. The term is often used to imply needless difficulty, inability to write clearly, or just incompetence; but sometimes the nature of a piece of writing demands treatment which is at first difficult for the reader but ultimately rewarding. *Johnson* disliked the *metaphysical* poets for their obscurity, *T.S. Eliot* was accused of it in THE WASTE LAND, and *Joyce* in FINNEGAN'S WAKE.

O'Casey, Sean (1880–1964): Irish playwright and autobiographer. As a young man he developed socialist and Republican sympathies. *Realism* and *tragi-comedy* were hallmarks of his early plays, which dealt with such matters as poverty, patriotism and survival. Later plays, beginning with THE SILVER TASSIE (1928), which was rejected by the Abbey Theatre, Dublin, and caused his rift with *Yeats*, are more *expressionist*. His six volume *autobiography* has been much admired. Other notable works include THE

SHADOW OF A GUNMAN (1923), JUNO AND THE PAYCOCK (1924), THE PLOUGH AND THE STARS (1926), THE STAR TURNS RED (1940), WITHIN THE GATES (1943).

occasional verse is *verse* written for a particular occasion, e.g. *Marvell*'s 'An Horatian Ode upon Cromwell's Return from Ireland', *Tennyson*'s 'The Charge of the Light Brigade'. The *poet laureate* especially might be expected to write such *verse*, as in the latter example. See *elegy, ode*.

occupatio is a rhetorical device, much loved of politicians, whereby a subject is raised by stating that it should not be raised, e.g. 'It is not appropriate to remind you that...'

O'Connor, Flannery (1925–1964): American novelist and *short-story* writer. With grim, ironic humour and in a clear, vivid *style* she deals with such subjects as religious fanaticism, spiritual poverty and violence. Her writing has variously been described as poetic and *gothic*. Notable works include WISE BLOOD (1952), THE VIOLENT BEAR IT AWAY (1960).

octameter: see *metre*.

octave, or octet, is a *stanza* or section of *verse* containing eight lines, usually defined by a unit of rhyme pattern.

octosyllabic couplet: in *verse*, a pair of rhymed *tetrameters*, usually *iambic* but occasionally *trochaic*. Among others *Chaucer, Milton, Coleridge, Wordsworth* and *Byron* used the *form*, and a good example is *Marvell*'s 'To His Coy Mistress'. See *metre*.

ode: a kind of *lyric* in which the poet reflects on a particular subject in a serious *tone* and a lofty *style*. The original odes were written by the Greek poet Pindar as hymns of praise to winners of the Olympic Games and other sporting events. The *genre* was developed by the Latin poet Horace, and made popular in England by Abraham Cowley (1618–67), since when many poets have written odes including *Dryden* ('Song for St Cecilia's Day', 1687), *Gray* ('Ode on a Distant Prospect of Eton College', 1747), *Coleridge* ('Dejection'), *Wordsworth* ('An Ode: Intimations of Immortality'), *Shelley* ('Ode to the West Wind'); and, of course, *Keats* wrote six famous odes.

Okara, Gabriel (b.1921): Nigerian poet and novelist. He is noted for his use of oral tradition in his writing, especially his *lyric* poetry. Notable works include THE VOICE (1964), THE FISHERMAN'S INVOCATION (1978).

Okpewho, Isadore (b.1941): Nigerian novelist and critic. His creative writing nearly always has a political agenda concerning his native land. Notable works include THE VICTIMS (1970), THE LAST DUTY (1976), MYTH IN AFRICA: A STUDY OF ITS AESTHETIC AND CULTURAL RELEVANCE (1983), TIDES (1993).

Okri, Ben (b.1959): Nigerian novelist, *short-story* writer and poet. His clear, concise *prose* conveys detailed observations of both individual and social responses to situations, often within the *context* of a strong sense of African place. Notable works include FLOWERS AND SHADOWS (1980), THE LANDSCAPE WITHIN (1981), INCIDENTS AT THE SHRINE (1986), STARS OF THE NEW CURFEW (1988), THE FAMISHED ROAD (1991), AN AFRICAN ELEGY (1992), DANGEROUS LOVE (1996).

Old English/Anglo-Saxon Period: generally taken to refer to literature written and language spoken in England between approximately 449AD (the arrival of the first English-speaking tribes on the shores of Britain) and 1066 (the Norman Conquest).

Oliver, Mary (b.1935): American poet. Through sharp descriptions and straight-forward language she explores the relationship between the individual and the natural world. Notable works include AMERICAN PRIMITIVE (1984), NEW AND SELECTED POEMS (1994), THE CHANCE TO LOVE EVERYTHING (2000).

omnibus edition: a collection of all an author's works in a single volume.

omniscient narrator: see *narrator/narrative voice.*

Ondaatje, Michael (b.1943): Canadian novelist and poet, born in Sri Lanka. His work is considered an important contribution to Canadian *post-modernist* writing. Much of his work explores the problems of an individual's past within a wider cultural history. His *poetry* is often dark and surreal, gaining the attention of the reader through arresting juxtapositions. In THE COLLECTED WORKS OF BILLY THE KID (1970) and RUNNING IN THE FAMILY (1982) he mixes *prose, verse* and photographs. Other notable works include THE DAINTY MONSTERS (1967), THE MAN WITH SEVEN TOES (1969), RAT JELLY (1973), RUNNING IN THE FAMILY (1983), THE SKIN OF A LION (1987), THE CINNAMON PEELER (1990), THE ENGLISH PATIENT (1992).

one-act play: a *drama* played with no interval and usually of less than an hour's duration. Although formerly much more popular than nowadays, some modern *dramatists* have excelled in the *genre*, e.g. *Pinter* with such plays as THE DUMB WAITER (1958) and LANDSCAPE (1970).

O'Neill, Eugene (1888–1953): American playwright. Influenced by Ibsen and Strindberg, his powerfully theatrical plays, which through *expressionism* and a variety of other *styles* tackle subjects such as self-deception and self-destruction, have had great influence on American theatre. Notable works include THE EMPEROR JONES (1920), ANNA CHRISTIE (1921), THE HAIRY APE (1922), ALL GOD'S CHILLUN GOT WINGS (1924), MOURNING BECOMES ELECTRA (1931), THE ICEMAN COMETH (1946), LONG DAY'S JOURNEY INTO NIGHT (1956).

one-man show: (or, more correctly, one-person show) see *monodrama.*

onomatopoeia is a term used in both a narrow and a broad sense:

- the narrow sense confines the term to the use of words whereby their sound closely represents what they mean, e.g. 'bang', 'smack', 'whisper'
- the broader definition allows the term to cover any way in which language closely suggests that which it denotes, extending beyond sound to, for instance, touch, appearance or movement. In 'Ode to Psyche' *Keats* describes the lovers as 'couched', which gives a tactile sense of softness not possible had he simply written 'lying'. In his 'Essay on Criticism' *Pope* talks of the sound echoing the sense (onomatopoeia is sometimes called 'echoism') and gives as an example:

> When Ajax strives some rock's vast weight to throw
> The line too labors, and the words move slow

open couplet: a *couplet* in *verse* where the sense is not complete by the end of the second line, but carries over into the following lines, e.g.

There anchoring, Peter chose from man to hide,
There hang his head, and view the lazy tide
In its hot slimy channel slowly glide;

(from *Crabbe*'s 'The Borough')

open stage: any *form* of staging whereby the audience is not separated from the actors by a *proscenium arch*. Open staging has become increasingly popular again over the past century after a break of almost three centuries.

open/closed texts: see Appendix 1.

opera: a *drama* in which all the words are entirely, or almost entirely, sung. Potentially a very powerful *form* of *drama*, few writers have been librettists, but opera has drawn much from *literature*, e.g. adaptations by the composer Benjamin Brittain (1913–76) of *Melville*'s BILLY BUDD, *Henry James'* THE TURN OF THE SCREW, and *Crabbe*'s story of Peter Grimes from 'The Borough'.

oral literature/tradition: the composing and passing on of *stories* by word of mouth, often in poetic *form*. A tradition of creating *epics*, *ballads* and *lyrics* (folk *songs*) has existed since primitive times, and is still practised today in illiterate or semi-literate communities. The *Anglo-Saxon epic* BEOWULF has its origins in such a tradition.

oration: a speech delivered at a formal public occasion, e.g. Mark Antony's oration at Caesar's funeral in *Shakespeare*'s JULIUS CAESAR (?1599).

organic form is where the *form* of a work arises naturally out of the writer's subject and *theme*, growing and taking shape like a living organism, rather than being imposed by a set of rules as in *mechanic form*. It has been noted that, among others, *Shakespeare* and his fellow *dramatists*, and *Coleridge* and his fellow Romantics, favoured organic *form*.

orientalism may loosely be described as western writing on, and fascination with, things of the East. Such an interest began during the *Renaissance* and gathered pace in the 18th century, Romantic poets such as *Coleridge* and *Byron* often turning to oriental *themes* and *settings*. The rise of the British Empire stimulated *novels* located in the East, e.g. the work of *Kipling, Forster, Paul Scott, Farrell;* and also much *travel literature* by such as *Stark, Theroux, Thesiger, William Dalrymple* (b.1965), *Naipaul*.

originality is the discovery and use of innovative writing and the rejection of *imitation* or *convention*, whether of *form* or subject-matter. Modern writers tend to consider originality to be more important than earlier writers such as *Shakespeare* and *Milton*.

Orton, Joe (1933–67): playwright and novelist. He explores violence, perversion, sex and corruption, among other aspects of human behaviour, to create sparkling, anarchic, deliberately tasteless and often farcical *black comedy*. Notable works include ENTERTAINING MR SLOANE (1964), LOOT (1965), WHAT THE BUTLER SAW (1969).

Orwell, George – real name Eric Arthur Blair (1903–50): novelist, essayist and journalist. In his clear and economic *style*, never using more words than necessary to convey his *meaning*, he writes of such matters as his deliberately chosen poverty in Paris and London, his observations of unemployment and his prophetic fears of the political manipulation of language (especially in his *essay* POLITICS AND THE ENGLISH LANGUAGE, 1946). He is best known for ANIMAL FARM (1945), an *allegory* on revolutions, and the grim NINETEEN EIGHTY-FOUR (1948), both *satires* about totalitarianism and state control. Other notable works include DOWN AND OUT IN PARIS AND LONDON (1933), THE ROAD TO WIGAN PIER (1937), COLLECTED ESSAYS, JOURNALISM AND LETTERS (1968).

Osborne, John (1929–94): playwright and autobiographer. Leader of the *Angry Young Men*, LOOK BACK IN ANGER (1956) changed the direction of mainstream theatre, moving it away from the *drawing-room comedy* and the *well-made play* towards *kitchen-sink drama*. Other notable works include THE ENTERTAINER (1957), LUTHER (1961), INADMISSABLE EVIDENCE (1964), A BETTER CLASS OF PERSON (1981), DÉJÀ VU (1992).

Osofisan, Femi (b.1946): Nigerian playwright and novelist. Influenced by *Soyinka*, but more interested in writing consciously politically plays in the widest sense. Notable works include A RESTLESS RUN OF LOCUSTS (1975), KOLERA KOLEJ (1975), THE CHATTERING AND THE SONG (1977), YUNGBA YUNGBA AND THE DANCE CONTEST (1995).

Osundare, Niyi (b.1947): Nigerian poet. Using oral and literary traditions, lyricism and *satire*, his much acclaimed *poetry* shows concern for social justice. He is a well known *performance poet*. Notable works include SONGS OF THE MARKET PLACE (1984), THE EYE OF THE EARTH (1986).

ottava rima: a *stanza* of eight ten-syllable *iambic* lines rhyming ababbcc, pioneered by *Wyatt* who imported the *form* from Italy. Used by *Keats* in 'Isabella' and *Yeats* in 'Sailing to Byzantium' (1928). It is sometimes known as a *byronic stanza* because *Byron* used it with great success in his *narrative* poem DON JUAN; he exploited the comic potential of the *rhyme scheme*, especially the final *rhyming couplet*, and the effect is enhanced by the *feminine endings* of the a and c *rhymes*.

Otway, Thomas (1652–85): playwright and poet. Influenced by French playwrights, especially Racine, he wrote *drama* in both *blank verse* and *heroic couplets*, some of his tragic writing achieving a power not heard on stage since the Jacobean Age. Notable works include DON CARLOS (1676), THE ORPHAN (1680), VENICE PRESERV'D (1682).

outsider: a term sometimes applied to writers such as *Kerouac*, or *characters* such as Holden Caulfield in *Salinger*'s THE CATCHER IN THE RYE, who are in some sense outsiders, detached from the society which surrounds them. The concept gained currency through THE OUTSIDER (1956) by Colin Wilson (b.1931).

over-reading: see Appendix 1.

Owen, Wilfred (1893–1918): poet. Usually regarded as one of the finest of the *war poets*, he writes with passion and compassion, and with technical mastery over *metre*, *assonance* and *rhyme*, of the futility of war and human suffering. Most of his best known *poems* were written between the summer of 1917 and his death shortly before the November 1918 armistice. Notable works include 'Dulce et Decorum Est', 'Strange Meeting', 'Futility', all in THE COMPLETE POEMS AND FRAGMENTS (1983). See *war literature*.

oxymoron: a *form* of *paradox* whereby apparently contradictory words are combined with arresting effect, e.g. 'loving hate' (from *Shakespeare*'s ROMEO AND JULIET) or 'marriage hearse' (from *Blake*'s 'London', 1794). See *antithesis*.

pageant: originally a cart or wagon upon which medieval *Mystery plays* were performed, the word has come to refer to a sometimes spectacular *dramatic* presentation of historical events.

palilogy is the rhetorical device of deliberately repeating a word or words for emphatic effect. See *amplification, device repetition.*

pamphlet: a short, unbound booklet, usually expressing a topical issue about which a writer feels strongly. The advantage of the pamphlet is that it is quite easy to produce and distribute, and is thus especially favoured by underground writers, political dissidents and revolutionaries. This means of communication has been used by many authors such as *Defoe, Dekker, Greene, Milton, More, Shelley, Jonathan Swift.*

panegyric: a speech or *poem* delivered in public fervently praising someone or something, e.g. Mark Antony's funeral *oration* in praise of Caesar in JULIUS CAESAR.

panoramic method: another term for *third person narrative.* See *viewpoint.*

paradox: a *witty* contradiction in terms. *Wilde* uses paradox to great effect in his plays, e.g. in his THE IMPORTANCE OF BEING EARNEST Algernon, upon hearing that a certain Lady Harbury has been widowed, comments that he 'hears her hair has turned quite gold from grief', paradoxically implying that her husband's death has had a rejuvenating effect upon her and her lifestyle. See *antithesis, oxymoron.*

paragraph: see *paragraphing,* Appendix 2.

paraliterature is a name given to works such as certain mass-market *romances* or *thrillers* which are not considered good enough to be called *literature.*

parallelism is where phrases or sentences of similar construction are set side by side in order to create an effect of balance or *antithesis,* e.g.

> I celebrate myself, and sing myself,
> And what assume you shall assume,
> For every atom belonging to me as good belongs to you.
>
> (*Whitman*'s 'Song of Myself', 1881)

There is also an example of *parallelism* in the second sentence of *paragraphing,* see Appendix 2.

pararhyme: see *half-rhyme.*

Park, Mungo (1771–1806): travel writer and explorer. A friend of *Walter Scott,* his intrepid adventures became famous as a result of his graphic TRAVELS IN THE INTERIOR DISTRICTS OF AFRICA… IN THE YEARS 1795, 1796 AND 1797 (1799).

Parkman, Francis (1823–93): American historian and travel writer who did much to chronicle the pioneering development of America by the French and English. Notable works include THE OREGON TRAIL (1849), HISTORY OF THE CONSPIRACY OF THE PONTIAC (1851), A HALF CENTURY OF CONFLICT (1892).

parody: the *imitation* of a particular *style* of writing or subject, usually for humorous effect, e.g. *Fielding*'s SHAMELA (1741) and JOSEPH ANDREWS are both parodies of *Richardson*'s novel PAMELA; *Austen*'s NORTHANGER ABBEY is a parody of the *gothic* novel; and *Gibbons*' COLD COMFORT FARM parodies popular steamy rural *romances*, especially those of *Webb*. See *burlesque*.

passion play: a medieval religious *drama* representing Christ's Crucifixion, usually performed on Good Friday, and sometimes incorporated into a cycle of *Mystery plays*.

pastiche: a patchwork made up from bits and pieces of the work of a writer which constitute a type of *imitation*, either as a tribute, an entertainment, or a *parody*.

pastoral, meaning 'to do with shepherds', refers in a literary sense to any work which paints a pleasant, idealised view of life in the countryside. The ancient Greek and Roman writings of Theocritus (early 3rd century) and Virgil (70–19BC) respectively provided models for *Renaissance* pastoral *poems*, plays and *prose* romances such as *Spenser*'s 'Shepheardes Calendar', *Sidney*'s ARCADIA, Thomas Lodge's (?1558–1625) ROSALYNDE (?1590), *Marlowe*'s THE PASSIONATE SHEPHERD TO HIS LOVE. Pastorals have always been popular as escape literature for those living in town or at court, and *Shakespeare*'s AS YOU LIKE IT (based on ROSALYNDE) is so named because Shakespeare wished to portray elements of rural life as people liked to see them. Various *forms* of the pastoral remained popular in succeeding centuries through the writings of *Pope*, *Wordsworth*, *Blake*, *Clare* and lesser writers, although there was an increasing tendency to portray country life with greater *realism*, as in *Crabbe*'s 'The Village' which sets out to portray aspects of rural life 'As truth will paint it, and as bards will not'. See also *romances*, *topographical poetry*.

pastoral elegy: a *form* of *elegy* derived from classical writers which developed an elaborate set of *conventions* whereby, among other things, all nature is involved in mourning someone, yet a spring-like reawakening is promised in part through the suggestion of the immortality of the dead one. Famous examples of this *genre* are *Milton*'s 'Lycidas' and *Shelley*'s 'Adonais'.

pathetic: 'worthy of *pathos*', 'poignant' or 'moving' is the true literary meaning of this word, which should never in a literary *essay* be used in the modern slang sense.

pathetic fallacy: a 19th century term for ascribing human qualities to nature. The most common example is the attribution of bad weather to a deliberate intention on the part of nature, e.g. in *Hardy*'s THE RETURN OF THE NATIVE the difficult conditions on Egdon Heath are for Eustacia Vye a result of deliberately hostile nature, whereas for the down-to-earth Thomasin they are merely the impartial actions of nature; and *Shakespeare*'s King Lear admits the possibility of pathetic fallacy when, battered by the storm, he directly addresses the elements at the beginning of Act III of KING LEAR.

pathos: an element in a work which evokes in an audience or reader feelings of grief, pity and sorrow, e.g. the death of the Duchess in Act IV, Scene 2 of *Webster*'s THE DUCHESS OF MALFI, the plight of the old man at the end of *Wordsworth*'s *narrative* poem 'Michael', the deaths of the children in *Hardy*'s JUDE THE OBSCURE. Sometimes pathos has been over-exploited, especially by novelists, an often cited example being the death of Little Nell in *Dickens*' THE OLD CURIOSITY SHOP (1840–1).

Paton, Alan (1903–88): South African novelist, *short-story* writer, biographer and auto-biographer. In CRY, THE BELOVED COUNTRY (1948) he brought the plight of Black South Africans to the attention of the world, and much of his subsequent writing concerns apartheid. Other notable works include TOO LATE THE PHALAROPE (1953), DEBBIE GO HOME (1961, published in the United States in 1965 as TALES FROM A TROUBLED LAND).

Patten, Brian (b.1946): one of the *Liverpool Poets*, his writing ranges from ironic social criticism to tender lyrical *love poetry*. Notable works include GRINNING JACK (1990), GARGLING WITH JELLY (1986) and THAWING FROZEN FROGS (1990) are highly regarded collections of *poetry* for children.

pattern poetry is an early type of *concrete poetry* in the *form* of a *stanza* which creates a design or picture on the page, e.g. *Herbert*'s 'Easter Wings' (1633).

Paulin, Tom (b.1949): Irish poet, literary critic and playwright. His work is sometimes bleak, concerned with the socio-political situation in Northern Ireland. He often uses the Ulster dialect and urban *settings*. Notable works include A SENSE OF JUSTICE (1977), THE STRANGE MUSEUM (1980), THE LIBERTY TREE (1983), IRELAND AND THE ENGLISH CRISIS (1984).

Peacock, Thomas Love (1785–1866): satirist, poet and essayist. Amusing, clever and radical, his stories and *settings* are sometimes *parodies* of the kind of *gothic romance* which was popular at the time. Notable works include HEADLONG HALL (1816), NIGHTMARE ABBEY (1818), MAID MARIAN (1822), CROTCHET CASTLE (1831), GRYLL GRANGE (1860–1).

penny dreadful was a name given in the late 19th century to a work of adventure, crime, action and/or mystery not intended to be great *literature*. It was printed on and bound in paper and sold for a penny. See *detective fiction, melodrama, thriller*.

pentameter: see *metre*.

perfect rhyme, sometimes known as 'full' or 'true' *rhyme*, is where the rhyming vowel and consonants are identical, but not the consonants preceding the vowel, e.g. launch/paunch.

performance poetry: *poetry* specifically written for public performance, e.g. see *Beat Movement* writers, *Liverpool Poets, Lochhead*.

performance poets: poets who do public readings of their own *poetry*, which may be *performance poetry*, but may originally have been written with the reader in mind.

period is a term used to categorise *literature* within a time-scale. A period may refer to:

- a general span of time (e.g. *Renaissance*)
- the reign of a monarch (e.g. *Victorian*)
- a movement (e.g. *Romantic*).

All are very general terms and imposed retrospectively, originating before and spilling beyond any defined starting or ending date. Even terms such as *Elizabethan* are imprecise (see *Elizabethan drama*).

periodic essay: an *essay* published in a *periodical*.

periodical: a magazine or *journal* which appears at regular intervals, e.g. weekly or monthly.

peripeteia is a reversal in the *hero* or *heroine*'s fortunes. In *tragedy*, for the worse; in *comedy*, for the better. The term is usually applied to the former, as when in *Shakespeare*'s KING LEAR the king is reduced by the actions of his daughters to a pitiful figure out in a raging storm. See *Aristotle*.

periphrasis: the use of indirect, long-winded language, e.g. Polonius in Act II, Scene 2 of *Shakespeare*'s HAMLET where he is trying to explain his theory regarding Hamlet's 'madness' to the King and Queen.

peroration: the conclusion or winding up of an *oration* or highly formal piece of writing, often used to imply pomposity.

persona: originally referring to a mask worn by actors and changed in order to assume a different *character*, the term has come to mean the identity assumed by the writer of a *story* or *poem*. See *narrator/narrative voice, persona*.

personification is the treating of an idea as if a person with human qualities, e.g. in 'Composed upon Westminster Bridge, September 3, 1802' *Wordsworth* writes of London wearing 'the beauty of the morn… like a garment'; and in the middle *stanza* of his 'Ode to Autumn' *Keat*'s deals with Autumn as if the season were an aging man.

perspective: see *narrator/narrative voice*.

Petrarch (1304–74): Italian poet and humanist, and friend of *Boccaccio*, who took a new look at the ancient Greek and Latin *literature*, and whose works had a marked influence upon English *Renaissance* writers such as *Wyatt* and *Surrey*, especially as regards the *sonnet* form and *lyric* love poetry.

Petrarchan sonnet: see *sonnet*.

Petrarchism: any *imitation* of the *manner* of the Italian poet *Petrarch*. Among his English followers were *Wyatt, Surrey, Sidney, Spenser* and *Shakespeare*.

phallocentric literature is a term from *feminist criticism* used to describe *literature* which reinforces the notion of society organised according to masculine priorities.

Phillips, Caryl (b.1958): West Indian playwright and novelist. His tense, naturalistic plays tend to focus on Caribbean families in Britain and the West Indies. Notable works include STRANGE FRUIT (1981), WHERE THERE IS DARKNESS (1982), THE FINAL PASSAGE (1985), HIGHER GROUND (1989), PLAYING AWAY (1987), CROSSING THE RIVER (1993).

picaresque is a term given to a *narrative* which relates the adventures of a likeable rogue ('picaro' is the Spanish for 'rogue') whose *character* develops little during the course of his escapades. DON QUIXOTE (1605) by the Spaniard Manuel Cervantes (1547–1616), although it does not conform in all respects and was not the first, is sometimes considered the father of the picaresque *novel*. The earliest example in English is THE UNFORTUNATE TRAVELLER (1594) by Thomas Nashe (1567–1601), later notable examples which are either typically or partly picaresque including *Defoe*'s MOLL FLANDERS (a rare case where the leading figure is female), *Fielding*'s TOM JONES, *Smollett*'s RODERICK RANDOM, *Twain*'s THE ADVENTURES OF TOM SAWYER, *Bellow*'s THE ADVENTURES OF AUGIE MARCH. An example of picaresque *narrative* in a *poem* is *Byron*'s DON JUAN.

picturesque: seeking out natural beauty in nature, or the picturesque, became almost a cult in the 18th century, many poets and other writers such as *Addison, Pope,*

Gray, various *gothic* novelists, *Walter Scott* and others incorporating picturesque descriptions into their work. It is related to *Romanticism,* although some say that it is a superficial manifestation of the true Romantic's deeper responses to the power of nature. *Austen* in MANSFIELD PARK and *Peacock* in HEADLONG HALL make fun of it.

Pinter, Harold (b.1930): playwright and screenplay writer. Heavily influenced by *Beckett* and *Theatre of the Absurd,* his plays consolidated a striking change in the direction of British *drama* in the 1950s. The histories and memories of his *characters* often play a key part in his plays, which sometimes contain a strong *subtext* of suppressed menace and vary in their level of *realism.* Notable works include THE BIRTHDAY PARTY (1957), initially little appreciated but now often regarded as a minor classic, THE CARETAKER (1960), A SLIGHT ACHE (1961), THE HOMECOMING (1965), OLD TIMES (1971), NO MAN'S LAND (1975), BETRAYAL (1978).

Pirandello, Luigi (1867–1936): Italian playwright, *short-story* writer and novelist. He challenged theatrical *conventions* of naturalism and influenced many playwrights including *Beckett* and *O'Neill.* Notable works include RIGHT YOU ARE, IF YOU THINK SO (1917), SIX CHARACTERS IN SEARCH OF AN AUTHOR (1921), HENRY IV (1922).

pirate edition: an edition of a *text* which has been copied for profit, e.g. the so-called 'bad' quarto of HAMLET was probably pirated by one of *Shakespeare's* own company so that the play could be performed elsewhere. There was at that time no copyright law to protect the *author;* nowadays such practice is illegal.

plagiarism is the unacknowledged and wholesale lifting of *text* from another source by a writer or an examination candidate. See *source,* and Appendix 2.

plaint: any poetic lament. See *complaint, elegy.*

Plath, Sylvia (1932–63): American poet and novelist. She separates herself from her *poetry* by the use of characteristically ironic and disturbing *tones* and undertones. Notable works include THE COLOSSUS AND OTHER POEMS (1960, the only work published before her suicide), the semi-autobiographical THE BELL JAR (1963), ARIEL (1965), CROSSING THE WATER (1971), THE JOURNALS OF SYLVIA PLATH (1982).

Plato (?427–?347BC): ancient Greek philosopher and writer. His profound thoughts and platonic *themes* have had a significant influence on subsequent writers. Books 2, 3 and 10 of his THE REPUBLIC are good introductions to the nature of *literature.* Other notable works include EUTHYPHRO, PROTAGORAS, GORGIAS (thought to be his earliest works), CRITO, APOLOGY, PHAEDO (thought to have been written between 371–367BC), THE LAWS. The dates of most of his writings are uncertain.

plot: the writer's organisation of a web of interconnected events in a play or *story* which build up the overall storyline. It is a more precise word than *story* because it denotes the deliberate act of organising the cause and effect of events within a scheme. *Forster's* book ASPECTS OF THE NOVEL contains some useful definitions of the word 'plot'. See *sub-plot.*

pluralism/plurality: the idea that there are a multiplicity of ways of reading *texts,* and that there is no 'correct' answer as to what a given text means. It is an essential awareness which students of *literature* must possess that different readers will read texts in different ways at different times, and that by taking into account varying perspectives a student will arrive at a personal response which, itself, may perfectly properly change over time. See also *assertion* (in Appendix 1), *deconstruction.*

pluralist criticism accepts a *plurality* of approach to texts. *Deconstructuralists* advocate this approach. *Structuralist criticism*, and attitudes which embrace a particular ideology such as *Marxist criticism*, tend to disapprove. See *deconstruction, structuralism*.

Poe, Edgar Allan (1809–49): American *short-story* writer and poet, sometimes regarded as an archetypal *gothic* horror writer: by taking rationality to the extreme, his heavily paradoxical *style* often explores the beauty of the dead or dying and split personalities through various types of storytelling. Notable works include THE FALL OF THE HOUSE OF USHER (1839), THE MURDERS IN RUE MORGUE (1841), THE MASQUE OF THE RED DEATH (1841–2), THE BLACK CAT (1843), THE PIT AND THE PENDULUM (1843), THE RAVEN AND OTHER POEMS (1845).

poem: any composition which may be described as *poetry* or *verse*.

poesie is an archaic term for *poetry* or, more specifically, the act of creating poetry. *Keats* uses the term in this sense in 'Ode to a Nightingale'. *Wordsworth* defines the act of creating poetry as 'emotion recollected in tranquillity'.

poet laureate is a largely honorary post awarded in Britain in recognition of a poet's achievements. Originally the holder was required to write *occasional verse* for particular events such as a monarch's coronation but nowadays this requirement, as the stipend, is nominal. Among former holders are *Dryden* (1668–89), *Wordsworth* (1843–50), *Tennyson* (1850–92), *Ted Hughes* (1984–99) and currently the holder is *Motion* (1999–). Various American states appoint a poet laureate (the first to do so was California in 1915), and since 1986 there has been a national laureate.

poetaster: a derogatory word for an inferior poet.

poetic diction refers to a choice of *diction* favoured by poets at any particular time. The phrase is most often applied in a condemning way to the idea, common among the *neo-classical* poets of the 18th century, that *poetry* should be written in an artificially elevated language which should not be debased by the use of everyday words. In general Latin-based words were preferred to direct Anglo-Saxon ones. *Gray* considered that 'the language of the age is never the language of poetry'. Examples of the poetic diction of this period are 'feathered breed' for 'birds', 'finny tribe' for 'fish', 'milky race' for 'cows', 'purple groves pomaceous' for 'orchards', 'rich saponeaceous loam' for 'good soil', and so forth. Some even considered it crude ever to use 'ever' (always 'e'er') or 'over' (o'er'). In the hands of the best poets of the period such as *Gray* or *Pope* such poetic diction can be effective and very *witty*. It was such language against which *Wordsworth*, *Coleridge* and other *Romantics* reacted, Wordsworth referring in his 'advertisement' which prefaced the LYRICAL BALLADS to 'the gaudiness and inane phraseology of many modern writers'; and elsewhere he declared his aim of writing in 'the ordinary language of ordinary men'. He did not always achieve his *naturalistic* aim (all art, is after all, by definition artificial); but his opinions have shaped the thinking of poets ever since.

poetic drama refers to any *drama* in which the *dialogue* is written in *verse*, usually *blank verse*. *Elizabethan drama* is the most famous of the type. Thereafter there was some *closet drama* written in *verse*, but little of note until the 20th century when there was a brave attempt to revive popular interest in the *form* by, among others, *T.S. Eliot*, e.g. MURDER IN THE CATHEDRAL, and Christopher Fry (b.1907), e.g. THE LADY'S NOT FOR BURNING (1949).

poetic licence is a term which covers:

- a taking of liberty with language and syntax by poets in order to create effects not strictly available according to the laws of *prose*
- mistakes, deliberate or through ignorance, made by writers in any medium which are trivial but which worry pedantic critics.

poetic prose: see *prose poem.*

poeticism is a term sometimes used pejoratively to denote the kind of artificial *poetic diction* against which *Wordsworth* reacted.

poetry is a term variously used to cover writing which:

- is written in any kind of *metre* (but this would not cover *free verse*)
- has any kind of pattern
- is written with a sense of the music of language, and not just for meaning.

Two definitions by famous poets:

- 'The spontaneous overflow of powerful feelings' (*Wordsworth*)
- 'The best words in the best order' (*Coleridge*).

A lesser-known poet once described poetry as 'words working overtime'. The word poetry tends to be used for more significant (but not necessarily more serious) writing than *verse.*

point of attack: the point in a *story* or play where the main *action* commences.

point of reference: taken from art, this term has come to denote a normal *character* who keeps a sense of perspective in a world of excessive behaviour. Kent in *Shakespeare's* KING LEAR may be regarded as such a figure.

point of view: see *narrator/narrative voice.*

polemic: a vigorously argued, non-objective piece of writing on a controversial subject such as politics or religion, e.g. *Milton's* AREOPAGITICA (1664). Other notable polemicists include *Jonathan Swift, Shaw.*

police procedural: *realistic* crime stories in which the central figure is a professional police officer (rather than the clever amateur detective of *detective fiction* who often makes the police appear incompetent), e.g. *P.D. James'* Dalgleish and Colin Dexter's (b.1930) Inspector Morse.

polyrhythmic refers to a *poem* which has various metrical patterns.

polysyndeton: the repeated use of conjunctions, e.g. *Hemingway's* frequent use of 'and' to string together phrases and clauses. The opposite of *asyndeton.*

Pope, Alexander (1688–1744): English poet, satirist and critic. His lively, *witty* and strictly metrical *verse* often focuses on the fashionable trends of his society and the landscape, and he is often cited as the most characteristic and best of neo-classical poets (see *neo-classicism*). Notable works include THE PASTORALS (1709), 'Essay on Criticism' (1711), 'The Rape of the Lock' (1712), THE DUNCIAD (1728), MORAL ESSAYS (1731–5).

popular novel: referring to any best-selling *novel*, the term often implies writing which is down-market and 'not proper *literature*'; yet many critically well-regarded writers such as *Le Carré* are also considered 'popular'.

pornography is writing which is of an explicitly sexual nature and designed to arouse sexual appetite. The term is often used to refer to writing which is merely obscene and has no literary merit, but there is a long history going back to ancient times of quality pornographic writing, and the definition of what is and is not pornographic depends very much on the public taste of the time. The trial in 1960 which resulted in the publication of *Lawrence*'s LADY CHATTERLEY'S LOVER (written 1928) is one example of a shift in such taste. Pornography is sometimes categorised into:

- erotica, concerning hetero-sexual activity
- exotica, covering a wide range of other sexual activities.

Post-colonial criticism seeks to place the literature and experience of former colonies within their cultural context, re-evaluating them and separating them from the assumptions of the previously dominant European colonial criticism which saw such continents as Africa from the European perspective. Post-colonial criticism has emerged alongside other *literary theory* such as *structuralism, post-structuralism, post-modernism, feminist* and *marxist theory.*

post-colonial literature is writing in English which originates in former colonies of Great Britain (or such writing in the mother tongue of any former colonial power), usually (but not always) written by natives of that colony after colonial times. A frequent mark of post-colonial language is the emergence of a variant *form* of the mother tongue (sometimes indicated by the use of lower case for english to distinguish it from the English of England). Some critics accept as 'post-colonial' any *literature* written in English which emerges at any time from such colonies, whether before, during or after colonial status. Such literature often concerns, explicitly or implicitly, the cultural, political and social impact of colonisation. The term is sometimes resented by those who regard the colonial period as a phase which they wish to forget. *Ngugi* writes in his native Gîkûyû where possible as an anti-imperialist statement; *Achebe* uses English in order to reach a global audience. Notable examples of post-colonial writers include:

- *Achebe, Coetzee, Gordimer, Ngugi, Okri, Soyinka* from Africa
- *Hulme, Mansfield, Stead, Patrick White* from Australasia
- *Atwood, Munro* from Canada
- *Naipaul, Walcott* from the Caribbean
- *Desai, Seth* from Asia.

See *Commonwealth literature.*

Post-colonial Realistic Period: a title sometimes used to cover American *literature* written between approximately 1865 and 1900.

post-modernism, simply put, refers to that which follows *modernism*. In general terms it covers *literature* written since 1945 (the end of the Second World War). Post-modernism continued the anti-tradition stance of modernism, but after the confidence in progress which is a feature of modernism, post-modernism reflects the kind of insecurity, doubt and sometimes nihilism caused by such as Nazi atrocities, environmental pollution and the threat of extinction under the shadow of the nuclear bomb. *Beckett*'s writings are characteristic of this *mood. Feminist, Marxist* and *psychoanalytic criticism* are all aspects of post-modernism, and it is closely related to *post-structuralism.* See also *literary theory.* Examples of post-modernist texts include

Lessing's CANOPUS IN ARGOS (1979), *Nabokov*'s PALE FIRE, V (1963) by Thomas Pynchon (b.1937), IN COLD BLOOD (1966) by Truman Capote (1924–84), SLAUGHTERHOUSE 5 (1969) by Kurt Vonnegut (b.1922), ZEN AND THE ART OF MOTORCYCLE MAINTENANCE (1974) by Robert Pirsig (b.1928), the *New Journalism* of *Wolfe* and others, and much of the work of *Carter* and *Rushdie*.

post-modernist: one whose artistic output shows features of *post-modernism*.

post-structuralism is an element of *post-modernism* which covers a whole range of ideas, some developed from and some in conflict with *structuralism*. Some post-structuralists argue that every word which a writer commits to paper is influenced by the historical, political and social culture of which s/he is a part, and nothing can be evaluated for its own sake. The most important aspect of *post-structuralist criticism* is *deconstruction*. The chief proponent of post-structuralism is the Frenchman Jacques Derrida (b.1930). See *feminist criticism, Marxist criticism, psychoanalytic criticism*.

post-structuralist criticism, the main aspect of which is *deconstruction*, is based on, among other things, the notion that the *meaning* of any *text* is unstable, and that it can mean an almost infinite number of things according to the varying perceptions of different readers.

pot-boiler: a derogatory term for a work written merely to make money.

Pound, Ezra (1885–1972): American poet. His *avant-garde* rhythmical and musical *verse*, which spans a wide range of cultural references, was influenced by *Robert Browning*'s dramatic monologues and was greatly admired by *T.S. Eliot*, whose own verse owes much to Pound's advice. Notable works include PERSONAE (1909, based on the impression *Yeats* made on him), LUSTRA (1916), THE CANTOS (from 1925).

Powell, Anthony (1905–2000): English novelist. By turns *witty* and satirical, light or black in his *humour*, his writings often capture a certain *zeitgeist*. Notable works include AFTERNOON MEN (1931), A DANCE TO THE MUSIC OF TIME (a sequence of 12 *novels*, 1951–75), TO KEEP THE BALL ROLLING (four volumes of *journals*, 1976–82), THE FISHER KING (1986).

practical criticism is a term used to describe the close reading of *texts* advocated by *Richards* and the *leavisite* approach to literary studies.

preface: an introduction to a literary work, e.g. *Wordsworth*'s 'advertisement' before his and *Coleridge*'s LYRICAL BALLADS, or *Shaw*'s prefaces to his plays.

Pre-Raphaelite Period: generally considered to cover *literature* written in England between approximately 1848 and 1860.

Pre-Raphaelites: a group of young English artists who in 1848 rejected the current fashion in art, returning to the ideals of simplicity and truthfulness which they regarded as existing before the time of the artist Raphael (1483–1529) and the Italian *Renaissance*. This interest in *medievalism*, influenced by *Spenser* and further stimulated by the *poetry* of *Keats* and *Tennyson*, spread to writers such as *Dante Gabriel Rossetti* (an artist and poet), *Morris, Swinburne* and *Christina Rossetti*, who focused upon sensuousness, *symbolism* and religious meaning in a *style* partly reminiscent of the medieval period. Significant works produced under this influence include *Christina Rossetti*'s 'Goblin Market' (1862), *Dante Gabriel Rossetti*'s 'The Blessed Damozel', *Morris*'s THE EARTHLY PARADISE (1868–1870).

prescriptive criticism occurs when a *text* is approached not with an open mind on the part of the reader, but with a bias that it should conform to certain rules or expectations. The opposite approach is *pluralist criticism*. All readers cannot to some extent help approaching a text with their own prejudices, even when trying to be pluralist. See also *reader-response theory*.

presupposition: the notions and preconceptions about the nature of the world which a reader brings to a *text*.

Priestley, J.B. (1894–1984): playwright, novelist, critic and broadcaster. A committed socialist, he was a prolific writer on such subjects such as the English social classes, his travels round England and his fascination with ideas of time, all of which proved very popular with readers and the theatre-going public of the day, a popularity which continues. His radio broadcasts did much to foster national morale during the Second World War. Notable works include THE GOOD COMPANIONS (1929), ANGEL PAVEMENT (1930), DANGEROUS CORNER (1932), TIME AND THE CONWAYS (1937), WHEN WE ARE MARRIED (1938), AN INSPECTOR CALLS (1946), SATURN OVER THE WATER (1961), ALL ENGLAND LISTENED (1968).

primitivism, in a literary sense, is a term applied to writers in every age who value the so-called 'natural' above the 'artificial', and who look back to a 'golden age' of the past when all was simple goodness. In the 18th century there emerged the cult of the 'noble savage' who was unsophisticated and non-intellectual, but had natural moral dignity. Many aspects of primitivism are present in *Romanticism*.

Pritchett, V.S. (1900–97): English novelist, critic and *short-story* writer. Drawing on his personal travelling experiences, his writing has an acute sense of observation. Notable works include MARCHING SPAIN (1928), DEAD MAN LEADING (1949), THE SPANISH TEMPER (1954), A CARELESS WIDOW (1989).

problem play: the term is applied to:

- a *drama* of *ideas*
- plays which are difficult to place into traditional categories such as *tragedy, comedy, history* and so forth, such as *Shakespeare*'s MEASURE FOR MEASURE (?1604), TROILUS AND CRESSIDA (?1602) or ALL'S WELL THAT ENDS WELL (?1604).

prolepsis is another term for *flashforward*. See also *anachorism, analepsis, flashback, in media res*.

proletarian novel: a *novel* about working-class life, at times a kind of *thesis novel*. Some of *Sillitoe*'s work may be so described.

prologue: either

- an introduction to a work which is an integral part of it, e.g. *Chaucer*'s 'General Prologue' to THE CANTERBURY TALES. In *drama* it tends to be in the *form* of a *chorus*, as in *Shakespeare*'s HENRY V; or
- the name of the *character* who speaks the *chorus*.

See *epilogue, induction*.

propaganda literature is any work such as a *thesis novel* or *thesis play* which sets out to advance a particular political, religious or sociological belief. See also *agitprop*.

proposition: a section of a work where the writer explicitly or implicitly states a main aim or *theme*, e.g. the opening lines of *Milton*'s PARADISE LOST.

proscenium arch: an architectural picture frame round the stage behind which the actors perform, with the audience seated in front of it. Theatres were thus constructed between 1660 and the 1900s, although since the mid-20th century the fashion has been a return to the *open stage* in order to bring the actors back into closer contact with the audience.

prose is the term used to describe language which seeks to communicate meaning without using any of the *devices* of *poetry*.

prose poem is a term given to *prose* which is close to *poetry* in its use of language, and of *devices* such as *rhythm* and *imagery*. Writers as varied as *Ashberry, T.S. Eliot, Faulkner, Joyce, Lee, Lowell, Wilde* and *Woolf* have all been described as writers of poetic *prose*.

prosody is the study of the art and science of every aspect of *versification*.

protagonist: the main *character* in a *story*. See *antagonist*.

protest literature is a term sometimes used to cover any kind of writing from *ballad* to funeral *oration* in which voices protest against a situation, e.g. *Shelley*'s 'The Mask of Anarchy' or *Bennett*'s address attacking the media at the funeral of the broadcaster Russell Harty.

Proulx, Annie (b.1935): American novelist, *short-story* writer and journalist. Her work has been variously described as *post-modernist*, feminist, accessible, popular, *witty* and comic, displaying both a regional and wider sense of 'Americanness'. Notable works include HEARTSONGS AND OTHER STORIES (1988), POSTCARDS (1991), THE SHIPPING NEWS (1993). See *regional novel*.

proverb: a short, pithy, saying which neatly sums up a widely accepted truth, e.g. 'Look before you leap'. Proverbs are popular in all cultures in all ages, printed *collections* ranging from THE BOOK OF PROVERBS in the Old Testament of the *Bible* to The OXFORD DICTIONARY OF ENGLISH PROVERBS (1935). See *maxim*.

pseudonym: a pen name or *nom de plume* adopted by an *author*, e.g. *Karen Blixen* wrote under the name *Isak Dineson*.

pseudo-statement: a term invented by *Richards* to denote poetic truth, which is imaginative and not verifiable by scientific, objective, logical means. The idea that *poetry* can convey truths which are not testable by intellectual means is very old. Much Romantic *literature* is devoted to this notion, e.g. *Shelley*'s 'To a Skylark'.

psychoanalytic criticism is an approach used by critics who consider a literary *text* as a product of a writer's psychology or as a way of analysing the human mind in general. The theories of Sigmund Freud (1856–1939) are particularly important to such critics. See *post-modernism, post-structuralism, surrealism.*

psychological novel: a loose term used to cover the hundreds of *novels* which are concerned with the psychological state of *characters* rather than with *action* and *plot*.

Ptolemaic system: the belief that the Earth is the centre of the universe and the sun, moon, stars and planets revolve around it. Devised by Ptolemaeus, a Greek astronomer and geographer of the second century AD. This idea was not superseded until the *Copernican revolution* in the 16th century.

puff: a brief uncritical piece in any medium designed to boost the sales of a book.

Pulitzer Prizes are American literary awards in various categories made every year since 1918. Winners include *Frost* (1924, 1931, 1937, 1943), *Tennessee Williams* (1948, 1955), *Morrison* (1988).

pulp literature: cheaply produced *paraliterature* in book or magazine *form*, often including *pot-boilers* and soft porn.

pun: a *witty* play upon words, where one word carries two or more meanings within a sentence. All ages have enjoyed puns, good and bad, and they are a favourite element in many jokes. The *Elizabethans* and *metaphysical* poets were particularly fond of employing them, e.g. Mercutio's dying pun in *Shakespeare*'s ROMEO AND JULIET when he says that tomorrow he will be 'a grave man', the kind of word-play which led *Johnson* to comment that a pun was the 'fatal Cleopatra' for which Shakespeare was content to lose the world. See *ambiguity*.

Purdy, Al (b.1918): Canadian poet, radio and television playwright, and novelist. Much of his writing is rooted in the landscape of rural Ontario and the impact it has upon the inhabitants' ways of thinking. Notable works include BEING ALIVE: POEMS 1958–78 (1978), THE COLLECTED POEMS OF AL PURDY (1986), THE WOMAN ON THE CHORE (1990).

purism: the insistence of absolute standards of 'correctness' in writing. The main problems for purists are that:

- agreement on what is 'correct' is difficult to establish
- language is always changing, and what was considered strange or slang yesterday is accepted usage today
- new ways of communicating such as emails are having an impact upon wider written usage.

'Appropriateness' is a much more useful notion than 'correctness'. The great strength of English, unlike perhaps French, is that it has always embraced new usage, regarding dictionaries as descriptive rather than prescriptive.

purple patch or **purple prose** are terms used to denote inappropriately ornate and over-written writing.

pyrrhic: see *metre*.

quantity: the length of the sound of a syllable which affects a poet's choice of words. For instance, 'bóók' is a long sound, 'blàck' a short one.

quarto: page size formed by a printer's sheet being folded twice, thus creating eight pages. The quarto editions of *Shakespeare*'s plays were printed in this size.

quatrain: a *stanza* or section of *verse* containing four lines, usually defined by a unit of rhyme pattern.

quintain: a stanza or section of verse containing five lines, usually defined by a unit of rhyme pattern.

quotation: the citing of a word, phrase or passage from a work. See *quotations, use of* in Appendix 2.

quotation titles are titles of works which use phrases taken from earlier *literature*, e.g. *Faulkner*'s THE SOUND AND THE FURY comes from Shakespeare's MACBETH and TENDER IS THE NIGHT (1934) by *Scott Fitzgerald* from *Keats*' 'Ode to a Nightingale'.

rabalaisian: reminiscent of the literary *style* of Rabalais (?1494–1553); that is, writing which is by turns coarse, boisterous, *satirical*, extravagant and obscene in one tradition of French writing of the day. The term is still applied to a kind of contemporary writing.

Ramanujam, A.K. (1929–93): Indian poet and translator. In his *poetry* he handles his subjects with gentle, sensitive insight and clarity of expression, often drawing inspiration from the blend of his Indian roots and his long years in America. Notable works include THE STRIDERS (1966), RELATIONS (1971), SECOND SIGHT (1986).

Rao, Raja (b.1909): Indian novelist and *short-story* writer. His work shows a strong awareness of the challenges of dealing with Indian themes and sensibilities through the medium of the English language, and some aspects of his writing anticipate *magic realism.* Notable works include KANTHAPURA (1938), THE SERPENT AND THE ROPE (1960), THE CAT AND SHAKESPEARE (1965), ON THE GANGA CHAT (1985).

Rattigan, Terence (1911–1977): playwright and screenplay writer. A very popular playwright in his time, he is often regarded as a master of the *well-made play.* His work is marked by compassion for his *characters.* His avowed target audience of the middle-aged and middle-brow (whom he called 'Aunt Edna') put him out of fashion during the ascendancy of the *Angry Young Men,* but since his death his plays have regained much critical regard. Notable works include FRENCH WITHOUT TEARS (1936), THE WILMSLOW BOY (1946), THE BROWNING VERSION (1948), THE DEEP BLUE SEA (1952), SEPARATE TABLES (1954), ROSS (1960).

readerly/writerly: terms invented by Roland Barthes (1915–80) indicating whether a *text* is 'readerly' in that it invites the reader to be passive and needing to make little effort (as, for example, in a *classic* realistic *novel* which is unchallenging because reliant upon *convention* and a fixed, closed meaning); or whether 'writerly' in that the reader must be active and work hard in order to respond, create meanings, almost 'write' her/himself (as, for example, in *Joyce*'s ULYSSES and similar texts where there is a focus, sometimes self-conscious, on language, *structure,* the mechanics of the writing, and so forth). Barthes points out that any text can be made either readerly or writerly: it all depends on the reader's approach to it. See also *authorial intention, intentional fallacy, post-structuralism.*

reader-response theory is the name given to various different approaches to *literature* which focus upon the reader's relationship with the *text,* e.g. *psychoanalytic criticism* and *structuralism.* The reader's response to a text is seen as crucial in determining any *meaning* that may be arrived at: different individuals and, indeed, different communities will respond in different ways, all of them valid. See also *cultural materialism, hermeneutics, implied reader, New Critics, reception theory, significance.*

realism has a range of possible definitions. Broadly speaking it can cover:

- writings from the 19th and 20th century which are concerned with focusing upon plain truths, often about the harsher aspects of life, which had previously not been considered fit subject-matter for *literature*

- insights into psychological truths, as distinct from *naturalism* which is concerned with the accuracy of *setting* and other surface details
- both psychological insights and attention to accuracy concerning all facts and details
- a writer's concern with the here and now rather than escapist fantasy
- working-class realities in the struggle for power (see *Marxist criticism*)

Realistic Period: often used of American *literature* to define the period between approximately 1865 (the end of the Civil War) and 1900.

reception theory is an aspect of *reader-response theory* which considers the changing reactions of different generations of readers to a *text* and in relation to those of the present day reader.

recognition: see *anagnorisis*.

recoil is when, in *tragedy*, the *protagonist* brings about her or his own downfall.

referential language is that which uses non-emotive, objective words in order to describe something with scientific precision. See *denotation*, and also *connotation*.

refrain: a line or lines repeated at regular points in a *poem*, often at the end of a stanza, sometimes with slight variations. Much used in *ballads*.

regional novel: a novel where the *setting* and society of a particular area is more than mere *local colour*, but an important ingredient in the fabric of the work. Among those who have made much use of regional aspects are *Gaskell, Hardy, Lawrence, Faulkner.*

regionalism: see *local colour/colourists*.

relativism is the notion that two opposing judgements can be equally valid. For instance, a piece of writing may be considered to be good or bad according to the taste of either the individual reader or the times in which s/he lives. In an examination what matters is less the relative judgement of the candidate, more the skill with which that judgement is argued and supported through a close reading of the *text*, together with an awareness that there is more than one valid way of reading text.

Renaissance: this was a time of 'rebirth of learning' following the Middle Ages, a period in which grew and flourished art, architecture, science, philosophy and *literature* such as had not been seen in Europe since Classical times. Some regard 14th century Italy as the cradle of the Renaissance, which then spread across Western Europe to England during the ensuing 200 years. The revival saw the appearance of great thinkers, scholars and writers, often *humanists*, such as Erasmus (?1467–1536) and *More* who re-kindled an interest in the achievements of Greece and Rome. Long held beliefs about the nature of God, man and the universe were challenged in many areas of learning: *Copernicus* and Galileo Galilei (1564–1642) overturned the *Ptolemaic* view of the universe which placed the earth at the centre; Martin Luther (1483–1546) and others led the Protestant Reformation against the domination of the Roman Catholic Church; Columbus (1451–1505) discovered the New World (1492); and the arrival of printing facilitated the spread of all these ideas. Important Renaissance writers include *Dante, Petrarch, Boccaccio*, Cervantes (1547–1616), *More, Wyatt, Spenser, Sydney, Shakespeare, Bacon.* The word 'Renaissance' is sometimes used to denote any revival in the arts.

Renaissance (or Early Modern) Period: generally considered to cover *literature* written in Europe between approximately 1500 and 1660.

repetend: a word or phrase which is repeated at irregular intervals in a *poem* (as opposed to the regularity of a *refrain*).

repetition of any kind, from individual sound through patterns of language to whole sections, from *allusions* to ideas, is a *device* frequently used in *literature*, especially *poetry*, and usually for emphasis. See *amplification, palilogy*.

resolution: the outcome of the *climax* of a play or *story*. See also *act, catastrophe, dénouement, plot*.

rest: a term borrowed from music, indicating where there is a pause in the *metre* in place of an unstressed syllable.

Restoration comedy: a type of English *comedy* which dominated the stage between the Restoration of the monarchy in 1660 and the appearance of *sentimental comedy* in the early 18th century. Also known as artificial comedy or *comedy of manners*, it was characterised variously by stylishness, *wit* and bawdiness. The plays lacked the broad appeal of the Elizabethan theatre, the audiences tending to be drawn from the higher classes who went to see portrayed on stage the ladies and galants drawn from their own social circle. The usual subject-matter was love, intrigue, social climbing and marital infidelity. In performance the plays can be very funny, but were described by *Meredith* as 'that weary feast where no love is'. The most gifted playwrights were *Congreve, Etherege, Farquar, Vanburgh, Wycherley*.

Restoration Period: generally considered to cover *literature* written in England between 1660 (the restoration of the monarchy under Charles II) until approximately 1700.

Restoration tragedy: a less enduring *genre* than *Restoration comedy*, and never reaching the heights of the *Elizabethan Age*. Nonetheless there were some notable tragedies written during the *Restoration Period* including *Dryden*'s blank *verse* ALL FOR LOVE and *Otway*'s VENICE PRESERV'D, both blank verse *dramas*. See *heroic drama/tragedy*.

revenge tragedy is a *genre* of *drama* which was very popular during the Elizabethan and Jacobean era. Derived partly from the tragedies of the Greek playwright Aeschylus (525–456BC) and the Roman playwright Seneca (?4BC–AD65), the plots revolve around a *hero* (or sometimes *anti-hero*) who sets out to right a wrong, usually the murder of a close relative, and who succeeds at the end of the play but dies in the *catastrophe*. One key to the success of such plays is that the emotions of the audience are torn: they know that morally revenge is unacceptable and should be left to God; yet dramatically they wish to see the revenger 'get his man' (or, in at least one instance, woman). The most famous play in this genre is *Shakespeare*'s *Hamlet*.

reversal: see *peripeteia*.

review is a journalistic term normally given to a brief survey of a book in a magazine or newspaper. It is also the name given to a *periodical* which specialises in such surveys and other critical or literary pieces of writing, e.g. CRITICAL QUARTERLY, QUARTERLY REVIEW.

revision: the act of altering or updating a *text*, or the revised text itself.

revisionism: the act of updating or altering *text* in order to distort history, which is Winston Smith's job in *Orwell*'s Nineteen Eighty-Four.

Revolutionary Age: sometimes used to cover American *literature* written between 1765 (the Stamp Act) and approximately 1790.

revue is a theatrical entertainment comprising a miscellany of short items such as sketches, *songs* and dance, sometimes with a unifying *theme* and often topical and/or satirical, e.g. *Coward*'s Apple Sauce (1940), Michael Flanders (1922–75) and Donald Swann's (1923–94) At the Drop of a Hat (1956), *Alan Bennett*, Peter Cook (1937–95), Jonathan Miller (b.1934) and Dudley Moore's (b.1935) Beyond the Fringe (1960).

rhetoric is the art of using language to persuade, both written and, especially, in speech. *Aristotle* defined rhetoric as the art of 'discovering all the available means of persuasion in any given case'. The Roman Cicero and others codified rhetoric into a series of *rules* which have changed little until relatively modern times, and which were divided into a logical sequence of five processes:

- *invention*, or the discovery of appropriate and relevant material
- disposition or arrangement; that is, the structured organisation of that material
- *style*; that is the manner appropriate to the situation or occasion (e.g. 'grand', 'neutral' or 'plain')
- memory, or how to remember speeches
- delivery, or method for delivering speeches to maximum effect.

A certain amount of insincerity may often be apparent to the reader of, or listener to, rhetoric. For the more specific impact of rhetoric on writing see *rhetorical figures*.

rhetorical criticism is the name given to a way of looking at *literature* which focuses upon the *devices* used by a writer in *prose* or *poetry* to guide the responses of the reader. This critical approach grew during the 1960s and 1970s, much influenced by The Rhetoric of Fiction (1961) by the American scholar Wayne Booth (b.1921).

rhetorical figures: any artistic arrangement of words in order to create an emphasis or other effect, e.g. *antithesis, chiasmus, rhetorical question, zeugma*. It is important to note that this term only refers to a non-standard rearrangement of words, bc it grammar or syntax, and not to such *figures of speech* as *metaphor*, which alters the literal *meaning* of words.

rhetorical question: a question asked for effect, not expecting an answer, e.g. 'If Winter comes, can Spring be far behind?', the final line of *Shelley*'s 'Ode to the West Wind'. It is a figurative *device* much loved of politicans ('Are we to accept this state of affairs?'). Sometimes the speaker or writer immediately offers an answer to the question, as when Falstaff in *Shakespeare*'s Henry IV Part 1 asks 'Can honour set to a leg? No. Or an arm? No. Or take away the grief of a wound? No.'

Rhone, Trevor (b.1940): Jamaican playwright. Sometimes employing historical *allegory*, his social *criticism* is conveyed realistically and with *humour* about such topics as Jamaican life today, with a good ear for types of dialect and speech patterns. Notable works include The Gadget (1969), Smile Orange (1971), Old Story Time (1975), If: A Tragedy of the Ruled (1983), Hopes of the Living Dead (1988).

rhyme, sometimes spelt 'rime', is the use in *poetry* of repeated vowel sounds, and is sometimes wrongly taken as the main indicator that what one is reading is poetry rather than *prose*. There was little use of rhyme in Anglo-Saxon poetry, *alliteration* being the dominant poetic *device*. Rhyme is used mainly, but not exclusively, at line endings to repeat identical or similar accented sounds, e.g. sow/low, beast/feast, tougher/buffer. There are various types of rhyme according to the number of syllables in the rhyming word, such as *masculine rhyme, feminine rhyme, triple rhyme*; these classifications are nowadays infrequently used in English poetry, but more useful categories are *end-rhyme, internal rhyme, eye-rhyme, perfect rhyme, half-rhyme* (or 'near' rhyme).

rhyme royal: a *stanza* of seven ten-syllable *iambic* lines rhyming ababbcc, sometimes known as a Chaucerian *stanza* because *Chaucer* used it in TROILUS AND CRISEYDE, THE PARLEMENT OF FOULES and several of THE CANTERBURY TALES. Others who have experimented with the *form* include *Wyatt,* Michael Drayton (1563–1631), *Spenser, Shakespeare.*

rhyme scheme is the term used to describe the pattern of *rhymes* in a *stanza*, usually indicated alphabetically, e.g. the *rhyme scheme* in *rhyme royal* is ababbcc.

rhyming couplets are pairs of rhyming verse lines (aabbcc...). See *alternate rhyme.*

Rhys, Jean (?1890–1979): novelist and *short-story* writer best known for her *novel* WIDE SARGASSO SEA (1966), a 'prequel' to JANE EYRE which deals with the early life in the West Indies of the first Mrs Rochester. Exploitation is a recurrent *theme* in her writing. Other notable works include SLEEP IT OFF LADY (1976).

rhythm is the sense of movement in a piece of writing created by various patterns of *stress* on the syllables. In *poetry* this is generated by the *metre.*

rhythmical pause: another term for a *caesura.*

Rich, Adrienne (b. 1929): American poet, essayist and critic. A radical feminist and discontented with American politics, in her technically accomplished and prolific output she often explores feminism with directness. Her writing has been called *confessional poetry.* Notable works include THE DIAMOND CUTTERS (1955), SNAPSHOTS OF A DAUGHTER IN LAW (1963), NECESSITIES (1966), ON LIES, SECRETS AND SILENCE (1979), BLOOD, BREAD AND POETRY (1986), DIVING INTO THE WRECK (1972), ATLAS OF THE DIFFICULT WORLD (1991), ARTS OF THE POSSIBLE (2001).

Richards, I.A. (1893–1979): literary critic who was one of the founders of the Cambridge University English *literature* degree course. His book PRACTICAL CRITICISM (1929) advocates precise *close reading* of the words on the page, divorced from considerations of history or *context.* Other notable works include THE PHILOSOPHY OF RHETORIC (1936). See *intrinsic attitude, leavisite.*

Richardson, Samuel (1689–1761): novelist who made a major contribution to the development of the *novel*, pioneering the *epistolary* form. PAMELA OR VIRTUE REWARDED (1741) is generally considered to be the first modern exploration in a novel of the emotions and psychology of *characters.* His other notable works include CLARISSA HARLOWE (1748) and SIR CHARLES GRANDISON (1754).

riddle: a word puzzle ending with a question, the answer to which is an object, person or idea. Riddles have been popular in all cultures, one of the most famous being the riddle of the Sphinx in *Sophocles'* OEDIPUS REX: 'What goes on four legs in the morning, two legs in the afternoon, and three legs in the evening?' – the answer being man, who crawls on all fours early in life, on two legs in the prime of life, and on three (by using a stick) when old. Riddles were frequent in Anglo-Saxon *literature* in which such objects as a shield or an onion were described in inventive ways so that listeners had to guess what was being described.

riding rhyme: see *heroic couplets*.

rime: an old spelling of *rhyme*.

rime riche, French for 'rich rhyme', occurs when rhyming words are identical in sound, e.g. stair/stare, threw/through, and even identical in *form*, for instance, when rhyming still/still and playing upon two different meanings of the word.

rising action is when the *action* of a play is rising towards its *climax*. See *act, anabasis*.

rising rhythm, in which most English *verse* is written, occurs when the final syllable of each *foot* is stressed, as with *iambic* and *anapaestic* metre. *Trochaic* and *dactylic* metre create *falling rhythm*. See *metre*.

Robinson Crusoe myth: the idea, ideal even, of being cast away on a desert island. Ever since *Defoe* drew on the experiences of Alexander Selkirk (1676–1721), writers, artists and broadcasters have elevated the castaway to *mythic* status through such works as *Cowper*'s poem 'The Castaway' (1803), *Golding*'s LORD OF THE FLIES and *Walcott*'s reworking of the Crusoe *story*. Ingenious use of the idea on radio and television has attracted fascinated audiences.

Rochester, Earl of: see *Wilmot*.

rocking rhythm is a term used by *Hopkins* to indicate a metrical *foot* (see *metre*) containing three syllables, the first and third being stressed, the middle one unstressed, as in the first three words of his THE WRECK OF THE DEUTSCHLAND:

> Bút he scóres…

rococo is an architectural term referring to elegant flourishes of decorative scrollwork. It is generally applied to writing which displays flourishes of verbal dexterity and *wit*, e.g. parts of *Pope*'s work, especially 'The Rape of the Lock'.

Roethke, Theodore (1908–63): American poet. Inspired by the locations and landscape of his childhood as a means of defining individual identity, he has written much *love poetry*. Notable works include OPEN HOUSE (1941), THE WAKING: POEMS 1933–1953 (1953), I AM! SAYS THE LAMB (1961), THE FAR FIELD (1964).

rogue literature is concerned with the criminal underworld, and was particularly popular in the 16th and 17th centuries, e.g. some of the writings of *Robert Greene* and *Dekker*.

roman à clef means, in French, 'novel with a key', and refers to a *novel* where apparently fictitious *characters* are thinly disguised portrayals of a real people, e.g. *Coleridge*, *Byron* and *Shelley* in *Peacock*'s NIGHTMARE ABBEY, *Lawrence* in *Huxley*'s POINT COUNTER POINT (1928). *Maugham* was notorious for failing sufficiently to disguise his models.

romance: an entertaining *story* written in *verse*, and later *prose*, about the world of *courtly love* and chivalry, e.g. Arthurian romances concerning the knights and ladies of King Arthur's court, and other stories of classical *heroes*. Such *tales* contrast with the *epic*, which is a story about war. Influenced by such *collections* as Richard Burton's (1821–90) translation of Oriental tales THE ARABIAN NIGHTS (1885–88), romances were not realistic stories but told of magical, almost fairy-tale worlds where knights perform such deeds as jousting in tournaments and battling with fantastical animals in order to save their ladies. Famous examples include the 14th century SIR GAWAIN AND THE GREEN KNIGHT in verse and *Malory*'s LE MORTE D'ARTHUR in prose. Later, 'romance' was extended to cover any kind of adventure story, often involving love – but by no means always: candidates must be very careful not to read this term in the 'Mills and Boon' sense. *Burlesque* mock-romances appeared such as *Beaumont*'s comedy THE KNIGHT OF THE BURNING PESTLE, where the 'hero' is a grocer's apprentice, *Fielding*'s *parody* JOSEPH ANDREWS, and *Samuel Butler*'s *mock-heroic* HUDIBRAS. Interest in chivalric romance re-emerged with such works as *Spenser*'s THE FAERIE QUEENE, *Keats*' 'The Eve of St Agnes', and *Tennyson*'s 'Idylls of the King'.

roman-fleuve: from the French meaning 'river novel', refers to a *saga* concerning the doings of a set of *characters* over a long period of time and can therefore run into several books or a series of *novels*. First appearing in France early last century, the most famous example of the type is A LA RECHERCHE DU TEMPS PERDU (REMEMBRANCE OF THINGS PAST) by Marcel Proust (1871–1922). A typical instance in English *literature* is *Galsworthy*'s THE FORSYTE SAGA.

romantic comedy denotes a kind of *drama* in which love is the main *theme* and where, after difficulties along the way, the lovers are united. The *genre* developed in popularity during Elizabethan times, *Shakespeare*'s AS YOU LIKE IT and A MIDSUMMER NIGHT'S DREAM being typical examples, and has remained so ever since.

romantic irony is a *device* whereby a writer builds up the illusion of reality in order deliberately to shatter it by intruding into the work as a *self-conscious narrator*, making the reader aware of the created *fiction* by commenting, often humorously, upon such matters as the *characters* and the problems of where next to take the *narrative*, e.g. *Sterne* in TRISTRAM SHANDY, *Byron* in DON JUAN.

Romantic Period: generally considered to cover *literature* written in Europe between approximately 1780 and 1830. In America the term is often used to refer to the period approximately from 1828 to 1865 (alternative terms being the *American Renaissance* or the *Age of Transcendentalism*). See *Romanticism*.

Romanticism is a term applied to a European-wide revolution in *literature* and other arts covering approximately the period 1780 to 1840. Romantics reacted against *neo-classicism*, 18th century rationalism, and the praise of pure intellect, celebrating the importance of feelings and the imagination. Among many other things, Romantics were variously interested in:

- nature-worship, especially of wild, lonely places
- primitivism
- *medievalism*, and the *gothic*
- Oriental, alien or vanished cultures (they would have enjoyed modern *science fiction*)
- the supernatural, bizarre or nightmarish
- idealism

- political and social revolution
- opposition to established institutions such as the monarchy and the church
- physical sensations and passion
- the notion of *carpe diem*
- above all, the importance of the individual creating his or her own relationship with the world.

The French writer Rousseau is generally regarded as the father of Romanticism. The most read English Romantic writers are *Wordsworth, Coleridge, Keats, Mary* and *Percy Shelley, Byron*. The most read European Romantic writers are Goethe, Schiller, Kant, Hegel, Hugo, Gautier, Dumas père, Stendhal. Among American writers are *Poe, Emerson, Thoreau, Hawthorne, Melville, Longfellow, Lowell, Whitman*. In music the best known composers are Berlioz, Mendelssohn, Schumann and, above all, Beethoven; and in painting Corot, Delacroix, Ingres, Millet. It is appropriate to write of the Romantic movement or writers with a capital 'R' in order to distinguish them from romantic writers who are concerned with sentimental love stories. At its best Romanticism is a celebration, a life-enhancing hymn of praise to the beautiful things in the world. The hippie movement of the 1960s was a neo-Romantic movement, and there have been and still are other manifestations of new Romanticism. We are all, in a sense, post-Romantics.

Rose Theatre, the: an Elizabethan theatre built by *Henslowe* and John Cholmley (?1550 – ?1595) near the River Thames at *Bankside* in Southwark, London, an area close to the Bear Garden and *the Globe Theatre*. The theatre features in the 1999 film SHAKESPEARE IN LOVE.

Rosenberg, Isaac (1890–1918): poet and artist, killed during the First World War. His *poetry* is characteristically *realistic*, sharp in its *imagery* and technically inventive. Notable works include NIGHT AND DAY (1912), YOUTH (1915), MOSES: A PLAY (1916).

Rossetti, Christina (1830–94): poet. Of Italian parentage and sister to the artist *Dante Gabriel Rossetti*, she is famous in two artistic respects: as a poet and as a model for the painters of the *Pre-Raphaelite* Brotherhood. She wrote *ballads*, hymns, carols, and childrens' *verse*, all of which showed her intense regard for detail, depth of emotion and her ability to use *symbolism* to great effect.

Rossetti, Dante Gabriel (1828–82): poet and translator. He was the brother of *Christina Rossetti*, and the leading light of the *Pre-Raphaelite* Brotherhood as a painter and a *lyric* poet. He translated works by various European writers, notably the lyrics of *Dante*. His own *poetry* contains detail of great depth, colour, mysticism and *fantasy*, his best known including THE BLESSED DAMOZEL (1846), THE HOUSE OF LIFE (1870), SISTER HELEN AND TROY TOWN (1851).

Roth, Philip (b.1933): American novelist and playwright. His novels mainly concern the American Jewish community. Notable works include GOODBYE COLUMBUS (1959), PORTNOY'S COMPLAINT (1969, controversial on account of its sexual subject-matter), SABBATH'S THEATER (1995).

Rotimi, Ola (b.1938): Nigerian playwright. His historical tragedies often contain social and political comment upon contemporary Africa. Notable works include OUR HUSBAND HAS GONE MAD AGAIN (1966), KURUNMI (1969), HOLDING TALKS (1979).

round characters, as defined by *Forster* in ASPECTS OF THE NOVEL, are *characters* who are rounded, three-dimensional and develop during the course of a *story*. He cites Becky Sharp from *Thackeray's* VANITY FAIR as an example. See *flat characters*.

roundel: an eleven-line *poem* in three *stanzas* with the opening words of the poem repeated as a *refrain* at the end of the first and third stanzas, thus: abaR(refrain), bab, abaR. The *form* was developed by *Swinburne* and published in his A CENTURY OF ROUNDELS (1883).

Rowley, William (?1585–?1637): playwright. As an actor he played fat clowns. Best known as collaborator with *Middleton* on A FAIR QUARREL (1616), and especially THE CHANGELING, and with *Dekker* and *Ford* on THE WITCH OF EDMONTON, he also wrote a few *citizen comedies* and other plays on his own. His plays remained popular during the 17th century.

Roy, Arundhati (b.1961): novelist whose first *novel*, THE GOD OF SMALL THINGS (1997) is, claims Roy, not specifically about India but about human nature. It has been variously described by critics as ambitious, fresh, highly wrought, poetic, over-rated.

Roy, Gabrielle (1909–1983): Canadian novelist. Her writing gives a realistic view of life from rural Manitoba to urban Quebec. Notable works include THE TIN FLUTE (1946), ALEXANDER CHENEVERT (1954), THE ROAD PAST ALTAMOUNT (1966), CHILDREN OF MY HEART (1979).

rules, in a literary sense, are a set of *conventions* and precepts, developed by custom which sometimes goes back to classical times (see *classic*), laying down how *novels*, *poems*, plays and so forth should be constructed. For instance, at some point rules have laid down that a novel should tell a *story* in a logical sequence, a sonnet should have 14 lines, and a play should observe the dramatic unities. A *sonnet* would not be a sonnet unless it consisted of 14 lines. However, in *Renaissance* times and later English playwrights such as *Shakespeare* often disregarded the rules of the *dramatic unities* which the French playwrights held dear (in much the same way as the French are stricter in adhering to the rules of language for which the English have a cheerful disregard).

run-on lines: another term for *enjambement.*

Runyon, Damon (1884–1946): an American *short-story* writer and journalist whose books include GUYS AND DOLLS (1932) in which Runyon brings to life *characters* of Broadway such as Nicely Niceley Johnson and Harry the Horse. He writes in the present tense and uses much Broadway slang which gives his work a great sense of vibrancy. The *style* is so individual that it is given the name Runyonese.

rural novel: a term sometimes used to define a sub-genre (see *genre*) of *stories* set in the countryside, and occasionally containing elements of the *pastoral*, such as *Hardy's* Wessex *novels* or *Webb's* PRECIOUS BANE, and *Gibbons'* *parody* thereof in COLD COMFORT FARM. See also *novel of the soil.*

Rushdie, Salman (b.1947): Anglo-Indian novelist, *short-story* and travel writer. His bi-lingual, post-colonial upbringing informs his work, much of which is characteristic of *magic realism*. As a result of THE SATANIC VERSES (1988) a charge of blasphemy against the Islamic religion was followed by a 'fatwa' (death sentence) imposed upon him by Ayatollah Khomeini (1902–89) of Iran, since when Rushdie has been in hiding. Other notable works include Midnight's Children (1981), Shame (1983), Haroun and the Sea of Stories (1990), East, West (1994), The Moor's Last Sigh (1995).

Ruskin, John (1819–1900): a critic and scholar of very varied interests extending from art, art history and architecture, social reform and politics to ornithology, geology and botany, he had an impact on nearly every sphere of cultural activity, including *literature*. His Modern Painters (1843) helped to define *Romanticism*, and his love of *gothic* architecture did much to further contemporary interest in *medievalism*. Other notable works include The Seven Lamps of Architecture (1849), The Stones of Venice (1851–3, including a famous *essay* entitled The Nature of Gothic).

Russell, Willy (b.1947): playwright who in much of his work writes with energy and *wit* about *characters* and their struggles in his native city of Liverpool. Notable works include Breezeblock Park (1975), Educating Rita (1980), Blood Brothers (1983), Our Day Out (1977), Shirley Valentine (1988).

S

Sackville, Thomas (1536–1608): playwright and poet. His best known work is the *tragedy* GORBODUC (1561), which he wrote with *Norton* and which some claim to be the first English *tragedy*. In some respects the plot foreshadows *Shakespeare's* KING LEAR.

Sackville-West, Vita (1892–1962): English poet, novelist and biographer. A close friend of *Woolf*, she favoured topics such as travel, gardening, history, literary topics. Notable works include THE LAND (1926), THE EDWARDIANS (1930), ALL PASSION SPENT (1931), COLLECTED POEMS (1933).

saga: medieval Norse *narratives*, originally oral but often later written down, about kings and other *heroes*. They have had some influence on later writings, for example *Longfellow's* SAGA OF KING OLAF (1863).

saga novel: a long *novel*, sometimes one of a series, concerning a family, e.g. *Galsworthy's* FORSYTE novels. See *roman-fleuve*.

Salinger, J.D. (b.1919): American novelist and *short-story* writer. Best known for THE CATCHER IN THE RYE (1951) with whose narrator successive generations of the young have identified. He has a good ear for the free-wheeling conversational *style* of his *characters*. Other notable works include FRANNEY AND ZOOEY (1961).

sapphic ode: a very complicated metrical *form* named after the ancient Greek poetess Sappho (7th century BC). Various English poets such as *Sidney, Cowper, Southey, Tennyson, Swinburne, Pound* experimented with it.

Saro-Wiwa, Ken (1941–95): Nigerian novelist, *dramatist*, and political writer. Before his execution in 1995 for violent political campaigning, his work explored modern Nigerian culture, often using strong *satire*. Notable works include SOZABOY: A NOVEL IN ROTTEN ENGLAND (1985), SONGS IN A TIME OF WAR (1985), PRISONERS OF JEBS (1988), ADAKU (1989).

Sassoon, Siegfried (1886–1967): poet and *prose* writer. Best know for his anti-war *poetry*, he highlights the true horrors of war by using an unpatriotic ironic tone. His later writings are more spiritual and autobiographical. Notable works include A SOLDIER'S DECLARATION (1917), MEMOIRS OF A FOX-HUNTING MAN (1928), MEMOIRS OF AN INFANTRY OFFICER (1930), VIGILS (1935), SIEGFRIED'S JOURNEY (1945). *Pat Barker's* REGENERATION is partly based on Sassoon's apparent psychological problems as a result of the First World War.

Satanic school is a term invented by *Southey* in his harsh attack on the life and morals of *Byron, Shelley*, and possibly *Keats*, in the preface to THE VISION OF JUDGEMENT.

satire, in *literature* or other arts, aims to make a moral point by mocking follies and vices, often through sometimes biting *humour*. Its *comedy* is not intended for mere entertainment, but for a purpose. The beginnings of *satire* may be traced to ancient Roman writers. Among others *Chaucer, Shakespeare, Jonson, Donne* all employed satire, but the great age of English literary satire is generally considered to be the late 17th and 18th centuries, notably in the writings of *Dryden, Pope* and *Jonathan Swift*. Later satirists include *Byron, Peacock, Shaw, Huxley, Orwell* and *Waugh*. See *burlesque, irony*.

satirical comedy is a *form* of *comedy* whose aim is to highlight the follies and vices of society. Sometimes the *characters* are grotesque rather than gently amusing, as in *Jonson*'s THE ALCHEMIST and VOLPONE. Later examples of the *genre* include *Sheridan*'s THE SCHOOL FOR SCANDAL, *Shaw*'s THE DOCTOR'S DILEMMA, *Bennett*'s FORTY YEARS ON, *Stoppard*'s JUMPERS, *Hare*'s TEETH 'N' SMILES, *Mamet*'s AMERICAN BUFFALO and GLENGARRY GLEN ROSS, *Churchill*'s SERIOUS MONEY.

scansion is the process of closely examining the stress pattern within each *foot* of each line of *verse*, and the overall *rhythm* and movement of the *poem* which is thereby created. See *metre*.

scene: the sub-division of an *act* which contains an *episode* normally separated in time sequence, and sometimes place, from the episode which follows. In *Elizabethan drama* a scene is normally deemed to have ended at a point when all the characters leave the stage, but act and scene divisions in editions of *Shakespeare* and his contemporaries have been supplied by later editors. Some modern plays consist of a continuous series of episodes with no breaks in the time sequence or change of scene.

school of writers is a term sometimes applied to a definable group who combine and have some influence on their contemporaries, e.g. the *Bloomsbury Group*.

Schreiner, Olive (1855–1920): South African novelist who broke *conventions* through her pioneering feminist writing, influencing such writers as *Brittain*. South African politics and the fight against the apartheid are also at the forefront of her *literature*. Notable works include THE STORY OF AN AFRICAN FARM (1883), DREAMS (1891), A SOUTH AFRICAN'S VIEW OF THE SITUATION (1898), WOMAN AND LABOUR (1911), FROM MAN TO MAN (1927).

science fiction is a type of *fantasy* literature, usually in the form of a *short story* or *novel*, which creates an alternative society based on the imagined technology of the future (and sometimes the past) and frequently involves such elements as space travel, alien beings, supernatural forces. *Science fiction* stretches the *imagination* by rooting the *fantastic* in reality. *Mary Shelley*'s FRANKENSTEIN is sometimes described as the key work in the development of the *genre*, later writers including *Wells, Huxley, Orwell, Burgess, Wyndham,* Isaac Asimov (1920–92), Ray Bradbury (b.1920), Arthur C. Clarke (b.1917), Brian Aldiss (b.1925), Frank Herbert (1920–86). The *genre* is often not regarded as 'serious' *literature*.

Scott, Dennis (1939–91): Jamaican poet and playwright. His *poems* often adopt several intimate voices, all of which tend to focus on the self. A recurring interest in his work is humorous behaviour in relation to racial and political oppression. Notable works include UNCLE TIME (1974), DOG (1981), DREADWALK (1982).

Scott, Paul (1920–78): novelist. Three years of living in India, Burma and Malaya, and experiencing the difficulties of Anglo-Indian relationships leading up to independence, gave him inspiration and *settings* for his works. His writings also show a preoccupation with historical perspectives. Notable works include BIRDS OF PARADISE (1962), THE JEWEL IN THE CROWN (1966) and three other novels which make up THE RAJ QUARTET (1966–74), STAYING ON (1977).

Scott, Walter (1771–1832): Scottish novelist, poet, critic and editor. His early work was nearly all *poetry*, *verse romances* on historical or legendary subjects such as THE LAY

OF THE LAST MINSTREL (1805). Partly prompted by the success of *Byron's* CHILDE HAROLD'S PILGRIMAGE, which he regarded as superior to anything he could achieve in *poetry*, he turned to historical romances in *novel* form. The great popularity of WAVERLEY (1814) confirmed the decision, turning Scott into the most read novelist of his time. His descriptions of ruins and landscape helped to define *Romanticism*, and his *settings* stimulated interest in *mediaevalism* and the *historical* novel, and restored to the Scottish nation the self-esteem lost after the 1745 uprising. His *characterisation, humour*, handling of history, and concern with political and social change all had an impact both upon writers such as the *Brontës, George Eliot, Gaskell* and upon the *reader-response* of the *Victorian Age* which followed. Twentieth century *Marxist criticism* interpreted his *novels* in the light of *historicism*. Other notable works include GUY MANNERING (1815), OLD MORTALITY (1816), ROB ROY (1817), THE HEART OF MIDLOTHIAN (1818), THE BRIDE OF LAMMERMOOR (1819), IVANHOE (1819), PEVERIL OF THE PEAK (1823), QUENTIN DURWARD (1823), REDGAUNTLET (1824).

Scottish Chaucerians: a name given to group of Scottish poets of the late 15th and early 16th centuries, such as *Dunbar* and *Henryson*, whose work may have been influenced by *Chaucer*, particularly in the use of *rhyme royal*.

second person narrator: see *narrator*.

selection: a term usually applied to a volume containing representative work of a single writer, often a poet, e.g. *Layton's* A WILD PECULIAR JOY: SELECTED POEMS 1945–82. See *collection, anthology*.

self-conscious narrator: see *narrator*.

self-reflexive writing is writing in which the author, often a self-conscious *narrator* and sometimes an autobiographer, incorporates into the *text* thoughts about the business of creating it, e.g. *Sterne's* TRISTRAM SHANDY, *Worsdworth's* THE PRELUDE.

semantics is the study of all aspects of words.

semiotics/semiology: the systematic study of all aspects of signs, including words.

senecan style of writing is concise and economic, after the *style* of the Roman writer Seneca (?4BC–65AD). It may be regarded as the opposite of a *Ciceronian style*.

Senecan tragedy, that is the *closet drama* of Seneca, had considerable influence on the *style* and subject-matter of much *Elizabethan drama* in its use of such features as a five act structure, *chorus*, the *revenge theme*, ghosts, messengers, sensational and often gory events (which the Elizabethans often showed on stage, whereas in Seneca they are reported events), *stichomythia*, grand (and sometimes tedious) speeches. Examples include *Norton* and *Sackville's* GORBODUC, *Kyd's* THE SPANISH TRAGEDY, *Shakespeare's* TITUS ANDRONICUS (1590). Influences are also apparent in his HAMLET and in *Webster's* THE DUCHESS OF MALFI.

Senior, Olive (b.1943): Jamaican essayist, *short-story* writer and poet. She tends to explore Jamaican political and social conditions. Notable works include THE MESSAGE IS CHANGE (1972), SUMMER LIGHTENING (1989), TALKING OF TREES (1985), WORKING MIRACLES (1991).

sense, in a particular meaning which developed in the 18th century, denotes a capacity for sound and intelligent judgement, which *Austen* contrasts with *sensibility* in SENSE AND SENSIBILITY.

sensibility is a term sometimes used to denote the ability to respond with feeling and *sympathy*, even *empathy*, to a text or other artistic *form*, especially in relation to:

- beauty
- the plight of others.

The term became popular in the late 18th century, and could refer to either the responses of reader or those of *characters* in the book. See *Sensibility, Age of*.

Sensibility, Age of: the term has been used to define a period of *literature* from 1744 (the death of *Pope*) until somewhere around 1784 (death of *Johnson*), 1789 (French Revolution) or as late as 1798 (publication of *Wordsworth* and *Coleridge*'s LYRICAL BALLADS). In general, this period sees a reaction against the cynicism of the *Restoration* and the writings of such as Thomas Hobbes (1588–1679), and the beginnings of the movement towards *Romanticism* and the elevation of feeling above *neo-classical* intellectualism and 'correctness'. Examples of relevant works are *Gray*'s 'Elegy', *Sterne*'s A SENTIMENTAL JOURNEY, *Goldsmith*'s 'The Deserted Village', *Cowper*'s 'The Task'. It was considered that to react with *sensibility* was proof of moral virtue in an individual; but this sometimes descended into *sentimentality*, *Sheridan* satirising hypocritical sentiment in THE SCHOOL FOR SCANDAL, and *Austen* criticising over-developed *sensibility* in SENSE AND SENSIBILITY. See *sense*.

sentimental comedy, in part a reaction against the perceived immorality of *Restoration comedy*, is a term used to denote the undemanding kind of play popular in the 18th century in which, typically, morally upstanding middle-class *heroes* and *heroines* utter fine sentiments in the face of adversity prior to a contrived happy ending, e.g. *Steele*'s THE CONSCIOUS LOVERS, *Goldsmith*'s THE GOOD-NATURED MAN (1768), THE WEST INDIAN (1771) by Richard Cumberland (1732–1811). *Sheridan*'s hypocritical Joseph Surface in THE SCHOOL FOR SCANDAL is a *parody* of such heroes.

sentimental novel: a type of *novel* which is always popular, in *literature* the term is especially applied to certain novels of *sensibility* written during the *Age of Sensibility* such as *Richardson*'s PAMELA, *Sterne*'s TRISTRAM SHANDY and A SENTIMENTAL JOURNEY. The ultimate excess of sensibility occurs in Henry MacKenzie's THE MAN OF FEELING where the *hero* is of such extreme sensitivity (a term which later replaced sensibility) that he dies as a result of pent-up emotion leading to a declaration of love. After the *genre* waned, the popularity of such sentimental episodes continued, an example being the death of Little Nell in *Dickens*' THE OLD CURIOSITY SHOP (1841).

sentimentality is when *sensibility* descends into a mawkish self-indulgence in a *manner* which students nowadays describe as 'cheesy'.

Sepamla, Sipho (b.1932): South African poet and novelist. He strongly promotes the arts in South Africa to create political awareness. His *style* is both subtle and direct and he uses his skill as a writer to voice his opinions on the political struggles of township life. Both THE SOWETO I LOVE (1977) and A RIDE IN THE WHIRLWIND (1981, banned in South Africa) deal with the Soweto uprising of 1976. Other notable works include THE ROOT IS ONE (1979), THIRD GENERATION (1986), FROM GORE TO SOWETO (1988).

septet: a *stanza* or section of *verse* containing seven lines, usually defined by a unit of *rhyme* pattern. See also *rhyme royal*.

sermon: an instructive talk on a moral or religious subject, as delivered from a church pulpit. *Renaissance* and *Victorian* literature in particular have many fine examples by such as *Donne* and Cardinal Newman (1801–90).

Serote, Mongane Wally (b.1944): South African poet and novelist. After being imprisoned in 1969 for nine months and released without charge, his strongly political works protest with a bitter and angry creative voice against the sufferings of urban blacks. Notable works include TSETLO (1974, banned in South Africa), NO BABY MUST WEEP (1975), THE NIGHT KEEPS WINKING (1983), TO EVERY BIRTH ITS BLOOD (1981).

serpentine verse is a line or *stanza* which begins and ends with the same word.

sestet: a *stanza* or section of *verse* containing six lines, usually defined by a unit of *rhyme* pattern.

sestina: a complicated and rare *verse* form consisting of six *stanzas* of pentameters followed by a three line *envoi*. The same six end words are used throughout, but in a different order according to a set pattern. The *form* was devised by troubadour poets in 13th century France. English poets who have used it include *Sidney* (in ARCADIA), *Swinburne* (in COMPLAINT OF LISA, 1870), *Kipling, Pound* (in SESTINA: ALTAFORTE, 1909), *Eliot, Auden, Ashberry.* See *sestet.*

Seth, Vickram (b.1952): Indian poet, novelist, *short-story*, children's and travel writer. With *wit* and technical skill he explores a variety of cultures and *themes.* Notable works include THE GOLDEN GATE (1986), ALL YOU WHO SLEEP TONIGHT (1990), A SUITABLE BOY (1993).

setting: the location or period within which a *story* or play is placed. For instance, in *Hardy*'s THE RETURN OF THE NATIVE Egdon Heath is of prime importance in the fabric of the *novel* as a whole. In *drama, setting* includes any stage scenery.

Shaffer, Peter (b.1926): playwright and novelist. His well-constructed *dramas* show compassionate philosophical and psychological insights into human yearnings. Notable works include FIVE FINGER EXERCISE (1958), THE ROYAL HUNT OF THE SUN (1964), BLACK COMEDY (1965), EQUUS (1973), AMADEUS (1979), THE GIFT OF GORGON (1992).

shaggy dog story: a long drawn-out joke, full of digressions, which usually has a laughably weak climax. *Heller*'s CATCH-22 has been described as a literary shaggy dog *story.*

Shakespeare, William (1564–1616): poet and playwright, he probably thought of himself primarily as the former and would be surprised to find that his fame rests mainly upon the latter. He is capable of a range of *lyric* poetry, most notably in his SONNETS (published 1609, but almost certainly written in the 1590s) which cover such subjects, *themes* and ideas as love, the effects of time, mortality, *carpe diem,* flattery, the pride of the great and meretricious. As his playwrighting career progressed he may be regarded as having taken on *Marlowe*'s mantle as the foremost developer of the *blank verse* line as a vehicle for the creation of powerful poetic *drama.* Shakespeare's combined skill with words (many of which he himself seems to have coined or at least brought into currency), poetic mastery, intuitive understanding and acceptance of the psychological complexities and contradictory nature of human beings (what

Keats later called *negative capability*), and a complete grasp of the theatre of his day make him, in the eyes of many, the master playwright of all time. He has had an impact on all art forms: his words, stories, *themes* and ideas are constantly recycled, updated and/or transposed into other media (film, opera, musical comedies and so forth). The stream of Shakespearean criticism and scholarship began soon after his death and has never ceased, commentators including *Dryden, Johnson, Coleridge, Hazlitt, Bradley, Shaw, Granville-Barker, Tillyard*. Attempts to edit and collate the various printed versions of his plays began early in the 18th century, editors including *Pope, Johnson, Boswell, Jon Dover Wilson, Kermode*. Other notable works include: *poems* – VENUS AND ADONIS (1593), THE RAPE OF LUCRECE (1594); histories – HENRY IV, PARTS 1 AND 2 (1597–8), HENRY V (?1599); comedies – AS YOU LIKE IT (?1599), TWELFTH NIGHT (?1600), A MIDSUMMER NIGHT'S DREAM (1594), MUCH ADO ABOUT NOTHING (?1598); tragedies – ROMEO AND JULIET (?1594), JULIUS CAESAR (C.1599), HAMLET (?1600), KING LEAR (1605), OTHELLO (?1603), MACBETH (?1606), ANTONY AND CLEOPATRA (?1607); late plays, sometimes classed as romantic *tragi-comedies* – THE TEMPEST (1611), THE WINTER'S TALE (?1610). The first collection of his works is the 1623 Folio edition which *Jonson* prefaces by the claim that Shakespeare 'was not of an age, but for all time'.

Shakespearean sonnet: see *sonnet*.

shavian: *characteristic* of the manner, attitudes and/or subject-matter of *Shaw*.

Shaw, George Bernard (1856–1950): Irish playwright, critic and novelist. Influenced by *Ibsen*, his plays wittily and irreverently entice the audience to think about socialist issues such as equal opportunities. In order to reinforce his points he often wrote long prefaces to his plays, and his *stage directions* are very detailed and demanding. He claimed that his *drama*, largely out of fashion nowadays, was superior to that of *Shakespeare*. Notable works include PLAYS UNPLEASANT (1893), PLAYS PLEASANT (1898), MAN AND SUPERMAN (1904), HEARTBREAK HOUSE (1920).

Shelley, Mary (1797–1851): novelist, biographer and editor. Time spent with her husband *Percy Shelley* and *Byron* in Switzerland and Italy influenced her choice of·*settings*, especially in her best-known work, the *gothic* novel FRANKENSTEIN, OR THE MODERN PROMETHEUS (1818), begun in 1816 as part of a *ghost story* competition suggested by Byron. She often used the type of historical *themes* which were characteristic of *Romanticism*. Other notable works include THE LAST MAN (1826).

Shelley, Percy Bysshe (1792–1822): poet, translator and playwright. His highly imaginative writing was much inspired by political views: he exemplifies the radical intellectual aspects of *Romanticism*, opposing tyranny, oppression and injustice wherever he came across it. 'Freedom!' and 'Liberty!' were his war-cries, and his technically masterful *poetry* is characteristically exuberant, humorous, fiery, high-soaring and visionary. He became friends with *Hunt, Keats, Hazlitt* and *Peacock*. Notable works include QUEEN MAB (1813), 'Ozymandias' (1818), THE MASQUE OF ANARCHY (1819, inspired by the Peterloo Massacre), 'Ode to the West Wind' (1819), THE CENCI (1819), DEFENCE OF POETRY (1820), 'To a Skylark' (1820), 'The Cloud' (1820), PROMETHEUS UNBOUND (1820), ADONAIS (1821), WHEN THE LAMP IS SHATTERED (1822).

Shepard, Sam (b.1943): American playwright. His *avant-garde* plays deal with popular culture surrounding family relations in America. Notable works include ICARUS'

MOTHER (1965), OPERATION SIDEWINDER (1970), THE TOOTH OF THE CRIME (1972), BURIED CHILD (1978), FOOL FOR LOVE (1983).

Sheridan, Richard Brinsley (1751–1816): playwright in the *comedy of manners* tradition. Notable works include THE RIVALS (1775, in which Mrs Malaprop's misuse of language gave the word *malapropism* to the English language), THE SCHOOL FOR SCANDAL (1777), THE CRITIC (1779).

Sheriff, R.C. (1896–1975): playwright and novelist whose best known work is JOURNEY'S END (1928), a powerful play about the effects upon different soldiers of trench life during the First World War. Laurence Olivier's performance of Stanhope in the original production helped to make him famous. Other notable works include BADGER'S GREEN (1930), THE WHITE CARNATION (1953).

Shields, Carol (b.1935): Canadian novelist. Often compared with *Atwood*, her common *themes* are developed through the use of skilful post-modern techniques. Notable works include HAPPENSTANCE: THE HUSBAND'S STORY (1980), HAPPENSTANCE: THE WIFE'S STORY (1982), THE REPUBLIC OF LOVE (1992), THE STONE DIARIES (1993).

short metre: a *quatrain*, usually *iambic*, composed of three *trimeters* and a third line which is a *tetrameter* and rhyming abcb or abab (see *metre*). Much used in *song*s, especially hymns, e.g. *Herbert*'s THE ELIXIR (1633):

> A man who looks on glass,
> On it may stay his eye,
> Or, if he pleaseth, through it pass,
> And then the heaven espy.

short novel: another term for *novella*.

short short stories: see *short story*.

short story: a brief work of *fiction* in which the basic elements are similar to the novel, but the writing is tighter in *form* and limited to fewer and sometimes only a single incident. Earlier forms were the *fable* and folktale, and relatively self-contained stories in the *Bible* such as Noah's Flood or Jonah and the Whale can be defined as short stories. *Poe* defined them as *prose* tales which could each be read at one sitting or in half to two hours (see *tale*). It is difficult to define when a short story becomes long enough to be classed as a *novella*, e.g. *Dickens*' A CHRISTMAS CAROL or *James*' THE TURN OF THE SCREW are at the least very long short stories. Certain modern writers such as *Carver* have specialised in what are sometimes known as *short short stories*, unelaborated *anecdotes* or *mood* pieces of a single page or less. Some critics divide short stories into two types:

- a traditional variety which is a tightly structured story with a twist at the end
- a modern variety which has less obvious form and aims to depict a mood and atmosphere rather than tell a clear story.

Short stories are a popular *genre* to this day in certain magazines, newspapers and *periodical*s. American writers seem to be particularly skilful at the *form*. Notable writers include *Poe, Hawthorne, Melville, Dickens, Hardy, Henry James, Bierce, Twain, Harte, Henry, Conrad, Mansfield, Doyle, Wells, Chesterton, Lawrence, Fitzgerald, Faulkner, Runyon, Dineson, Hemingway, Carver, Naipaul, Kingsley Amis, Theroux, Trevor, Carter, Graham Swift.*

showing and telling: in a *narrative*, a writer is 'showing' the *characters* when their *actions*, *dialogue* and thoughts are presented to the reader, who then has to make up her or his judgement about those characters. 'Telling' occurs when the author intervenes to tell the reader about the characters and thus influences the reader's opinions. It is sometimes considered a superior technique to 'show', but some great writers tend to 'tell'. *Henry James* tends to 'show'; *Austen*, to 'tell'. See *characterisation*.

sibilance: *alliteration* of the letter 's'. See *sigmatism* for an example.

sick verse: humorous *poems* of deliberately bad taste, sometimes macabre, leaving the reader with a sense of unease. Examples may be found in the poetry of, among others, *Poe* ('The Sleeper', 1831; 'The Raven', 1845; 'The Bells', 1849), *Browning* ('The Laboratory', 1845; 'Childe Roland to the Dark Tower Came', 1855), *Swinburne* ('Faustine; After Death', 1862), *Auden* ('Miss Gee', 1940) and *Plath* ('In Plaster, Surgeon at 2.a.m.', 1961). See also *black comedy, graveyard school of poetry*.

Sidney, Philip (1554–86): poet, literary critic and prose writer. He came to be regarded as the idealised *Renaissance* courtier of the *Elizabethan Age*, both in his life (and the noble manner of his death) and through the *style* and subject matter of his *poetry*. He experimented in a variety of *forms*, and English *literature* owes a considerable debt to him. Notable works include ARCADIA (1590, seen by some as the ancestor of the English *novel*), ASTROPHEL AND STELLA (1591, the first English *sonnet cycle*), AN APOLOGY FOR POETRY (1595).

sight rhyme: see *eye rhyme*.

sigmatism: repeated use of the letter 's' in order to create *sibilance*, e.g.

All shod with steel
We hissed along the polished ice in games...

(from *Wordsworth*'s THE PRELUDE)

sign: any symbol, such as a word, which stands for something. In the case of a word, the 'signifier' is the word itself, the 'signified' is the concept or *meaning* which it conveys.

signified: see *sign*.

signifier: see *sign*.

significance is the impact which a work of *literature* has upon an individual reader. See *meaning, reader-response*.

Silko, Leslie Marmon (b.1948): American novelist and screenwriter. Her writings are heavily based on her own experiences of growing up as half White and half Indian and explore identity struggles consequent upon not fitting entirely into one culture. Notable works include LAGUNA WOMEN (1974), CEREMONY (1977), ALMANAC OF THE DEAD (1991), GARDENS IN THE DUNES (1999).

Sillitoe, Alan (b.1928): British novelist and poet. His writing, often of a political nature, is frequently set in or near his home town of Nottingham, and depicts working-class struggles within a modern industrial society. Notable works include SATURDAY NIGHT AND SUNDAY MORNING (1958), THE LONELINESS OF THE LONG DISTANCE RUNNER (1959), A TREE ON FIRE (1976), LOST LOVES (1990).

silver-fork novel, or 'fashionable *novel*', is a slightly mocking term for works written by *Frances Trollope* and others during the period 1810–50 and which concern the manners and etiquette of the upper classes.

simile: a comparison between two things not usually compared in order to illuminate or provoke thought in the reader through the striking nature of the comparison. A simile is usually heralded by 'as' or 'like', e.g. 'The road wound like a snake up the mountain-side'. Similes have been common in both *poetry* and *prose* since the earliest *literature* in English. See *epic* or *extended simile*, *metaphor*.

sincerity: the notion that to be sincere is a most important aspect of writing. With characteristic Victorian moral solemnity *Arnold* considered that *literature* could not be great unless it showed that 'high seriousness which comes from absolute sincerity'. *De Quincy* found *Pope* to be devoid of 'a sincere thought or a sincere emotion'. However, it is often impossible to be clear about the intentions of a writer, and most critical thinking nowadays suggests that readers should stick to an objective assessment of what they see on the page, ignoring what the author's intentions may or may not have been. See *intentional fallacy*.

single rhyme is another term for *masculine rhyme*.

Skelton, John (?1460–1529): poet and satirist. His *verse* conveys a lively picture of the political and social life of the time, and he was highly regarded by his contemporaries, Erasmus (?1467–1536) calling him 'the light and glory of English letters'. See *skeltonics*. Notable works include THE BOWGE OF COURT (1498), A BALLAD OF THE SCOTTISH KING (printed 1513), MAGNYFYCENCE (1516), THE TUNNING OF ELINOR RUMMING (1517).

skeltonics: fast-moving, helter-skelter *verse* in short lines with frequent rhyming effects and similar to *doggerel*. Named after such *poems* by *Skelton* as THE WORLD NOWADAYS (?1512) and COLIN CLOUTE (1519–20).

sketch: a term used variously to describe:

- a short piece of drama to begin an entertainment, a 'curtain raiser', popular in late 19th and early 20th century
- an item within a *revue*, often satirical and topical
- a short piece of prose, e.g. *Dickens'* SKETCHES BY BOZ (1836–7), sometimes amounting to a short story
- an article in a newspaper or magazine.

slant rhyme: another term for *half-rhyme*.

Slessor, Kenneth (1901–71): Australian poet and journalist. His formal but imaginative *verse* frequently covers such subjects as war (he was the official war correspondent between 1940–44), friends and sea stories. Notable works include EARTH-VISITORS (1926), DARLINGHURST NIGHTS AND MORNING GLORIES (1933), FIVE BELLS (1939).

slice of life, from the French 'tranche de vie', is a term sometimes used to refer to writing which describes life in a realistic way, presenting the facts in a direct, raw, apparently unvarnished fashion. The term was applied to *novels* such as *Braine's* ROOM AT THE TOP and *Sillitoe's* SATURDAY NIGHT AND SUNDAY MORNING at around the same time as the phrase *kitchen-sink drama* was applied to *drama*. 'Slice of life' sometimes suggests that the work does not have a conventionally artistic shape, but aims to replicate real life in its seeming randomness.

Smart, Christopher (1722–71): poet. Most of his work, written whilst imprisoned for debt or in hospital for insanity, contains elaborate religious language and praises the natural order of the divine world in an unusually prophetic and public voice, sometimes using the Old Testament rhythms of Hebrew *verse*. The celebratory nature of much of his *poetry* has sometimes caused him to be called an early *Romantic*. Notable works include 'Song to David' (1763), 'Jubliate Agno' (published 1939).

Smith, Stevie (1902–71): British poet and novelist. Her work is often illustrated with simple line drawings, and her humorous *style* takes her heavily autobiographical subjects from the absurd to the light-hearted to the serious and theological. Notable works include NOVEL ON YELLOW PAPER (1936), A GOOD TIME WAS HAD BY ALL (1937), 'Not Waving But Drowning' (1957).

Smollett, Tobias (1721–71): Scottish novelist, critic, poet and playwright. His largely autobiographical works, not always successful with the reading public of his day, range from political *satires* to travel *journals*. He is sometimes loosely referred to as *picaresque*. Notable works include RODERICK RANDOM (1748), THE REPRISAL (1757), THE EXPEDITION OF HUMPHRY CLINKER (1771).

Snyder, Gary (b.1930): American poet. His eight years spent in Japan studying Zen Buddhism is at the heart of his free, detailed and philosophical *verse*, which is centrally concerned with ecology, spiritualism and human culture in relation to everyday life. See *Beat Movement*. Notable works include THE BACK COUNTRY (1968), REGARDING WAVE (1969), TURTLE ISLAND (1974), EARTH HOUSE HOLD (1969).

socialist realism is the belief that *literature* (and other arts) should present the world from the Marxist viewpoint. See *Marxist criticism*.

society verse: see *vers de société*.

sociological novel: see *thesis novel*.

sociology of literature: the idea that all *literature* is a product of social, cultural and historical *contexts*. See AS/A level Assessment Objective 5 in Appendix 3 and the various aspects listed under *literary/critical theory*.

Socrates (469–399BC): Greek philosopher. Although he himself wrote nothing down, his teachings on ethics have been handed on to us via *Plato*, *Aristotle* and Xenophon (?420–?355BC), and have thereby had a considerable influence upon western writers and thinkers. A key to his theories is that virtue is knowledge and wickedness is a result of ignorance.

Sofola, Zulu (b.1938): Nigerian *dramatist*. Ranging from the tragic to the comic, her combination of local dialects and standard English explores both western and African cultures. Notable works include WEDLOCK OF THE GODS (1970), KING EMENE (1974), SONG OF A MAIDEN (1991).

soliloquy: a *device* much used in the Elizabethan theatre whereby a *character* communicates thoughts directly to the audience by speaking aloud when no other character is present on the stage. It is a *convention* that the audience can accept the complete honesty of a character's thoughts so revealed, as there can be no motive for deception (unless the character is self-deceived). Hamlet's soliloquies are probably the most famous in English *literature*. See also *aside*.

solo play: see *monodrama*.

song: in a literary sense, a *lyric* poem written with the purpose of being set to music, some of the best of which were written during the *Elizabethan Age*. Songs appear in *Shakespeare*, and were included in *masques* in the early 1600s. After this time 'song' in a literary sense increasingly refers to a *verse* lyric *form* rather than any intention that the words should be set to music. Other writers of songs include *Wyatt, Jonson, Donne, Milton, Dryden, Herrick, Goldsmith, Sheridan, Smart, Burns,* (SONG TO DAVID, 1793), *Blake* (SONGS OF INNOCENCE AND OF EXPERIENCE), *Yeats, O'Casey, T.S. Eliot, Auden, Arden.* See *ballad, lyric*.

sonnet: a 14-line *lyric* poem composed in *iambic pentameter* and organised in one of several possible *rhyme* schemes:

- Petrarchan (or Italian) *sonnet*, developed by the Italian poet *Petrarch*, consisting of an octave (rhyming abbaabba) and a *sestet* (rhyming cdecde or cdcdcd). The *octave* tends to contain the posing of a situation or problem, the *sestet* its resolution
- Shakespearean (or English) sonnet, consisting of three *quatrains* (rhyming abab, cdcd, efef) and a concluding couplet (rhyming gg). The three quatrains tend carefully to construct a situation or problem, climaxing in an underlining of it (or occasionally an undercutting of it) in the final couplet
- Spenserian sonnet, a slight variant of the *Shakespearean sonnet* with the interlinking rhyming pattern abab, bcbc, cdcd, ee (hence it is sometimes known as a 'linked sonnet').

Wyatt and *Surrey* are credited with importing the sonnet form into England. After the Elizabethan heyday (see *sonnet cycle*) Milton revived it (although he dispensed with the Petrarchan turning point at the beginning of the *sestet*, within which his rhyme scheme was more flexible); and then the *Romantics* and 19th century poets rekindled an interest, notably *Wordsworth, Keats, Percy Shelley, Elizabeth Barrett Browning, Christina Rossetti*, most of whom favoured the Petrarchan form. Among other subjects Wordsworth wrote many sonnets on capital punishment. More recent sonneteers include *Yeats, Frost, Auden, Dylan Thomas* and *Seth*. See also *metre*.

sonnet sequence: a series of *sonnets* on a *theme*, usually love, and addressed to a particular individual. Each poem is complete in itself. The most famous example is *Shakespeare's* SONNETS. Other notable sequences include *Sidney's* ASTROPHEL AND STELLA and *Spenser's* AMORETTI (?1592). An example on a *theme* other than love is *Donne's* HOLY SONNETS (1635–9). Notable later writers of sonnet sequences include *Wordsworth, Dante Gabriel Rossetti, Elizabeth Barrett Browning* and *Dylan Thomas*.

Sophocles (496–406BC): playwright. One of the three great Athenian writers of Greek *tragedy* (the other two being Aeschylus (525–456BC) and Euripedes (485–406BC), only seven of his hundred or so works survive, the best known being OEDIPUS REX and ANTIGONE (together with OEDIPUS AT COLONUS making up the *trilogy* known as the Theban plays) which have had considerable influence over the centuries on writers as varied as *Milton, Dryden*, Percy, *Shelley, Arnold, Swinburne, Yeats* and *Heaney*.

sound poetry, fashionable in the 1960s and relevant mainly as *performance poetry*, sets no store by logical meaning and merely celebrates sounds for their own sake, e.g. by saying any single word in as many ways as possible.

source: a work from which another writer has made reasonable use (unlike *plagiarism*) in the development of the *plot, story* or *ideas* of his own work. For instance, *Shakespeare* uses ROSALYNDE (1590) by Thomas Lodge (1558–1625) as a source for AS YOU LIKE IT, and he and other Elizabethan *dramatists* use Raphael Holinshed's (?1525 – ?1580) CHRONICLES (1577) for their history plays.

Southey, Robert (1774–1843): poet, historian, essayist, biographer and prolific man of letters. A friend of *Coleridge*, they married sisters and planned a 'Pantisocratic' community in America which came to nothing. He was on the fringe of the *Lake Poets*, although his poetic output is little akin to that of *Wordsworth* and *Coleridge*. However, like Wordsworth, he changed politically from being a radical to a Tory as he grew older, and this did not endear him to the second phase of *Romantics*: he attacked them (especially *Byron* and *Shelley*) and they in turn (especially Byron, *Hazlitt* and *Peacock*) attacked him. He was *poet laureate* from 1813–43. Notable works include JOAN OF ARC (1796), PALERMIN OF ENGLAND (1807), A VISION OF JUDGEMENT (1821).

Soyinka, Wole (b.1934): Nigerian playwright, novelist and poet. He expresses his unease about a Nigeria under military rule by capturing a traditional African spirit through *comedy*, mime and dance. Notable works include THE LION AND THE JEWEL (1959), A DANCE OF THE FORESTS (1960), KONGI'S HARVEST (1965), MADMEN AND SPECIALISTS (1970).

Spark, Muriel (b.1918): Scottish novelist, *short-story* writer, poet, literary critic and autobiographer. Her writing contains much black humour (see *black comedy*) and irony, and she often focuses upon the stranger aspects of human behaviour, and critics have remarked upon the elegance of her style. Several of her novels are set in Italy, where she lived for a while. She has had a considerable influence upon other writers. Notable works include THE BALLAD OF PECKHAM RYE (1960), THE PRIME OF MISS JEAN BRODIE (1961), GIRLS OF SLENDER MEANS (1963), THE MANDELBAUM GATE (1965), COLLECTED STORIES (1967), COLLECTED POEMS (1967).

Spender, Stephen (1909–95): English poet, playwright and critic. Politically conscious, he was very concerned with using his work as a public voice, where he combines *realism* and idealism. Notable works include THE DESTRUCTIVE ELEMENT (1935), TRIAL OF A JUDGE (1938), POEMS OF DEDICATION (1947).

Spenser, Edmund (c.1552–99): poet. He admired *Chaucer*, and his use of an archaic medieval language adds charm to his great allegorical heroic *romance* THE FAERIE QUEENE (1590–1596) but was criticised by *Sidney* and *Jonson*. The Sherpheardes Calender (1579) has been regarded as one of the best *pastoral* sequences in English. His *poetry* has been admired in all ages which followed him, and he especially influenced *Milton*, who responded to his intellectual didacticism, and *Keats*, the Romantic poets loving his sensuousness and *medievalism*. Other notable works include AMORETTI (1595), EPITHALAMIUM (1595), COLIN CLOUT'S COME HOME AGAIN (1596), PROTHALAMIUM (1596).

Spenserian sonnet: see *sonnet*.

Spenserian stanza: a nine-line *iambic stanza* in which the first eight are *pentameter* and the final line a *hexameter* (or *Alexandrine*), rhyming ababbcbcc. Devised by *Spenser* for THE FAERIE QUEENE, and in some ways a development of *ottava rima*, the form has been used to good effect by such as *Byron* in CHILDE HAROLD'S PILGRIMAGE, *Keats* in 'The Eve of St Agnes', *Shelley* in ADONAIS (1821) and *Tennyson* in THE LOTUS EATERS (1832).

spondee: see *metre*.

spontaneity: the notion that writing is the result of *inspiration* rather than hard work. The *Romantics* highly regarded spontaneity: *Wordsworth* talks of *poetry* as 'the spontaneous overflow of powerful feelings'; *Keats* that the creation of *poetry* should be 'as natural as the leaves on a tree'; and *Percy Shelley* might have been thinking of the act of writing poetry when he calls the song of the skylark 'unpremeditated art'. He rejected the idea that fine poetry was the result of 'labour and study' whereas *Auden*, while accepting the notion of initial *inspiration*, considered that thereafter writing was 'slogging away'.

sporting verse/fiction may be regarded as a minor *genre* and it has been observed that, given the British love of sport and invention of so many games, it is surprising that there is little great sporting *literature* written in English. Sporting episodes of various kinds feature in, among others, the writings of *Abse* and *Ted Hughes* (football), *Betjeman* (golf and tennis), *Byron*, *Crane* and *Swinburne* (swimming), *Coleridge* (climbing), *Dunn* (running), *McGough* (*concrete poetry* on tennis), *MacNeice* (cycling), *Masefield* (fox-hunting), *Nicholson* (cricket), *Pound* (fencing), *Wordsworth* (skating), *Yeats* (horse-racing).

spots of time: *Wordsworth*'s term for a *moment* or *epiphany*.

sprung rhythm: a form of poetic rhythm pioneered by *Hopkins* whereby the metrical *foot* consists of one stressed syllable and any number of unstressed syllables, and a *verse* line contains a variable number of feet. See also *metre, rocking rhythm*.

spy story: *fiction* concerning any kind of espionage. Although there were earlier stories, the popularity of the *genre* has its origin in *novels* such as Anthony Hope's (1863–1933) THE PRISONER OF ZENDA (1894), BARONESS ORCZY'S (1865–1947) THE SCARLET PIMPERNEL (1905) and *Conrad*'s THE SECRET AGENT. The World Wars and Cold War of the 20th century encouraged the proliferation of spy stories, most famously those of Ian Fleming's (1908–64) James Bond and *Le Carré*'s Smiley.

stage directions: instructions other than speech in the *text* of a play which indicate to actors or readers *setting*, movements, *tone* of voice, gestures, sounds or other non-verbal instructions. In early plays these were non-existent, and many in the texts of writers such as *Shakespeare* have been added by later editors. Some playwrights, such as *Shaw*, incorporated very full and precise stage directions which leave little to the imagination.

standpoint: see *narrator/narrative voice, showing and telling*.

stanza: sections of *poetry* of regular length, usually repeating the same metrical and rhyming pattern and number of lines. Sections of poetry of irregular length (as, for example, in *Wordsworth*'s TINTERN ABBEY) should be called 'sections' or *verse paragraphs*, and not stanzas.

Stark, Freya (1893–1993): travel writer. Her strong *style*, exploring landscapes and history, focuses on her many solitary travels mainly to the Middle East. Notable works include BAGHDAD SKETCHES (1933), THE VALLEYS OF THE ASSASSINS (1934), A WINTER IN ARABIA (1940), TRAVELLER'S PRELUDE (1950).

Stead, Christina Ellen (1902–83): Australian novelist. Her extensive travelling around America and Europe is conveyed through the variety of *settings* of her work, which often explores her left-wing politics partly through autobiographical and psychological studies. Notable works include THE SALZBURG TALES (1934), THE MAN WHO LOVED CHILDREN (1940), DARK PLACES OF THE HEART (1966, published in the UK as COTTER'S ENGLAND, 1967).

Steele, Richard (1672–1729): Irish essayist and *dramatist*. He wrote in several *periodicals* and papers such as THE GAZETTE, SPECTATOR, THEATRE and THE TATLER (which he founded), often collaborating with *Addison*. His *dramas* pointed the way towards the *sentimental comedy* which became popular later in the 18th century. Notable works include THE FUNERAL (1701), THE IMPORTANCE OF DUNKIRK CONSIDER'D (1713), THE CONSCIOUS LOVERS (1722).

Steinbeck, John (1902–68): American novelist. With a tone of striking *realism* he explores the struggles of rural working life in his homeland, especially California. Notable works include TORTILLA FLAT (1935), OF MICE AND MEN (1937), THE GRAPES OF WRATH (1939), THE WINTER OF OUR DISCONTENT (1961).

Sterne, Laurence (1713–68): British novelist. Made famous by the experimental novel TRISTRAM SHANDY (1759 67), he breaks all *narrative conventions* making him a pioneering writer well ahead of his time. His *stream of consciousness* technique, later picked up by writers such as *Joyce*, denies the reader the comforting, reliable narrator (see *narrator/narrative voice*). This innovative shifting, fragmentary *style* always carries a unique shrewd *wit* which makes Sterne's work comic, yet thought-provoking through psychological exploration. Other notable works include THE SERMONS OF MR YORICK (1760–69), A SENTIMENTAL JOURNEY THROUGH FRANCE AND ITALY (1767).

Stevens, Wallace (1879–1955): American poet. His writing explores the Romantic notion of the imagination against a more modern sense of reality through elaborate, metaphoric and fanciful language. Notable works include SUNDAY MORNING (1915), THREE TRAVELLERS WATCH A SUNRISE (1916), THE MAN WITH THE BLUE GUITAR AND OTHER POEMS (1937).

Stevenson, Robert Louis (1850–94): Scottish novelist, essayist and poet. His adventurous nature is reflected in his light-hearted story-telling, which often touches on a darker side through his admiration for morally dubious *characters*. Notable works are TREASURE ISLAND (1883), THE STRANGE CASE OF DR JEKYLL AND MR HYDE (1886), KIDNAPPED (1886), THE BLACK ARROW (1888).

stichomythia: alternate lines of dialogue in *drama*, often using antithesis and/or repeated patterns. It is an excellent *device* for argument or building up tension. For example:

Queen Elizabeth:	Shall I be tempted of the devil thus?
King Richard:	Ay, if the devil tempt you to do good.
Queen Elizabeth:	Shall I forget myself to be myself?
King Richard:	Ay, if your self's remembrance wrong yourself.

| Queen Elizabeth: | But thou didst kill my children. |
| King Richard: | But in your daughter's womb I bury them. |

(from *Shakespeare*'s RICHARD III, ?1594)

stock characters/response/situations: these are terms for easily recognisable and accepted features:

- stock characters are jealous husbands (as Simkin in *Chaucer*'s THE REEVE'S TALE), ignorant country fellows (as William in *Shakespeare*'s AS YOU LIKE IT), swaggering soldiers (as Pistol in Shakespeare's HENRY V), and so forth
- stock responses are such as when we are encouraged to hiss the *villain* (often another stock character)
- stock situations are familiar patterns in *literature* such as the eternal triangle (as in Chaucer's THE MERCHANT'S TALE) or confusion caused by identical twins (as in Shakespeare's THE COMEDY OF ERRORS (?1594).

Stoppard, Tom (b.1937): British playwright, radio, television and screenwriter. Both his stage and television plays challenge and explore literary *conventions*, and ask philosophical questions through *puns* and *parody*. Some praise his plays for their verbal ingenuity and grand flights of intellectual daring; others complain that they display *style* but lack *content*. Notable works include ROSENCRANTZ AND GUILDENSTERN ARE DEAD (1966), JUMPERS (1972), PROFESSIONAL FOUL (1977), NIGHT AND DAY (1978), THE REAL THING (1982), ARCADIA (1993), SHAKESPEARE IN LOVE (1999, a film script).

storm of association: a term used by *Wordsworth* to describe the power of *inspiration* which drives a poet to write.

story: a sequence of events, which does not become a *plot* until those events are structured into a *narrative*.

story-within-a-story: a *story* which is a digression from the main *narrative*, e.g. 'The Story of a Goblin who Stole a Sexton' is told to the assembled party on Christmas Eve in *Dickens*' THE PICKWICK PAPERS.

Stow, Randolph (b.1935): Australian novelist and poet. His work often involves journeys of self-discovery. Notable works include A HAUNTED LAND (1956), THE BYSTANDER (1957), THE MERRY-GO-ROUND IN THE SEA (1965), VISITANTS (1979), THE SUBURBS OF HELL (1984).

stream of consciousness is a *narrative* technique whereby a writer attempts to recreate in words the natural free-wheeling thought processes of a person's mind. Works such as *Sterne*'s TRISTRAM SHANDY and *Coleridge*'s 'Frost at Midnight' are forerunners of the *technique*, but the term is generally associated with 20th century experiments in *novel* form in such works as *Joyce*'s ULYSSES, *Woolf*'s TO THE LIGHTHOUSE and *Faulkner*'s THE SOUND AND THE FURY. A LA RECHERCHE DU TEMPS PERDU (1913–27, translated as REMEMBRANCE OF THINGS PAST, 1922–31) by Marcel Proust (1871–1922) is probably the most famous European stream of consciousness novel. The *device* has become a common narrative method. See also *anti-novel*, *interior monologue*.

stress refers to the syllables in words upon which emphasis naturally falls, the use of which is essential in developing *rhythm* in *poetry*. See *metre*.

Strindberg, August (1849–1912): Swedish playwright and novelist. His writings show his neurotic reactions to class, sex and religion and, later on, his search for salvation. He influenced among others *O'Neill* and the *Theatre of the Absurd*. Notable works include THE FATHER (1887), MISS JULIE (1888), THE DANCE OF DEATH (1901), THE GHOST SONATA (1909).

structural irony is created when the author employs a structural *device* which creates *irony*. For instance, there may be a *fallible* or *naïve narrator* (see *narrator/narrative voice*) whose *point of view* is misguided, the knowing reader being aware of the writer's *intention* and thus of the irony.

structuralism, as a theory applied to *literary theory*, argues that no *text*, or aspect of the language of a text, has any existence or significance on its own, but only makes sense when considered as part of a whole language system. Structuralists argue that, far from the traditional view that *literature* reflects reality, all writing is made up of a system of *signs*, *codes* and *conventions*. Some structuralists go on to argue that there is no point of contact between the writer and reader (see *death of the author*), that the former creates a *persona* through which s/he writes the text, and that persona is as much a literary construction as the *characters* created in a *novel* or play. Structuralism emerged from its roots during the 1960s, the key advocate being the Frenchman Roland Barthes (1915–80), who argued that the author is never fully conscious of what s/he is doing. Structuralism has been superseded by the *post-structuralist* theories of *deconstruction*.

structure is the overall organisation of a work. Some regard the word as interchangeable with the word *form*; others consider the latter to be confined to the shaping of parts within the structure of the whole. Many modern critics only use structure as a specialist word in connection with *literary/critical theory*. See *structuralism*.

style is how a writer conveys subject-matter, and covers every characteristic aspect of *manner* such as *attitude*, *diction*, *figurative language*, *form*, *imagery*, *narrative* technique, *structure*, *syntax* and so forth. Writers who are typical of the *style* of a period or reminiscent of a previous writer's style may be given an *epithet* such as *Augustan* or Dickensian.

stylistics: the scientific analysis of written and spoken *style*.

stylometrics is computer-aided *stylistics*, by which means it is easier to detect, for instance, which of *Shakespeare's apocryphal* works are more or less likely to have been written by him.

subjectivity is the idea that the perception and interpretation of every work of *literature*, indeed of all things abstract or concrete, is affected by the individual reader's experience of the world. See *objectivity*, and also Assessment Objective 4 in Appendix 3.

sublime: a term used, sometimes rather pompously, to suggest various kinds of lofty literary excellence in *style* and/or subject-matter. Many *Romantics* apply the term to the emotions evoked by the *gothic* and descriptions of the grandeur of nature. Some critics value *Chaucer* and *Shakespeare* for their ability to move between the sublime and the earthy.

sub-plot: a secondary *plot* in a play or *story* which in some way reflects, echoes, parallels, contrasts with or in other ways enhances the main plot. The *device* was popular in *Elizabethan drama*. Examples are the Gloucester family sub-plot in relation to the Lear family main plot in *Shakespeare*'s KING LEAR, the Falstaff scenes in his HENRY IV plays, or *Rowley*'s madhouse scenes in THE CHANGELING. See *double plot*.

substitution, in *verse*, is the replacement of a regular *foot* with one of a different *metre*. The most common substitution in English *verse* is the use of a *trochee* at the beginning of an otherwise *iambic* line, as in *Surrey*'s

> Cálm is / the séa / the wáves / work léss / and léss
>   (from the *sonnet* 'Complaint by Night of the Lover not Beloved')

sub-text is, in general terms, the hidden agenda behind the surface of the text, what *Pinter* has called 'the pressure behind the words'. It is that which is implicit rather than explicit. It may take the *form* of a reader or member of an audience working out, or imagining, what lies behind words or *actions*. Some *Marxist* critics consider that authors themselves may be unaware of the sub-text which they are creating, often the result of the cultural, social and political climate in which they are writing. See *literary theory*.

subversion occurs when any *text* or idea sets out to undermine or subvert an established way of looking at things. For instance:

- *feminist criticism* aims to subvert what it sees as the traditionally *phallocentric* nature of *literature*
- *leavisites* argued that there is an established *canon* of great literature, and that the function of the literary critic is to pursue and interpret the true *meaning* of each text. Structuralists and *post-structuralists* subvert this idea by arguing that the established canon is merely an accident of history, that any one text can be read in an almost infinite number of valid ways, that *authorial intention* is irrelevant, and that anyway true meaning is impossible to establish.

There are many other kinds of political, social and cultural subversion. Most begin by being *avant-garde*, then themselves become an established way of looking at things, and are then subverted by new approaches to literature. See also *alternative literature, underground literature*.

succès d'estime: a work which is praised by the critics but not popular with the public at large. e.g. *Hulme*'s THE BONE PEOPLE.

suggestion is the stimulation of ideas, feelings, impulses and/or meanings beyond the surface *meaning* through such as *allegory, association, symbolism*. See also *connotation, subjectivity*.

surprise (ending): a turn in the *tale* which the direction of events or *conventions* of a *story* has not led us to expect. It is a *paradox* that in the case of traditional kinds of *short story* a surprise ending is expected. In an effective story the exact nature of such a twist in the tale should not be foreseen by the reader, but should in retrospect be perceived as prepared for by the author. See *suspense*.

surrealism refers to a movement in art and *literature* which explores 'beyond the real' in order to depict the workings of the unconscious mind. Influenced by the writings of Freud (1856–1939), among key artists were Giorgio de Chirico (1888–1978), Rene Magritte (1898–1967) and Salvador Dali (1904–89), and key writers were mainly French. The movement has had a lasting and important impact upon all the arts. American writers such as *Burroughs* in *prose, Albee* in *drama* and *Ashbery* in *poetry* have experimented with surrealism. See *expressionism, Theatre of the Absurd.*

Surrey, Henry Howard, Earl of (?1517–47): poet and translator. Often linked with *Wyatt* as an early experimenter with the Petrarchan *sonnet* in English, he helped to adapt it into what became known as the *Shakespearean sonnet.* He is credited with introducing *blank verse* into English *poetry.* Notable works include 'Complaint by Night of the Lover not Beloved' (1557), 'So Cruel Prison' (1557).

suspense: a lack of certainty as to what is going to happen in a *story*, and an eagerness to know what will happen. An interplay between suspense and *surprise* is an important element in many stories.

suspension of disbelief occurs when a reader or member of an audience knows that, however natural they may seem, the *setting* and/or events of a book or play are not 'real'; and that the perceived reality thereof depends upon going along with the writer in an imaginative act of willing acceptance. *Shakespeare*'s Chorus at the beginning of HENRY V urges us to do just this. *Coleridge* coined the phrase 'willing suspension of disbelief' in BIOGRAPHIA LITERARIA.

Sutherland, Efua (b.1924): Ghanaian playwright. Her writing is mainly concerned with the attempt to merge traditional and contemporary social cultures. Notable works include ROADMAKERS (1961), FORIWA (1962), EDUFA (1967), THE MARRIAGE OF ANANSEWA (1975).

Swift, Graham (b.1949): novelist and *short-story* writer. Much of his work deals with the history and memories of his *characters*, and shows elements of *magic realism.* He creates and sustains complex psychological states, and is skilled in evoking a sense of place and atmosphere, such as the Fens in WATERLAND (1983). Other notable works include THE SWEET SHOP OWNER (1980), SHUTTLECOCK (1981), LEARNING TO SWIM (1982), LAST ORDERS (1996).

Swift, Jonathan (1667–1745): Irish satirist, essayist and poet. *Congreve* was a schoolfellow, *Dryden* a cousin, *Addison, Pope* and *Steele* friends. His prolific output is very varied: he wrote on political and religious matters, and attacked social and intellectual abuses, injustices and stupidity of all kinds, often with great satirical *wit*, and became a noted Irish patriot. His works were disliked in the 18th and 19th centuries by such as *Johnson* and *Thackeray* for what was regarded as his harsh, coarse misanthropy; but the 20th century saw a revival of interest in his common sense, intelligence and sharply observed *satire.* Notable works include THE BATTLE OF THE BOOKS (1704), A TALE OF A TUB (1704), GULLIVER'S TRAVELS (1726), A MODEST PROPOSAL (1729).

Swinburne, Algernon Charles (1837–1909): poet, playwright, novelist and critic. Influenced by *Dante Gabriel Rossetti* and *Whitman*, and by both classical and romantic traditions, he has a command over a great range of poetic *forms.* He was a part of the aesthetic movement (see *Aestheticism*), and his writings were often highly individualistic and offended Victorian sensibilities. Notable works include 'Atalanta in Calydon' (1865), POEMS AND BALLADS (1866), POEMS AND BALLADS: SECOND SERIES (1876).

syllabic verse is *metre* which is measured by the number of syllables in the line, regardless of the stress pattern.

syllepsis is an alternative term for *zeugma*.

symbol: a kind of *metaphor* where something stands for something else. For instance:

- in *Blake's poem* 'The Sick Rose' (1794) the rose is an *emblem* which stands for perishable loveliness and love as embodied by the woman's body
- *Coleridge* wrote of objects in the outside world, especially in nature, as symbols of what he was feeling
- in THE GLASS MENAGERIE by *Tennessee Williams* the collection of glass animals is symbolic of Laura's state of mind.

symbolism/symbolist movement: any writer who uses *symbols* in a persistent planned way may be called 'symbolist', or as one who makes much use of symbolism. For instance:

- several of the Romantics such as *Blake* and Percy *Shelley* make much use of recurrent symbols
- symbolism was prominent in the writings of various 19th century Americans such as *Hawthorne, Melville, Emerson, Poe.*

The symbolist movement as a term specifically defines a group of French 19th century writers including Charles Baudelaire (1821–67), Arthur Rambaud 1854–91), Paul Verlaine (1844–96), Stéphane Mallarmé (1842–98), and Paul Valéry (1871–1945) who had a considerable influence upon later writers in English such as *Yeats, T.S. Eliot, Pound, Joyce* and *Faulkner.*

sympathy is a term used in *literature* to indicate feelings of understanding which a reader or audience has towards the situation of a *character*, whilst remaining detached. See *empathy*.

synaeresis: the combining of two separate vowels to create a single syllable as in 'seest' for 'see-est'. The *technique* is common in *poetry* in order to preserve the regular *metre* of a line. See *elision*.

synaesthesia is the mixing of two or more senses within one image, common in writers such as *Keats* who frequently use sensuous *imagery*, e.g. in 'Ode to a Nightingale' he implies all five senses in describing wine as:

> Tasting of Flora and the country green,
> Dance, and Provençal song, and sunburnt mirth...

and later in the poem he describes sight in terms of touch:

> But here there is no light,
> Save what from heaven is with the breezes blown...

In *Spender's* 'Seascape' (1946) he writes of the sea as 'burning music for the eyes'.

syncope: the reduction of a word by missing out letters as in 'o'er' for 'over'. See *elision*.

synecdoche: a figure of speech in which a part stands for a whole, e.g. in LYCIDAS Milton refers to the unseeing and greedy clergy as 'blind mouths'. The *device* is often used in everyday speech, e.g. 'Liverpool (for 'Liverpool Football Club') won the cup'. See *metonymy*.

Synge, J.M. (1871–1909): Irish playwright. Influenced by *Yeats*, he spent much time gathering background material about Irish peasant life, language and landscape for his plays, which are a curious mixture of lyrical depictions of illusion and harsh reality. Notable works include THE RIDERS OF THE SEA (1904), THE PLAYBOY OF THE WESTERN WORLD (1907), DEIRDRE OF THE SORROWS (1910).

systrophe: a rhetorical *device* by which something is defined by an accumulation of phrases or by *repetition*, e.g. Macbeth's *apostrophe* to Sleep:

> ...the innocent sleep,
> Sleep that knits up the ravell'd sleave of care
> The death of each day's life, sore labour's bath,
> Balm of hurt minds, great nature's second course,
> Chief nourisher in life's feast, ...

(from Shakespeare's MACBETH II.3.37–41)

tale: a type of *short story* or short *narrative poem* which concentrates more on *action* and incident than *atmosphere* and *character*. It often draws upon an oral rather than a literary tradition. Among others *Conrad* and *Faulkner* have been noted writers of tales. See also *yarn*.

tapinosis is a figurative *device* which ridicules something by ludicrously exaggerating it, e.g. in the following extract from a description of a game of cards:

> An Ace of Hearts steps forth: the King unseen
> Lurked in her hand, and mourned his captive Queen.
> He springs to vengeance with an eager pace,
> And falls like thunder on the prostrate Ace.
> (from Pope's THE RAPE OF THE LOCK, 1712)

See *hyperbole*.

taste, in a literary sense, has come to refer to subjective preferences for certain kinds of *literature*, often influenced by fashion. In the 18th century the word denoted objective aesthetic and critical judgement concerning what was defined as good or bad literature (and many at that time considered that *Shakespeare*'s plays lacked taste). See also *aesthetics, objectivity, subjectivity*.

technique is the particular craft and *method* employed by a writer. It is often not appropriate to separate technique from *content*, as what a writer wishes to say will largely dictate technique (although some *devices* are purely decorative). For example, *Shelley*'s colourful and soaring *imagery* in 'To a Skylark' is integral to the *meaning* of the poem.

telling: see *showing*.

ten year test: a term used by the literary critic Cyril Connolly to denote a book which is still highly regarded ten years after its publication, e.g. *Farrell*'s THE SIEGE OF KRISHNAPUR or Graham *Swift*'s WATERLAND.

Tennyson, Alfred Lord (1809–92): poet and playwright. As an undergraduate at Cambridge he formed a close relationship with Arthur Henry Hallam, whose early death in 1833 so affected Tennyson that, after a 17-year gestation period, he published the series of moving *poems* IN MEMORIAM A.H.H. (1850), probably the longest *elegy* in the English language. His technically masterful *poems* range from the melancholy, solitary, and /or lyrical; to the confident, moral, *epic* and/or imperialist. Highly popular in his lifetime, later critical opinion has valued him more for his former range than the latter to which he devoted so much energy. He was *poet laureate* from 1850–92. Notable works include POEMS (1842, including 'The Lady of Shalott' and 'The Lotus-Eaters'), THE PRINCESS (1847), MAUD AND OTHER POEMS (1855, including 'The Charge of the Light Brigade'), IDYLLS OF THE KING (1872–85), DEMETER AND OTHER POEMS (1889, including 'Crossing the Bar').

tenor and vehicle: a *metaphor*, the tenor is the subject and the vehicle is the metaphoric *image* which conveys the subject. For example, in 'the high, steep mountain of Achievement', 'Achievement' is the tenor and 'the high, steep mountain' is the vehicle. The terms were coined by *Richards* in THE PHILOSOPHY OF RHETORIC.

tension occurs when any kind of conflict is created in the reader or audience. It may be, for example, between the literal and metaphorical, or the emotional and the intellectual. An instance of the latter might be in *Shakespeare*'s HAMLET where emotionally and dramatically an audience might wish to see Hamlet take *revenge*, at the same time intellectually knowing that revenge is wrong in the eyes of the law and God; thus tension is created. One might also talk of a tension created in the reader/audience who on the one hand might empathetically regard *characters* as 'real', yet at the same time realise that they are 'unreal' literary constructions.

tercet: a *stanza* or section of three lines of *verse*, often rhyming.

terza rima consists of *tercets* interlinked by a *rhyme scheme* whereby each second line rhymes with the succeeding first and third line (aba, bcb, cdc and so on). Used by Italian poets such as *Dante* and *Petrarch*, *Wyatt* introduced it into England. Among others *Chaucer, Milton, Byron, Browning* and *T.S. Eliot* all used the form, as did *Shelley*, notably in 'Ode to the West Wind':

> O wild West Wind, thou breath of Autumn's being
> Thou, from whose unseen presence the leaves dead
> Are driven, like ghosts from an enchanter fleeing
>
> Yellow, and black, and pale, and hectic red,
> Pestilence-driven multitudes: O thou,
> Who chariotest to their dark wintery bed...
> and so forth.

tetralogy: four related novels or plays, e.g. *Shakespeare*'s RICHARD II (1595), HENRY IV PART 1, HENRY IV PART II and HENRY V.

tetrameter: see *metre*.

tetrapody: a *verse* line containing four feet (see *metre*).

tetrastich: a section or *stanza* of *verse*, or complete *poem*, of four lines; another word for a *quatrain*.

text may mean:

- the words of a book
- the main body of a book, discounting such matter as preface, introduction, acknowledgements, list of contents, bibliography, appendices and so forth
- a piece of *literature* prepared for critical analysis
- a passage taken from the Bible as a *theme* for a sermon.

textual criticism is the analysis of the various existing *texts* of a work in order to attempt to determine:

- the best possible (or definitive) text for publication
- authorship, if it is uncertain or in dispute.

texture refers to the surface qualities of a work rather than its *form, structure* or *meaning*, e.g. its *diction* or *imagery* which may create a particular atmosphere.

Thackeray, William Makepeace (1811–63): novelist, journalist, sketch and travel writer. Influenced by his admiration of 18th century writers, his social awareness led to a satirical edge in much of his writing, but this is tempered by compassion for his *characters* and a fine comic energy. A great critical and popular success in his day, his standing has since declined, but he is still much admired by some. VANITY FAIR (1847–8), a title taken from *Bunyan*'s PILGRIM'S PROGRESS, is generally considered to be his masterpiece. Other notable works include THE YELLOWPLUSH PAPERS (1837–8), THE HISTORY OF PENDENNIS (1848–50), THE HISTORY OF HENRY ESMOND (1852), THE NEWCOMES (1853–5).

Theatre of Cruelty is a term applied to a *genre* of 20th century plays which deliberately set out to make the audience think through the shock of horror, violence and sensation, e.g. Peter Weiss's THE MARAT SADE (1964).

Theatre of Silence is a term applied to the notion that the silences in plays are often as important as the dialogue. *Chekhov* and *Pinter* are examples of playwrights who have used prolonged pauses to good effect, e.g. especially *Pinter*'s LANDSCAPE (1970) and SILENCE (1970).

Theatre of the Absurd: see *Absurd, Theatre and Literature of.*

theatre-in-the-round describes an auditorium where the audience are all round the actors, or at least in a horse-shoe, rather than separated from the *action* by a *proscenium arch*. This *style* of presenting plays, probably common with medieval *Mystery* and later *Morality plays*, became increasingly popular again during the 20th century; and theatre architecture in recent decades has often taken account of the need for a flexible stage in order to present plays within auditoria of various shapes.

thematic imagery is *imagery* which runs through a work, helping to bring out a central *theme*. For instance, repeated clothing *imagery* in *Shakespeare*'s MACBETH underwrites the idea that Macbeth has taken the clothing of kingship which does not belong to him, and *images* of imprisonment and darkness in *Webster*'s THE DUCHESS OF MALFI emphasise the claustrophobic world which closes in upon the Duchess.

theme: a central or essential idea in a *text*. The term is much abused, students sometimes using the word as an all-purpose catch-all (see, for instance, *emblem, motif, setting*).

theories of criticism: see *literary/critical theory.*

Theroux, Paul (b.1941): novelist, journalist, travel and *short-story* writer. He is a very versatile writer who is able to turn his hand to various subject-matter in different *genres* and *styles*. Notable works include THE GREAT RAILWAY BAZAAR (1975, one of three books about railway journeys), THE OLD PATAGONIAN EXPRESS (1978), RIDING THE IRON ROOSTER (1988), THE HAPPY ISLES OF OCEANIA (1992).

Thesiger, Wilfred (b.1910): travel writer and autobiographer. He writes of his experiences in energetic, direct *prose*, rejecting *modernist* concepts of technological progress. Notable works include ARABIAN SANDS (1959), THE MARSH ARABS (1964).

thesis: this can refer to:

- a long scholarly work presented to a university for a higher degree
- a main line of argument in a literary work (see *dissertation*)
- any proposition, against which is set its *antithesis*
- the unstressed syllable in an *iambic* or *trochaic* foot (see *metre*).

See *discourse, tract, treatise.*

thesis novel: sometimes called a sociological novel, this refers to a *didactic* novel which by means of its storyline advances a sociological, political, religious or other moral point or *thesis*. Examples include Stowe's UNCLE TOM'S CABIN (1852), *Dickens'*

HARD TIMES (1854), *Samuel Butler's* THE WAY OF ALL FLESH, *Holtby's* SOUTH RIDING, *Steinbeck's* THE GRAPES OF WRATH, *Paton's* CRY, THE BELOVED COUNTRY. See also *documentary novel, proletarian novel.*

thesis play is another term for *drama of ideas.*

Thiong'o, Ngugi wa: see *Ngugi.*

third person narrator: see *narrator/narrative voice, viewpoint.*

Thomas, Dylan (1914–53): Welsh poet, broadcaster, *short-story* and scriptwriter, he is famous for his extravagant behaviour and hard-drinking lifestyle (which eventually killed him) as much as his writing. His *poetry* was very popular in his lifetime, but some critics since have considered him over-rated. His *verse* is variously exuberant, mystical and psychologically complex, and the *imagery* of his later poetry is influenced by his Welsh coastal home. Notable works include PORTRAIT OF THE ARTIST AS A YOUNG DOG (1940), COLLECTED POEMS (1953), UNDER MILK WOOD (1953).

Thomas, Edward (1878–1917): poet, critic, biographer and *topographical* writer. Influenced and encouraged by *Frost*, his *poetry* includes loving observations of the English countryside, and he attempts to use natural, and sometimes colloquial, language within a metrical *structure*. Notable works include THE WOODLAND LIFE (1897), AN ANTHOLOGY OF NEW VERSE (1917), LAST POEMS (1918).

Thomas, R.S. (1913–2000): Welsh poet, *prose* writer and priest. His *poetry* gives a *realistic*, stark, uncompromising yet paradoxically beautiful picture of the harsh Welsh hill-farming life and a strong sense of the landscape. He also brings his sharp intellect to bear on personal and spiritual issues, and on Welsh cultural and linguistic matters. Notable works include THE STONES OF THE FIELD (1946), NOT THAT HE BROUGHT FLOWERS (1968), H'M (1972), SELECTED PROSE (1986), COMPLETE POEMS 1946–1990 (1993).

Thoreau, Henry (1817–62): essayist, travel writer and poet. A friend of *Emerson*, he was much influenced by *transcendentalism*. He challenged authority, materialism and the work ethic, and has been regarded as a pioneer ecologist. Notable works include A WEEK ON THE CONCORD AND MERRIMACK RIVER (1849), ON THE DUTY OF CIVIL DISOBEDIENCE (1849), WALDEN, OR LIFE IN THE WOODS (1854).

threnody nowadays refers to any work of lamentation, e.g. *Tennyson's* IN MEMORIAM. See *complaint, dirge, elegy, monody.*

thriller: a loose term which covers many kinds of *fiction* written for sensational effect, but most often used as another word for the *crime novel.* See also *detective fiction, police procedural, spy story, whodunnit.*

Thurber, James (1894–1961): American *short-story* writer. Through gentle, humorous *satire*, illustrated by his own cartoons, he often shows the innocent individual under threat in a bewildering world. Notable works include THE SECRET LIFE OF WALTER MITTY (1932), FABLES OF OUR TIME (1940), MY WORLD – AND WELCOME TO IT (1942).

time novel is a term sometimes used to define *novels* in which time is a major factor or of central thematic importance, and in which *stream of consciousness* is often employed, e.g. *Joyce's* ULYSSES.

time play is a vague term for any kind of play in which time is an important factor. This could be through:

- a gap in the time sequence, as in *Shakespeare*'s THE TEMPEST where there is a time gap of 16 years while Perdita grows up
- the sequence of the play not being strictly chronological, incorporating *flashbacks* or *flashforwards*, as in *Priestley*'s TIME AND THE CONWAYS.

Literary *genres* other than *drama* have, of course, been pre-occupied with time, especially *science fiction*.

Times Literary Supplement: a notable literary paper published weekly which reviews books of all sorts from *fiction* and academic scholarship to politics, music, science and other arts.

Tillyard, E.M.W. (1889–1962): scholar and literary critic who specialised in the Elizabethan period. Notable works include THE ELIZABETHAN WORLD PICTURE (1943) in which he set out to consider the *viewpoints* and assumptions, such as the *Great Chain of Being*, of the Elizabethans who watched *Shakespeare*'s plays. Among other things he also considers *John Davies*'s poem ORCHESTRA.

Tolstoy, Count Lev Nikolaevich (1828–1910): Russian novelist, playwright, *short-story* writer, essayist and philosopher who much influenced 19th century writing, especially the novel. Notable works include WAR AND PEACE (1863–69), ANNA KARENINA (1873–77).

tone covers the *attitude* taken by a writer towards both the reader and the *content* of the writing, and conveyed by such factors as language and syntax. For example, the tone may be *witty*, angry, compassionate, sombre, detached and so forth, as with a *tone* of *voice* in speech. See also *ambience, atmosphere, mood*.

topographical poetry: *poems* written about specific places, usually rural landscapes but sometimes urban or other locations. Examples include *Gray*'s 'Elegy Written in a Country Churchyard', *Wordsworth*'s 'Tintern Abbey' (1798), *Ted Hughes*' 'River' (1983) and much of the *poetry* of *Edward Thomas*, *MacCaig* and *Nicholson*. See also *pastoral*.

touchstone: a hard stone used to test the purity of gold; in a literary sense, a standard or yardstick. In his essay THE STUDY OF POETRY (1880), *Arnold* uses the term to indicate passages of literary excellence against which other works may be judged. He regarded this as more objective than personal judgement or assessment by historical importance.

Tourneur, Cyril (?1575–1626): playwright. Little is known about him, and some critics think that THE REVENGER'S TRAGEDY (?1607), an intense, bloody, *witty* piece with elements of *black comedy*, possibly a *parody* of the *revenge tragedy* genre and usually ascribed to him, was written by *Middleton*. Other notable works include THE ATHEIST'S TRAGEDY (?1611).

tract: a *pamphlet* or *essay* on a contentious issue, usually religious or political. See *discourse, dissertation, thesis, treatise*.

tradition: the concept that past writings influence later writers. However innovative or experimental a work may be, to a large degree its interest lies in a comparison with what has gone before. Writings which consider the impact of tradition include *T.S. Eliot*'s TRADITION AND THE INDIVIDUAL TALENT (1919) and *Leavis*'s THE GREAT TRADITION.

tragedy is a term which has come to describe a *drama* which ends disastrously, usually in the death of the *protagonist* and others. Broadly speaking there are two types:

- Greek tragedy, where fate brings about the downfall of the *character*(s) involved, e.g. in *Sophocles*' OEDIPUS REX, it is fated by the gods that Oedipus will kill his father and marry his mother, and he cannot escape this fate
- Shakespearean tragedy, where a *character* has free will and a fatal flaw causes the downfall, e.g. in *Shakespeare*'s OTHELLO it may be said that it is the *protagonist*'s inability to control his jealousy which brings him down.

However, these are over-simplifications: there are also flaws in Oedipus' character, and unlucky circumstances of fate surrounding Othello's situation, which contribute towards their respective falls. The *manner* of the unfolding of both kinds of tragedy involves a sense of inevitability. Usually a tragic protagonist should be of sufficient moral stature to make his or her fall worthy of *pathos*; however, not all central characters in tragedy are good, e.g. Shakespeare's Macbeth or Richard III. Tragic figures in modern plays sometimes come from humbler areas of society, and the *dénouement* does not necessarily result in death, e.g. in *Miller*'s THE PRICE. Tragedy is a term which is strictly speaking restricted to plays, but the word has become extended to *poetry* and *prose*, e.g. some of *Hardy*'s *poems* and *novels*.

tragedy of blood is another term for *revenge tragedy*. After Bosola has carried out his revenge in *Webster*'s THE DUCHESS OF MALFI he is called 'thou wretched thing of blood'.

tragic flaw: a weakness of *character*, or *hamartia*, which brings about a person's downfall. The critic *Bradley* was foremost in advancing the theory of the 'fatal flaw' in the character make-up of a tragic *protagonist*, pointing to Hamlet's speech in Act I Scene 4 of *Shakespeare*'s HAMLET concerning men who carry 'the stamp of one defect'. See *hubris*, *tragedy*.

tragic irony is *dramatic irony* when it specifically relates to *tragedy*, with the *protagonist* moving towards the recognition (*anagnorisis*) of a truth of which the audience is already aware.

tragi-comedy decribes plays (or sometimes other *literature*) which involve a mixture of *tragedy* and *comedy*. It may be used of plays which are 'bitter-sweet' in that they threaten tragedy, perhaps contain some unfortunate circumstances which are unresolved at the end, but conclude more or less happily. *Shakespeare*'s THE MERCHANT OF VENICE (?1597) and THE WINTER'S TALE have been placed in this category. Plays such as Shakespeare's TWELFTH NIGHT or MUCH ADO ABOUT NOTHING, while classed as comedies, contain respectively dark tones and the potential for tragedy. The term may also be used of plays which contain elements of comedy but which are ultimately grim – or at least bitter – such as Shakespeare's TROILUS AND CRESSIDA. Modern plays which have been placed in this *genre* include *Beckett*'s WAITING FOR GODOT and *Hare*'s SECRET RAPTURE (1989).

transcendentalism was an American New England movement active between the 1830s and 1860s which stressed the importance of the individual's conscience and intuition as a basis for morality, creativity and spiritual renewal. It was a continuation of aspects of *Romanticism* in its reaction against *neo-classicism* and against modern materialism, advocating a return to nature for inspiration. *Emerson* was a foremost member, and others associated with it included *Hawthorne* and *Thoreau*.

transferred epithet: sometimes called 'hypallage', this is a common *device* whereby an *epithet* is transferred from the noun to which it should apply (sometimes understood but not stated) and attached to another noun to which it does not apply. For instance, in the phrase 'a sleepless night' the epithet 'sleepless' has been transferred from the person who cannot sleep and attached to the night. The intended sense is easily understood.

travel literature is writing in which the author sets out to record experiences moving in a part of the world and culture which is different from her/his native place. It has been said that the job of a travel writer is to provide a new way of looking at the world, and a search for the truth about a particular culture and its people; but also that travel writing is one culture reporting on another and, as such, is never objective. It is usually non-fiction, but is sometimes *fiction* (or at least *faction*) or *poetry*. It may be written in a straightforward *narrative*, or in a *diary* or *epistolary* form. It may be some kind of literary or personal quest, a pilgrimage towards a spiritual goal, contain elements of *autobiography* (or at least *autobiographical memoir*), be a kind of escapism (for writer and reader) or wish for freedom from the restraints of a settled life (and, for a native of Britain, from the physical limitations of an island), and/or be an attempt to record a way of life about to be lost. Often an element of risk is an important stimulus for the writer. The *genre* has a long history from classical times, through the writings of Elizabethan discoverers such as Walter Raleigh (1554–1618), the 18th and 19th century travelogues of *Boswell, Johnson, Smollett, Sterne*, Richard Burton (1821–90) and *Stevenson*, to notable modern travel writers including *Chatwin*, William Dalrymple (b.1965) (IN XANADU: A QUEST, 1989), *Fermor*, Norman Lewis (b.1908) (A DRAGON APPARENT, 1951), *Murphy*, Eric Newby (b.1919) (A SHORT WALK IN THE HINDU KUSH, 1958) Jonathan Raban (b.1965) (OLD GLORY, 1981), *Theroux, Thesiger*, Colin Thubron (b.1939) (BEHIND THE WALL, AMONG THE RUSSIANS, 1983).

treatise: a substantial and systematic written examination of every aspect of a subject, often on a philosophical, political, religious, scientific or academic matter, e.g. *Sidney's* APOLOGIE FOR POETRIE, SYSTEM OF LOGIC (1843). See *discourse, dissertation, thesis, tract*.

Trevor, William (b.1928): Irish novelist and *short-story* writer. A technically very accomplished writer, his work often involves aspects of life in Ireland, and his *themes* include microcosmic worlds which are faded or in decay, loss of innocence, the condition of old age. Notable works include THE OLD BOYS (1964), MRS ECKDORF IN O'NEILL'S HOTEL (1969), THE CHILDREN OF DYNMOUTH (1976), FOOLS OF FORTUNE (1983), THE NEWS FROM IRELAND (1986) THE COLLECTED STORIES (1992), FELICIA'S JOURNEY (1994).

trilogy: three related *novels* or plays, e.g. *Golding's* historical sea stories RITES OF PASSAGE (1980), CLOSE QUARTERS (1987) and FIRE DOWN BELOW (1989).

trimeter: see *metre*.

triple metre occurs when each foot (see *metre*) is made up of three syllables, as in *anapaest*s and *dactyls*. It is not as common in English verse as *duple metre*, although used to effect in some 19th century verse by *Byron, Tennyson* and others.

triple rhyme occurs when accented rhyming syllables are followed by two identical syllables (silvery/coppery, mothering/bothering, wittily/prettily), and is most often used for comic effect.

triple rhythm: another term for *triple metre*.

triplet: an alternative term for *tercet*.

trochaic: see *metre*.

trochee: a single *trochaic* foot. See *metre*.

Trollope, Anthony (1815–82): novelist, biographer, autobiographer, travel and *short-story* writer. His output was prolific. He modestly called himself a 'grocer of words', but he was meticulously professional in his approach to his work. He shows a clear understanding of human motivation, and writes with low-key *irony* about Victorian life and institutions. THE BARSETSHIRE NOVELS (1855–67), of which THE WARDEN (1855) is the first in a series which developed *characters* and their lives within the same community, focused upon the clergy and represented a new kind of *regional novel*. THE PALLISER NOVELS (1864–80), including THE EUSTACE DIAMONDS (1873), deal with political life. Other notable works include THE WAY WE LIVE NOW (1874–5), which some consider to be his masterpiece.

Trollope, Frances (1780–1863): novelist and travel writer, mother of *Anthony Trollope*. Much of her work, documentary and *fiction*, looks at social, religious, industrial and other aspects of life in Victorian England. Notable works include DOMESTIC MANNERS OF THE AMERICANS (1832), THE VICAR OF WREXHILL (1837), THE LIFE AND ADVENTURES OF MICHAEL ARMSTRONG, THE FACTORY BOY (1840).

trope: in a general sense, any rhetorical or figurative use of language such as *metaphor, metonymy, personification, simile*.

Tudor interludes: see *interlude*.

turning point: any kind of change (for instance of subject-matter, *theme, mood* or direction of a *story* or *drama*), e.g. in a *poem*, a shift between the *octave* and *sestet* in a *sonnet* (sometimes known as the 'volta').

Twain, Mark (1835–1910): American novelist, *short-story* writer, autobiographer and journalist, working as the latter at some point with *Harte*. His most famous works, THE ADVENTURES OF TOM SAWYER (1876) and HUCKLEBERRY FINN (1884), draw greatly on his own Mississippi childhood. Much of his writing has a moral and/or humorously satirical quality. The energy and innovation of his earlier works, partly dissipated by personal troubles, converts to a sombre but arresting pessimism in his later writings. Other notable works include THE CELEBRATED JUMPING FROG OF CALAVERAS COUNTY (1867), THE INNOCENTS ABROAD (1869), ROUGHING IT (1872), THE PRINCE AND THE PAUPER (1882), A CONNECTICUT YANKEE IN THE COURT OF KING ARTHUR (1889).

type is a term which may refer to:

- a stereotypical *character* (what *Forster* called a *flat character*)
- a *genre*.

ubi sunt is Latin for 'Where are they now?', and denotes a frequent elegiac *motif* in *literature*, especially in *lyric* poetry where the writer laments a vanished past. Among notable examples are the *Old English* poems THE SEAFARER and THE WANDERER, and IN TIME OF PESTILENCE (1600) by Thomas Nashe (1567–1601). The motif is recurrent in *Tennyson's* work. Although strictly speaking the term relates to *poetry*, one can detect passages in *prose* works which may be described in the spirit of ubi sunt, e.g. in *Brittain's* TESTAMENT OF YOUTH.

Udall, Nicholas (1504–56): playwright. His RALPH ROISTER DOISTER (?1552) is considered to be the first English *comedy*. Influenced by the Roman comedies of Plautus (?254–184BC) and Terence (?190–159BC), his play may in turn have influenced Elizabethan comedies such as *Shakespeare's* THE TAMING OF THE SHREW (?1592) and THE COMEDY OF ERRORS (?1594).

underground literature is a term used to describe any *literature* which is subversive or anti-establishment, and which circulates in other than standard published *form* (e.g. in privately printed documents or through public readings). Under a suppressive political system it is necessary for writers to operate in this way, but in western-style democracies such literature soon becomes a part of established studies, e.g. the *Beat Movement*, the *Liverpool Poets*. See *alternative literature*.

understatement: see *litotes*.

unities, dramatic: three guidelines for the construction of plays, which are:

- unity of action laid down that there should be one main *action* of a play and no *sub-plots*
- unity of place ruled that the action should occur in one place, and not keep shifting location
- unity of time ruled that the action of a play should not cover events exceeding a 24-hour period.

Unities of action and time were described by *Aristotle* in his POETICS as being features of Greek tragedies, to which later theorists added the unity of place. This formula for the construction of *tragedies* remained in use until *Shakespeare* and his contemporaries increasingly disregarded them (as did Spanish playwrights), often extending the action to multiple *plots* ranging over many years in different places. French and Italian playwrights tended to regard the unities as fixed rules until the 19th century. In his PREFACES TO SHAKESPEARE (1765) *Johnson* rejected the whole idea (upon which the supposed importance of the unities was based) that the stage presentation should necessarily give audiences the illusion of reality. See *rules, suspension of disbelief*.

unity is the concept that a work has complete structural coherence with nothing within it that is superfluous, and that the adding or taking away of anything will damage the whole.

universality is the quality which gives a piece of *literature* appeal beyond the time and culture in which it is written. In general, modern critical thinking holds that this is impossible, all writing being culture-bound. However, writing which focuses upon the unchanging aspects of human nature is more likely to achieve *universality*. Among notable writers in English who are held in part to have achieved this are *Chaucer, Shakespeare, Jonson, Dryden, Jonathan Swift, Pope*, often through satirising the aforementioned human traits such as greed, hypocrisy and lust for power.

University Wits: a name given to a group of Elizabethan Oxford and Cambridge educated poets and playwrights who were active in London towards the end of the 16th century, including *Lyly, Marlowe*, Thomas Nashe (1567–1601). It is reputed that they met in the Mermaid Tavern off Cheapside. *Shakespeare* pokes gentle fun at this group in LOVE'S LABOURS LOST (?1595).

unreliable narrator: see *narrator*.

Unsworth, Barrie (b.1930): novelist whose writing often has an historical dimension, empire featuring as a recurrent *theme*. Notable works include THE PARTNERSHIP (1966), SUGAR AND RUM (1990), SACRED HUNGER (1992), MORALITY PLAY (1995), AFTER HANNIBAL (1996).

untranslatableness, in the sense used by *Coleridge* in BIOGRAPHIA LITERARIA, is the notion that it is impossible to 'translate' the words of *poetry* in the same language without damaging the *meaning*. Attempts to do this are normally done with the misguided intention of making the meaning clearer, and perhaps those who try to render *Shakespeare* into 'plain English' should mark *Coleridge*'s words.

Updike, John (b.1932): American novelist, journalist, *short-story* and children's writer, and poet. His *novels* explore middle-class American life in a *witty*, urbane *style*. Notable works include THE POORHOUSE FAIR (1959), RABBIT RUN (1960), RABBIT IS RICH (1981), THE WITCHES OF EASTWICK (1984), RABBIT AT REST (1990), ELECTRIC LIGHT (2001), LICKS OF LOVE (2001).

urtext: a lost early version of a *text*, e.g. textual analysis suggests that *Shakespeare*'s HAMLET is based on an urtext, possibly by Kyd.

utilitarianism is, in general terms, the doctrine that the value of things may only be weighed by their strict usefulness to the greatest number of people. Hence *literature* was considered of little practical use. Jeremy Bentham (1748–1832) and James Mill (1773–1836) were leading exponents of this philosophy, the emotionally crippling effects of which were attacked by *Dickens* in HARD TIMES (1845), where Gradgrind values facts and rejects imagination. The economist John Stuart Mill (1806–73), son of James, describes in his AUTOBIOGRAPHY (1873) such effects in his own upbringing, and goes on to record the spiritual awakening he experienced upon first reading the *poetry* of *Coleridge* and *Wordsworth*. *Oscar Wilde*'s notion of one who 'knows the price of everything and the value of nothing' may be taken as a cynic's definition of an utilitarian.

utopias: in *literature*, these are writings which construct an ideal state where the inhabitants lead a completely well-governed life which approaches perfection on earth. The word is derived from *More*'s UTOPIA (a conflation of the Greek words for 'good place' and 'no place') where, typical of subsequent literary utopias, an adventurous traveller discovers a distant fictional utopian state. The *genre* is a good vehicle for *satire*, as in Jonathan Swift's GULLIVER'S TRAVELS in which Gulliver visits various countries which display both utopian and *dystopian* characteristics. Modern fiction more often depicts *dystopias* than utopias.

Vanburgh, John (1664–1726): playwright of *Restoration comedy*, writer of *adaptations*, and architect. Notable works include THE RELAPSE, OR VIRTUE IN DANGER (1696, a satirical sequel to *Cibber*'s LOVE'S LAST SHIFT), THE PROVOK'D WIFE (1697).

valediction: a farewell speech, e.g. *Donne*'s poem 'A Valediction: Forbidding Mourning' (1633).

vehicle: see *tenor*.

Venus and Adonis stanza: a six-line *stanza* rhyming ababcc, as used by *Shakespeare* in VENUS AND ADONIS (1593).

verisimilitude occurs when, in the opinion of the reader, a writer has succeeded in depicting things with truth and *realism*, when there are *fantastic* elements in a work. For example, it is claimed that *Jonathan Swift* achieves this in GULLIVER'S TRAVELS notwithstanding Gulliver's travels into fantastic worlds.

verism: a verist believes that literature and all art should depict reality, however harsh or difficult that reality might be.

vernacular: the language of one's native country, the term is often used to distinguish between 'literary' English and writings in a local dialect, e.g. some of *Burns*' poems are written in Lowland Scots vernacular, William Barnes' (1801–86) in Dorset, *Walcott*'s in Caribbean Creole.

vers de société refers to *witty*, light-weight *verse* which deals with the trivial aspects of society. Much of *Betjeman*'s verse is considered to be of this type, and other notable exponents are *Pope, Belloc, Chesteron, Auden. Larkin* produced an example actually called 'Vers de Société' (in HIGH WINDOWS).

verse is a term used to refer to:

- a line written in *metre*
- a *stanza*
- a unit of writing in the *Bible*
- *poetry* in general as distinct from *prose* (it is sometimes used to suggest light-weight poetry).

verse drama describes any *drama* written in *verse*. *Elizabethan* and *Jacobean drama* was predominantly written in *verse*, but from the *Restoration Period* onwards *prose* was the main medium. In the mid-20th century an attempt was made to revive verse drama by *T.S. Eliot*, Christopher Fry (b.1907) and others, but its success was short-lived.

verse paragraph: is a defined section of (usually *blank verse*) lines which make up a distinct unit as found in *Milton*'s PARADISE LOST or *Wordsworth*'s THE PRELUDE.

verset: a flexible *form* of verse written in groups of long lines, often of irregular length, forming short *verse paragraphs*, as in *Lawrence*'s KANGAROO (1923). It is derived from the type of Old Testament biblical *verse* to be found in THE SONG OF SOLOMON.

versification can mean:

- the act of composing a *verse*
- studying verse *form*
- putting a *prose* work into verse.

Vice: a stock, buffoonish character who often appeared in *Morality plays* and *interludes* as a tempter of mankind. *Shakespeare*'s Falstaff in HENRY IV PARTS 1 AND 2 is in many ways a re-creation of the Vice figure.

Victorian Age: generally considered to cover *literature* written in England between approximately 1830 and 1901, comprising the reigns of William IV (1830–7) and Victoria (1838–1901).

viewpoint: see *narrator/narrative voice, showing and telling.*

vignette: originally a small decorative design on a blank page in a book at the beginning or end of a chapter, often of foliage and branches or a small rural scene, in a literary sense the word has come to describe a part or whole of *prose* work which skilfully creates an image of something as though it were a small picture, e.g. *Woolf*'s short story KEW GARDENS (1919).

villain: the evil person in a story. The term often indicates a rather *flat character* type, although there are plenty of more complex villains such as Iago in *Shakespeare*'s OTHELLO. The villain is more often associated with *drama* than other *genres*. Sometimes the *antagonist*, he (rarely 'she') develops from the devils of medieval *Mystery plays*, through the *Vices of Morality plays*, into the megalomaniacs of *Elizabethan drama* such as *Shakespeare*'s Richard III and *Marlowe*'s Tamburlaine. There are many villains in *revenge tragedy* and later in Victorian *melodrama*. Satan in *Milton*'s PARADISE LOST is sometimes regarded as the villain of all villains because he brings about the Fall of Man.

villanelle: a poem consisting of five *tercets* followed by a *quatrain*, with an interlinking *rhyme* scheme using only two rhymes: the first and third line of each tercet rhyme consistently throughout, as does each second line, the final quatrain using the same rhyme as *alternate* rhyming couplets (thus each tercet rhymes aba, and the concluding quatrain abab). This *form* originated in the Middle Ages, and experienced a revival of interest in the mid-20th century, e.g. *Auden*'s 'If I Could Tell You' (1940) and *Dylan Thomas*'s 'Do Not Go Gentle into that Good Night' (1952).

virgule: a forward slash indicating *foot* divisions in a line of *verse*, e.g. 'The cur/few tolls/ the knell/ of part/ing day' (the opening line of *Gray*'s 'Elegy') indicates the divisions between the five *iambic* feet. See *metre*.

voice may refer to either:

- the persona created by the writer through which a *poem* or a narrative is communicated to the reader
- the authorial voice itself which emerges behind the *content*.

The two may sometimes be the same thing; that is, it is clear that the writer himself is speaking directly to the reader, not using a persona to give voice to the content. See *narrator/narrative voice, persona, viewpoint*.

volta: see *turning point*.

vowel rhyme is another term for *assonance*.

Walcott, Derek (b.1930): Caribbean poet and playwright. He often uses a range of *verse* forms to explore the Caribbean experience, making use of both West Indian and European traditions. His plays draw on Creole language and use both *prose* and verse. Notable works include Henri Christophe (1950), In a Green Night (1962), The Castaway (1965, see *Robinson Crusoe myth*), Another Life (1973), The Dream on Money Mountain and Other Plays (1970), Collected Poems 1948–84 (1986), The Odyssey (1993).

Walker, Alice (b.1944): Black American novelist, *short-story* writer and poet. She cites her mixed racial background and *Hurston* as important influences in her work. She writes with understanding and passion of women's struggles against racism and sexism, considering herself to be 'womanist' rather than feminist. Notable works include In Love And Trouble (1973), Revolutionary Petunias and Other Poems (1973), You Can't Keep a Good Woman Down (1981), The Color Purple (1982, a good example of an *epistolary novel*), Horses Make the Landscape Look More Beautiful (1984), The Temple of my Familiar (1989), Possessing the Secret of Joy (1992), The Complete Stories (1994), The Light of my Father's Smile (1998), The Way Forward is with a Broken Heart (2001).

Walpole, Horace (1717–97): letter-writer, novelist, editor and writer of *verse drama*. It is clear that his charming letters were written with an eye to publication and posterity, and over 4,000 of them have been gathered together in the 48 volume Yale edition (1939–83). He was a friend and editor of *Gray*. The gothicisation of his house in Middlesex encouraged the Gothic Revival, and his *gothic* novel The Castle of Otranto (1764) is a forerunner of the *Romantic* interest in the *genre*. See *Mary Shelley, Beckford*.

Walsh, Jill Paton (b.1937): novelist and children's writer. She often uses historical *settings*, and some of her books are *detective fiction*. Notable works include Farewell The Great King (1972), The Emperor's Winding Sheet (1974), A Chance Child (1978), Lapsing (1986), The Wyndham Case (1993), A Piece of Justice (1995).

war literature refers mainly to *poetry* written as a result of the First World War, some of which is patriotic (e.g. *Brooke*), but most expresses horror and some can be classed as *protest literature* which deglamorises war (e.g. *Owen, Sassoon*). Other notable writers include *Blunden, Rosenberg, Edward Thomas* and *Jones*, whose In Parenthesis (1937), *epic* in scale, is a combination of *poetry* and *prose*. Novels, short stories, autobiographies, memoirs, diaries, escape stories and many other kinds of *literature* by the aforementioned and others came out of the war. Two notable memoirs are *Graves*' Goodbye to All That and *Sassoon*'s Memoirs of an Infantry Officer, and a notable novel based on his experiences as an ambulance driver in Italy is *Hemingway*'s A Farewell to Arms. Some minor literature came out of the Second World War, notably from *Alun Lewis, Fuller, Causley*.

war poets: see *war literature*.

Washington, Booker T. (1856–1915): African-American writer. He conflicted with *Du Bois* over his conciliatory approach concerning the way to advance the situation of Blacks. Notable works include his *autobiography* UP FROM SLAVERY (1901), FREDERICK DOUGLASS (1907, a *biography*).

Wasserstein, Wendy (b.1950): American playwright and essayist. Her innovative plays have been produced off- and off-off-Broadway, and she is sometimes concerned with the world from a particular female perspective. Notable works include UNCOMMON WOMEN AND OTHERS (1975), THE HEIDI CHRONICLES (1989).

Waugh, Evelyn (1903–66): novelist, travel writer and journalist. His *style* is *witty* and his *satire* is often a cynical and trenchant view of his times. Notable works include DECLINE AND FALL (1928), A HANDFUL OF DUST (1934), SCOOP (1938), BRIDESHEAD REVISITED (1945) and the SWORD OF HONOUR trilogy (1952–61).

weak ending: an extra unstressed syllable added to the end of a *blank verse* line. Sometimes known by the rather sexist term 'feminine ending'. The most famous example is 'To be, or not to be: that is the question' (from Act III Scene 1 of *Shakepeare*'s HAMLET) where repeated weak endings in the following lines generate a sense of Hamlet's hesitancy as he tries to make sense of his situation. See also *metre*.

Webb, Mary (1881–1927): novelist whose passionate rustic *romances* were famously parodied by *Gibbons* in COLD COMFORT FARM. Notable works include GONE TO EARTH (1917), PRECIOUS BANE (1928, which has some emotional power and is evocative of the Shropshire landscape).

Webster, John (?1578–1632): playwright. Some critics consider that his two great tragedies, THE WHITE DEVIL (1612) and, especially, THE DUCHESS OF MALFI (?1614), are the best plays of the period after those of *Shakespeare*. One of his hallmarks is the use of striking and often contrasting *imagery*, and a powerful sense of mortality. He collaborated with several other playwrights of the period.

Welch, James B. (b.1940): North American Indian novelist and poet. He sees himself as more in the western novelist *tradition* than as the Indian story-teller. Notable works include RIDING THE EARTH BOY (1971), WINTER IN THE BLOOD (1974), THE DEATH OF JIM LONEY (1979), FOOL'S CREW (1986).

well-made play: a neatly constructed play, e.g. by such as *Rattigan*. By the 1950s the term was used by the *Angry Young Men* and others as an expression of contempt, implying that such plays were mechanical in *plot*, and superficial and bland in subject matter.

Wells, H.G. (1866–1946): novelist and *short-story* writer. His prolific output varies from comic *novels* inspired by his youth such as LOVE AND MR LEWISHAM (1900), KIPPS (1905) and THE HISTORY OF MR POLLY (1910) to *science fiction* (a *genre* upon which he had a considerable influence) such as THE INVISIBLE MAN (1897). His later writings, often socialist in *tone* and some of which may be classed as *novels of ideas*, become increasingly pessimistic with warnings of political and scientific doom. Other notable works include THE TIME MACHINE (1895), THE WAR OF THE WORLDS (1898).

Welty, Eudora (1909–2001): American *short-story* writer and novelist with a particular interest in the past of the Southern States. Notable works include THE ROBBER BRIDEGROOM (1942), DELTA WEDDING (1946), THE OPTIMIST'S DAUGHTER (1972), COLLECTED STORIES (1980).

Wendt, Albert (b.1939): West Samoan novelist, *short-story* writer, literary critic and poet whose works explore the diversity of Polynesian culture. Notable works include LEAVES OF THE BANYAM TREE (1979), BLACK RAINBOW (1992).

Wertenbaker, Timberlake (b.1951): playwright, television script-writer and translator. Predominant *themes* in her work are a belief in the power of the creative imagination to enhance the lives of all people, not just artists; and concern for the position of women in male-dominated societies. Notable works include OUR COUNTRY'S GOOD (1988, adapted for the stage from *Keneally*'s *novel* THE PLAYMAKER).

Wesker, Arnold (b.1932): playwright, television script-writer, essayist and autobiographer. Much of his early work is committed to the idea of popularising culture and the creation of a socialist *utopia*; more recent work, while retaining its left-wing *tone*, is broader in scope and less obviously *didactic*. Notable works include CHICKEN SOUP WITH BARLEY (1958), ROOTS (1959), I'M TALKING ABOUT JERUSALEM (1960), CHIPS WITH EVERYTHING (1962), THE FOUR SEASONS (1965), THE OLD ONES (1972), LOVE LETTERS ON BLUE PAPER (1976), THE MERCHANT (1977, a re-working of aspects of *Shakespeare*'s THE MERCHANT OF VENICE).

West, Nathaniel (1903–1940): American novelist and screen-writer who focuses upon the illusions and emptiness of contemporary American life. Notable works include MRS LONLEYHEARTS (1933), A COOL MILLION: THE DISMANTLING OF LEMUEL PITKIN (1934),THE DAY OF THE LOCUST (1939).

Wharton, Edith (1862–1937): American novelist and *short-story* writer. She was much influenced by her close friendship with *Henry James* with whom she shared an interest in *witty* and *satiric* observation of the difference between American and European 'tribal behaviour', as she called social customs. She has been increasingly regarded as important in the development of the modern American *novel*. Notable works include THE HOUSE OF MIRTH (1905), ETHAN FROME (1911), THE CUSTOM OF THE COUNTRY (1913), XINGU AND OTHER STORIES (1916), THE AGE OF INNOCENCE (1920).

White, Antonia (1899–1979): novelist, *short-story* writer, essayist, diarist and translator. Much of her writing is autobiographical, concerning such matters as her experiences of mental instability, relationships with men, and loss and regaining of her Catholic faith. Notable works include FROST IN MAY (1933), THE LOST TRAVELLER (1950), THE SUGAR HOUSE (1952), BEYOND THE GLASS (1954), AS ONCE IN MAY (1983), DIARIES (1991, 1992).

White, E.B. (1899–1985): American essayist, journalist, literary critic and children's writer. Notable works include IS SEX NECESSARY (1929, in collaboration with *Thurber*), STUART LITTLE (1945), CHARLOTTE'S WEB (1952).

White, Gilbert (1720–93): naturalist and letter-writer whose NATURAL HISTORY AND ANTIQUITIES OF SELBOURNE (1788–9), lovingly describing the nature and wildlife of his native place, is highly regarded for its combination of scientific content and lyrical literary charm.

White, Patrick (1912–90): Australian novelist, playwright, poet, *short-story* writer and essayist. Influenced by German *Romanticism* and showing a persistent interest in the Australian landscape, he is considered to be one of Australia's finest novelists and playwrights. Notable works include THE TREE MAN (1955), VOSS (1957), RIDERS IN THE CHARIOT (1961) and A SEASON AT SARSAPARILLA (1961).

Whiting, John (1917–63): playwright, *drama* critic and essayist. His plays often powerfully portray spiritual struggles in a way which was ahead of its time and not always appreciated by critics or the theatre-going public. Notable works include A PENNY FOR A SONG (1951), SAINT'S DAY (1951), MARCHING SONG (1954), THE DEVILS (1961).

Whitman, Walt (1819–92): American poet and journalist. He creates a distinctively American *literature* through his *free verse*, written in everyday language and covering the extensiveness of his country, its landscape, its people, the influences of the Civil War, and his frank approach to homosexuality. Notable works include LEAVES OF GRASS (1856–92), DRUM TAPS (1865), SEQUEL (1865–6), MEMORANDA DURING THE WAR (1875), NOVEMBER BOUGHS (1888).

whodunnit: (that is 'who did it?') a *thriller* which depends upon suspense as regards who committed a crime.

Wilde, Oscar (1845–1900): playwright, novelist, essayist, poet and *short-story* writer. He is associated with the aesthetic movement (see *aestheticism*) and was famous for his *wit*, which was often carefully studied and not as spontaneous as he pretended. His plays in the *comedy of manners* tradition were hugely successful and have remained popular. Notable works include THE HAPPY PRINCE AND OTHER TALES (1888), THE PICTURE OF DORIAN GRAY (1890), LADY WINDERMERE'S FAN (1892), A WOMAN OF NO IMPORTANCE (1893), THE IMPORTANCE OF BEING ERNEST (1895), AN IDEAL HUSBAND (1895), THE BALLAD OF READING GOAL (1898).

Wilder, Thornton (1897–1975): American novelist and playwright. His plays sometimes blend *realism* with *expressionism*, and his priority is an attempt to depict psychological truth rather than *naturalistic* presentation. Notable works include BRIDGE OF SAN LUIS REY (1927), HEAVEN'S MY DESTINATION (1934), OUR TOWN (1938), THE SKIN OF OUR TEETH (1942), THE MATCHMAKER (1954, later adapted as the musical HELLO DOLLY).

Williams, Raymond (1921–88): Welsh critic and novelist. An influential figure in *Marxist criticism* of *literature*, his concerns include literature's place alongside other media and means of communication within culture and society as a whole. Notable works include CULTURE AND SOCIETY, 1780–1950 (1958), THE ENGLISH NOVEL FROM DICKENS TO LAWRENCE (1970), MARXISM AND LITERATURE (1977).

Williams, Tennessee (1911–83): American playwright, novelist and *short-story* writer. He explores human feelings and desires with understanding and sympathy, often through *symbolism* and *expressionism*. Some of his writing examines the characteristics and prejudices of the deep South and its culture. Notable works include THE GLASS MENAGERIE (1944), A STREETCAR NAMED DESIRE (1947), THE ROSE TATTOO (1951) and CAT ON A HOT TIN ROOF (1955).

Williams, William Carlos (1883–1963): American poet, novelist and *short-story* writer. Always an experimenter, his *poems* range from the minimalist to the long, from *imagist* through *objectivist* to *modernist* (he has been described as a master of *modernism*). However *free* his *verse* may appear, *rhythm* is always important. He is a great observer of ordinary everyday events and things. Notable works include SPRING AND

ALL (1923), PICTURES FROM BRUEGHEL AND OTHER POEMS (1963), COLLECTED POEMS (2001, edited by Litz and MacGowan).

Williamson, David (b.1942): Australian playwright and screenplay-writer. A naturalistic writer whose *witty*, observant and often satirical plays of Australian life have contributed to Australia's 'New Wave' of writers. Notable works include THE COMING OF THE STORK (1970), DON'S PARTY (1971), THE CLUB (1977), TRAVELLING NORTH (1979), COLLECTED PLAYS (in two volumes, 1986 and 1994).

willing suspension of disbelief, a phrase coined by *Coleridge*, means that when responding to art one knows that it is not 'real', but one conspires with the creator to believe in the truth of what s/he is presenting. For instance, a person watching a play is aware of accepting theatrical *conventions* such as *soliloquy*; or when in the cinema, that real people are not moving on the screen; or when reading a *novel*, that the story contained therein is not actually happening.

Wilmot, John (1647–80): poet. An intellectual libertine, described variously as *metaphysical* and one of the first *Augustans*, his poems are *witty*, satirical, scurrilous, sceptical and/or bluntly pornographic. Notable works include A SATIRE AGAINST REASON AND MANKIND (1675), COMPLETE POEMS (1968, ed. D.M. Veith).

Wilson, A.N. (b.1950): novelist, biographer and literary critic. His tragi-comic stories often explore religious beliefs and human dilemmas, at times with slightly caustic *wit*, at others with gentle *satire*. Notable works include THE SWEETS OF PIMLICO (1977), THE HEALING ART (1980), WHO WAS OSWALD FISH? (1981), WISE VIRGIN (1982), PENFRIENDS FROM PORLOCK (1988), THE VICAR OF SORROWS (1993).

Wilson, Angus (1913–91): novelist, *short-story* writer and critic. He co-operated with *Bradbury* in the setting up of a unique creative writing course at East Anglia University. Through various *narrative* techniques he explores a range of human affairs with *wit* and sharp, sometimes satiric, observation. Notable works include THE WRONG SET (1949), SUCH DARLING DODOS (1950), HEMLOCK AND AFTER (1952), ANGLO-SAXON ATTITUDES (1956), NO LAUGHING MATTER (1967), AS IF BY MAGIC (1973), SETTING THE WORLD ON FIRE (1980).

Wilson, John Dover (1881–1969): Shakespearean scholar and editor who had a considerable appeal to the general reader and was passionate that *literature* should be made accessible to all. Notable works include NEW CAMBRIDGE SHAKESPEARE (1921–66, editor), THE ESSENTIAL SHAKESPEARE (1931), WHAT HAPPENS IN HAMLET (1935).

Winterson, Jeanette (b.1959): novelist. Among other *themes* she explores *feminism* and lesbianism, employing *magic realism* and various *narrative devices*. Notable works include ORANGES ARE NOT THE ONLY FRUIT (1985), BOATING FOR BEGINNERS (1985), SEXING THE CHERRY (1989), ART AND LIES (1994).

Winton, Tim (b.1960): Australian novelist, *short-story* and children's writer. He writes with compassion of ordinary people in small Western Australian communities, and of the land and sea by which they live. Notable works include AN OPEN SWIMMER (1982), SHALLOWS (1984), CLOUDSTREET (1991), THE RIDERS (1995).

wit has come to mean an intelligent, clever, neat and usually humorous way of putting a point. Among poets, *Chaucer* and *Pope* have been noted for their wit, and *metaphysical* poets such as *Donne* and *Marvell* are noted for their ability to combine surprising verbal dexterity (that is, wit) with seriousness. *Hazlitt* rated wit as artificial and inferior to the naturalness of *imagination*. Broad, unsubtle verbal humour does not count as wit.

witty: see *wit*.

Wodehouse, P.G. (1881–1975): novelist, *short-story* writer and playwright. His output was prolific. He characteristically uses light, genteel *humour* and *romance*, and he is now best known for the creation of the resourceful butler Jeeves and his master Bertie Wooster. Notable works include THE INIMITABLE JEEVES (1923), CARRY ON, JEEVES (1925), BLANDINGS CASTLE (1935), THE CODE OF THE WOOSTERS (1938).

Wolfe, Tom (b.1930): American novelist and journalist. A foremost proponent of *New Journalism*, which he once claimed 'would wipe out the *novel* as *literature*'s main event' – but this did not stop him writing novels. Notable works include THE KANDY-KOLORED TANGERINE FLAKE STREAMLINE BABY (1966), THE PUMPHOUSE GANG (1968), THE ELECTRIC KOOL-AID ACID TEST (1968), THE BONFIRES OF THE VARIETIES (1987).

Wolff, Tobias (b.1945): American *short-story* writer identified with the Dirty Realism style. Notable works include THE GARDEN OF THE NORTH AMERICAN MARTYRS (1981, published in UK in 1982 as HUNTERS IN THE SNOW), THE BARRACKS THIEF (1984), BACK IN THE WORLD (1985).

Woolf, Virginia (1882–1941): novelist and literary critic. A leading member of the *Bloomsbury Group*, she is identified with the development of the *stream of consciousness* technique. One of the 20th century's major novelists, her importance is increasingly recognised as a leading exponent of *modernism* and in the advance of *feminist criticism*. Notable works include MRS DALLOWAY (1925), TO THE LIGHTHOUSE (1927), ORLANDO (1928), A ROOM OF ONE'S OWN (1929).

Wordsworth, Dorothy (1771–1855) was a significant literary influence upon her brother William, with whom she lived most of her life. She did not write for her publication, but it is clear that *William Wordsworth* drew extensively on her *diaries* as a literary source, most famously in the composition of his *poem* 'I Wandered Lonely as a Cloud'. Notable works include her GRASMERE JOURNAL (edited by W. Knight 1896, 1904) which covers the period 1800–03.

Wordsworth, William (1770–1850): poet. A key figure in English *Romanticism*, the political radicalism of his youth (he thought it 'very heaven to be alive' during the French Revolution) and the conservatism of his age is reflected in his writings. He did much to change the course of English *poetry* in two crucial ways:

- he rejected the poetic *diction* of *neoclassicism* and aimed to write in 'the ordinary language of ordinary men'
- he wrote about everyday things and people he saw around him and came across.

He is closely associated with the topography and people of his native Lake District where he spent most of his life. His best work was written before 1810, after which he re-worked much of his early poetry, often to its disadvantage. He was *poet laureate* from 1843–50, a post he only accepted on condition that he did not have to write anything. Notable works include LYRICAL BALLADS (1798, in collaboration with *Coleridge*), 'Resolution and Independence' (1802), 'Ode: Intimations of Immortality from

Recollections of Early Childhood' (1802), 'I Wandered Lonely as a Cloud' (1807), THE EXCURSION (1814), THE PRELUDE (1799–1850).

Wright, Judith (b.1915): Australian poet and essayist. Her passionate concern for wildlife, the environment and the Aboriginal community is reflected in her *poetry*. Notable works include THE MOVING IMAGE (1946), ALIVE (1973), THE CRY FOR THE DEAD (1981).

Wright, Kit (b.1944): poet. A writer of light comic *verse*, he shows inventiveness and tenderness. Notable works include THE BEAR LOOKED OVER THE MOUNTAIN (1977), BUMP-STARTING THE HEARSE (1983), GREAT SNAKES (1995).

Wright, Richard (1908–60): Black American novelist, social critic, *short-story* writer, radio *dramatist*, poet and essayist. One of the most influential Black writers of the 20th century, he explores the social causes of racism and oppression generally, especially in the Southern States. Notable works include NATIVE SON (1940), BLACK BOY (1945, an autobiography), THE OUTSIDER (1953), BLACK POWER (1954), WHITE MAN, LISTEN! (1957).

writerly: see *readerly/writerly*. See also *authorial intention, intentional fallacy, post-structuralism*.

Wyatt, Thomas (1503–43): A poet, courtier and diplomat who was much influenced by *Petrarch*, translating him and, with *Surrey*, adapting the *sonnet* to English usage, and developing the typical final *rhyming couplet*. He experimented with other new *forms* in English such as *terza rima*. Notable works include 'They Flee from Me' (1557), 'My Lute Awake' (1557), 'Stand Whoso List' (1557), 'Whoso List to Hunt' (1557).

Wycherley, William (1641–1715): his plays contain sharp observation of the manners of the period, especially sexual morality and marriage *conventions*. He is best known for THE COUNTRY WIFE (1675). See also *comedy of manners* and *Restoration comedy*.

Wyndham, John (1903–69): novelist and *short-story* writer of *science fiction*. Influenced by *Wells* and Jules Verne (1828–1905), he writes what he called 'logical fantasy': that is, convincingly vivid stories about people's struggles with terrifying and bizarre situations. His *novels* have been described as defining a characteristically English response to disaster. Notable works include THE DAY OF THE TRIFFIDS (1951), THE KRAKEN WAKES (1953), THE CHRYSALIDS (1955), THE MIDWICH CUCKOOS (1957), THE TROUBLE WITH LICHEN (1960), CONSIDER HER WAYS AND OTHERS (1961).

yarn is a colloquial word for *tale* originating in nautical slang. Sometimes in a *short story* a narrator will 'spin a yarn' as a *story* within the story, which often gives a feeling of informality. Notable yarners include *Conrad, Kipling, Stevenson, Twain, Faulkner,* whose THE LIAR (1925) is a good example.

Yeats, W.B. (1865–1939): Irish poet, playwright and editor. Influenced by, among others, *Spenser, Blake*, the *Pre-Raphaelites* and French *symbolism*, he became fascinated by Irish folklore and legend, and by the mystic and supernatural in general. An Irish nationalist, he helped to found Irish literary societies in Dublin and London, and an Irish national theatre. His early *poetry* of the 1890s was elaborately *Pre-Raphaelite* in *style*, but later work became increasingly simplified, achieving a clear, rich, lyricism. Notable works include THE COUNTESS CATHLEEN (1892), THE CELTIC TWILIGHT (1893), THE GREEN HELMET AND OTHER POEMS (1910), THE WILD SWANS AT COOLE (1919), MICHAEL ROBARTES AND THE DANCER (1921), THE TOWER (1928), NEW POEMS (1938), LAST POEMS AND TWO PLAYS (1939).

yellow book: a quarterly *periodical* published between 1894 and 1897. Associated with *Aestheticism* and *Decadence*, its contributors (including the artist Aubrey Beardsley) sometimes deliberately set out to shock.

zeitgeist is the spirit of the times, and is applied to what is sometimes regarded as the prevailing *mood* of an age, e.g. much *Elizabethan* and *Victorian* literature is upbeat and patriotic; much *Jacobean* literature is downbeat and morbid.

zeugma: a *figure of speech* whereby a word or words are used to apply in differing senses to two or more other words in a sentence, e.g. 'He put out his cigar, the milk bottles and the light.'

APPENDIX I
EXAMINERS' TERMS

The terms below are of two types:

- terms you are likely to encounter within the wording of examination questions
- terms examiners use when talking to each other.

It is likely that you will come across many of them in the classroom.

It is helpful for you to be acquainted with the former so that you are familiar with the language of question-setting and what examiners are looking for when they use certain terms. Although the question papers within a particular specification tend to adopt a common language, Principal Examiners for each examination board favour their own terms with which they consider their candidates should be familiar. It is for this reason, rather than to spot likely questions, that it is worth a careful look at the style of question paper which is usual (although not guaranteed) for the examination papers which you are to sit.

By gaining some knowledge of the language which examiners use when discussing scripts you will enable yourself to understand better how to prepare for, and then write, the examination itself.

analyse: *examine* closely the various parts of something (usually going on to draw conclusions about the whole).

answering the question: the most important task of a candidate, but one easily forgotten in the attempt to show how much is known. See *relevance, twisting the question, unloading information.*

appreciation: an appreciation is much the same as a *commentary,* but by using this word an examiner wishes to emphasise that more is required than a mere line by line mechanical analysis of a piece of writing.

argument: the views which an *essay* or literary work sets out to *discuss.*

assertion: a statement which purports to be an objective and incontestable fact. Whilst some assertions about texts are indeed objective (e.g. 'Hamlet does not kill Claudius until near the end of the play'), others are subjective and disputable (e.g. 'Hamlet's problem is that he cannot make up his mind') and, with AS/A level AO4 in mind (see Appendix 3), should be avoided in critical essays, especially if unsupported by textual reference. A better way of approaching an idea is to emphasise its subjectivity (e.g. 'One way of reading of Hamlet's problem is that he is simply unable to make up his mind; on the other hand, it could be argued that he is quite able to be decisive but that circumstances are against his taking action').

AQA: Assessment and Qualifications Alliance. It is one of the three English AS/A level examination boards.

assess: see *discuss.*

assessment objectives: see Appendix 3.

at risk: a candidate is said by senior examiners to be 'at risk' if:

- the *predicted grade* for a particular paper is markedly different from the grade achieved
- the overall predicted grade for the entire syllabus is markedly different from the grade achieved
- a candidate is very close to a borderline having just failed to achieve the higher grade.

BTEC: Business Training and Enterprise Council.

by close reference to: it may seem obvious to state that this phrase means exactly what it says, but it is remarkable how often candidates fail to notice it as *key words* in a question, giving a strong prompt to AS/A level AO3 (see Appendix 3).

by what means...? indicates that you must show with illustrations exactly how a writer conveys, for instance, an aspect of the text, e.g. 'By what means does Keats achieve his effects in the following poem?' or 'By what means does Shakespeare build up dramatic tension in this scene?'

closed text examination: an examination where set texts are not allowed to be taken in and used in the examination room.

comment: see *discuss*.

commentary: if you are asked to write a commentary on a piece of writing, you must give a close reading of it, considering all aspects of style and content, discussing the piece from all relevant points of view. Some questions may be qualified by asking you to write a commentary from specific angles, in which case you must focus upon *key words* and not write a generalised commentary.

compare/compare and contrast: the latter is a common formulation when two passages or whole texts are set side by side for *commentary* and thus AS/A level AO5 (see Appendix 3) is targeted. The two words are similar, but 'contrast' is present in the question in order to remind candidates that despite similarities in, for example, *theme* or subject-matter, the style or treatment may be different.

concern: you might be asked to consider a writer's concerns, and this is almost the same as *themes*.

consider: see *discuss*.

consider the view...: a combination of *discuss* and *do you agree?*.

continuous assessment is a rather inexact phrase for *coursework*, because coursework is invariably a selection of the best work achieved during a course, and not a continuous assessment of everything assessed during the course.

contribute/contribution: the contribution which an aspect makes to a text amounts to the same thing as its *importance*.

coursework refers to all work contributing to a candidate's final assessment which is done in the student's own time and marked by a teacher, rather than under timed examination conditions.

describing is when a candidate merely describes what is going on, but fails to comment upon it (*commentary* being the aim of every question).

descriptors: a term used by some examination boards to refer to assessment objectives (see Appendix 3).

discuss: this is the word most commonly used to invite a close consideration of a topic. Other words which mean much the same may be used in order to vary the vocabulary of questions:

- assess
- comment
- consider
- examine (see *analyse*)
- explore
- evaluate (more rarely used).

do you agree?: this formulation is likely to follow a quotation or statement of a viewpoint about a text. It is a genuinely open invitation to *discuss*, and in a subjective discipline such as English it will be rare that you unreservedly agree or disagree. A likely response might be 'up to a point', followed by a supported, balanced discussion weighing up the points for and against the view posited in the question.

do you find...? is an invitation to *discuss* a proposition, similar to *do you agree?*.

dramatic effect/effectiveness are phrases which can cause some unease when used in an examination question because, it is claimed, there is lack of clarity as to what is actually meant. If you are asked about the dramatic effectiveness of a particular passage or aspect of a play, you should *consider* all factors such as situation, significance in plot development, *presentation* of character, dramatic irony, stage directions, sub-text, language, poetic effects (in a verse drama) and anything else you can think of which *contributes* towards the impact created upon an audience by a piece of drama.

dramatic impact means much the same as *dramatic effect*.

dramatic interest means much the same as *dramatic effect*.

dramatic tension is a part of *dramatic effectiveness*, namely *dramatic effect* which might create a tense atmosphere for the audience.

EDEXEL Foundation is an examination board formed by the combining of *BTEC* and London Examinations. It is one of the three AS/A level examination boards.

effectiveness is a word which, when it appears in a question, invites you to *consider* how well certain devices used by a writer succeed (success to be defined by you, the critic).

embedding is a term sometimes used to describe the seamless weaving of words and phrases from the original text into a candidate's own sentences. This is often the most effective form of quoting. See *quotations, use of* in Appendix 2.

essay: see *essay* under E in main entries.

essay plan: see Appendix 2 under 'In the examination room'.

evaluation is the process of judging the merit of literary work, citing examples which demonstrate the ways in which it may be considered worthwhile or poor.

examine: see *discuss*.

explore: see *discuss*.

evaluate: see *discuss*.

expression refers to the language skills with which a writer (including an examinee) communicates her/his subject matter. In an examination poor powers of expression can mar the quality of an answer.

from your reading of...: if these words appear in a question, they are there to emphasise that an examiner wishes to draw out your personal responses to a text. However, the sub-text behind those words is an encouragement to show your appreciation that there may be other valid ways of reading the text than yours (see AS/A level AO4 in Appendix 3).

function: how an aspect of a piece of writing works in relation to the whole. (A question may also explicitly or implicitly invite the candidate to consider the *importance* of a particular aspect.)

generalisation: see Appendix 2 under 'In the examination room'.

grammar: the *rubric* on many English literature examination papers warns candidates that the quality of their grammar and sentence construction will be taken into account when arriving at an overall mark for an answer (see AS/A level AO1 in Appendix 3).

handling means much the same as *method* (see under M in main entries).

how helpful...? is another way of asking '*Discuss* the suggestion that...'.

how...: if this word is used in a general way with no qualifications (such as *how effectively*), you should pause and reflect exactly what is being asked (such as whether it means *in what ways...* or *by what means...*).

how effectively...? is another form of *how successfully...?*.

how far...? signals a similar invitation to *do you agree?* (and is sometimes followed by these words).

how fair is it...? is a similar invitation to *do you agree...?*.

how helpful do you find...? is a similar prompt to *do you agree?*.

how important...?: see *importance*.

how relevant...? is another way of asking you to *consider* the *function* of an aspect of the text.

how successfully...? invites a candidate to *consider* how well a writer has set out to achieve something which it is assumed is an objective of the writing. Sometimes the question is focusing on an issue upon which there are well established differences of opinion, but more often the question is simply inviting you to debate the issue highlighted.

how valid...: a variation on *how far do you agree...?*.

how would you respond...? is a similar invitation to *consider the view* or *do you agree?*.

importance: one of the best ways of approaching a question which asks you to *consider* what one aspect of a text *contributes* to the overall work is to imagine the loss if that aspect was missing: that loss will be a good measure of its *importance*.

IB: the International Baccalaurate.

(in the light of) your reading...: see *from your reading of...*.

in what ways...?: note that, unless the question includes *how far*, you are not allowed to *consider* whether factors other than the main thrust of the question are more important in the text as a whole. For instance, the question 'In what ways may Alice Walker's THE COLOR PURPLE be read as a feminist text?' does not invite you to suggest other ways of reading the text (that is, the question is not a strong prompt for AS/A level AO4 – see Appendix 3). However, 'How far, and in what ways, is it limiting to read Alice Walker's THE COLOR PURPLE as a feminist text?' invites both a consideration of the book as a possible feminist text and alternative ways of reading it (that is, this question is a strong prompt for AO4). This is a good example of how important it is to note the *key words* in a question.

in your opinion/do you consider...: a variation on *from your reading of....*

key words: see Appendix 2, *questions*, under 'In the examination room'.

language: by this an examiner means a close reading of the words in particular which make up the language in general of a text or part of a text. When used on an examination paper 'language' is sometimes linked with a consideration of imagery.

literal interpretation: used by examiners when describing a script where a candidate's reading remains on a literal level and fails to perceive sub-text or metaphorical aspects.

mechanical accuracy: see Appendix 2, under 'In the examination room'.

narrative is when the candidate merely tells the story of a text, or part of a text, without explicitly answering the question. The examiner will try to discern implicit relevance in this, but it is not enough for the candidate to leave the examiner to do the work: it is up to the candidate to make explicit why narrating some of the story is relevant to the question in hand.

OCR: Oxford Cambridge and RSA Examinations. It is one of the three English examination boards.

open text examination: an examination where set texts must be taken in and used in the examination room.

over-reading occurs when a candidate strains a point of view further than is sensibly sustainable through reference to the text.

paragraphing: see Appendix 2 under 'In the examination room'.

paraphrase is when an answer, or part of an answer, is merely a rewriting of a set passage in the candidate's own words. By doing this a candidate will demonstrate understanding of content, but no more; and is unlikely to have shown an ability to *comment* upon it.

passage-based questions are those which feature a printed passage on the examination paper (in a *closed text examination*) or a page reference to an extract from a set work (in an *open text examination*), and which usually ask you to closely read (AO3 – see Appendix 3) and *comment* upon a specific aspect of the extract. It is very important indeed, as always, to note the exact terms of the question, which may ask you:

- to confine your consideration to this passage (and such a prompt towards AO3 is often underlined or printed in bold on the paper)
- to relate the passage, or specific issues in it, to the work as a whole.

plagiarism: examiners are constantly on the alert for any form of unfair practice. They are aware of most of the standard introductions to and critical works on set texts, and can usually quickly detect the unfair and unacknowledged use of such material. It has even happened that an examiner has read his own published words written down and passed off as a candidate's own. All secondary sources must always be acknowledged. If an examiner has the faintest suspicion of plagiarism the matter is passed to higher authority for investigation. The penalties for such proven malpractice are severe – see Appendix 2 for more details, and see also *plagiarism* under P in main entries.

predicted grade: after the examination papers have been marked, senior examiners look at the grades which centres have predicted for their candidates in order to judge which candidates may be particularly *at risk*. It is important to stress that this process is a safeguard for the candidate: it is extremely rare for a candidate's script to be re-read and the mark reduced if s/he has apparently done better than a centre predicted; the focus is upon those candidates who seem not to have done as well as predicted, and their scripts are re-read in order to check that a fair mark has been awarded. For these reasons it is extremely important for centres to send predicted grades to the examination board.

presentation:

- when printed in the *rubric*, refers to the fact that poor presentation of work by the candidate may lead to deduction of marks
- when used in a question title, usually invites the candidate to *discuss* the presentation of a character, issue or aspect in the work as a whole or in a particular extract (see *passage-based questions*).

punctuation: poor punctuation can make reading a script hard work for an examiner, and will badly impair the communication of the candidate's ideas and inevitably diminish the mark awarded (see AS/A level AO1 in Appendix 3).

quotations, use of and quoting: see Appendix 2 under 'Preparing for the examination' and 'In the examination room'.

register is a term frequently used to refer to the formality or informality of the language in which something is written. You must ensure that you write literary *essays* in an appropriate register and terminology, and not use a casually colloquial style (AO1 – see Appendix 3). This does not mean that you should write in a stiff, pompous or old-fashioned language: the vitality of your own language is important. However, it does mean recognising that an examination script is a relatively formal document. For instance, it would be inappropriate to refer to Sir Toby Belch in *Shakespeare*'s TWELFTH NIGHT as a 'laid-back' character, even if you considered that modern colloquial term adequately sums up his attitude: you must find a more formal term. The period of the text on which you are writing may have an effect upon the style in which you write (for instance, you may find subtly different language becomes automatically appropriate when you write about Chaucer, Congreve, Wilde, or Duffy).

relevance is when the material used by a candidate is all focused upon the requirements of answering the question set. Irrelevance is penalised, however interesting the material in its own right. See 'answer the question asked' in Appendix 2, *question* under 'In the examination room'.

repetition is when an answer covers ground, however briefly, which it has already dealt with. To an examiner this indicates a poorly planned and presented essay.

what is you response to...? is another variation on *do you agree...?*, but the wording will possibly appear to be more neutral, and less specific in its advocacy of a point of view.

rôle is a term often used in connection with the *function* of a character within a work as a whole. The word is usually there to indicate that what you are being asked to do is more than a mere character study.

rubric: the instructions on the front of a question paper or before sections of the paper or individual questions. These must be read carefully before you start writing or, for instance, you might answer the wrong number of questions.

significance is another word for *importance*.

spelling: the *rubric* on many English literature examination papers warns candidates that the quality of their spelling will be taken into account when arriving at an overall mark for an answer (see AS/A level AO1 in Appendix 3).

straining means much the same as *over-reading*.

starting with a detailed examination of... implies that there must be a fairly close consideration of that which is specified before moving on to the rest of the question; but see also *taking as a starting point....*

stretching means much the same as *over-reading*.

summary: a synopsis of the main points or story of a text, and which in an examination should usually be avoided, or used very sparingly, in a very focused way and only if strictly relevant in answering a question.

supposition is when a candidate makes assumptions which are not supported by the evidence in the text. Often this is an attempt to show a personal interpretation which goes too far.

syntax is a word sometimes written by examiners in the margin of an answer when confusion has been created as a result of poor word arrangement in a sentence.

taking as a starting point... is a formula still used, but finding less favour among examiners because it can be ambiguous to candidates, who may be unsure of how much time to spend considering the 'starting point' and how much on the rest of the question. Generally speaking, the 'starting point' should be given a paragraph or so of consideration, but the rest of the question should form the bulk of an answer. However, see *starting with a detailed examination of....*

tendentious questions: a tendentious examination question is one which is phrased in such a way that it encourages agreement with a critical opinion. English literature examiners try to avoid setting such questions, but sometimes they find their way onto an examination paper. For example, 'By what means does Shelley achieve a passionate intensity in his poetry?' assumes that a candidate will accept that Percy Shelley's poetry is passionately intense. Such questions are best avoided, if possible.

to what extent...? is similar to *how far....*

theme: see under T in main entries.

twisting the question is when a candidate fails to focus upon the exact question asked, but distorts the answer in order to make it fit what the candidate wants to say (often a previously prepared essay). However skilfully a candidate may think s/he is 'adapting' the question, it is very clear to an examiner when a candidate is saying to her/himself 'Never mind your question – this is the one I'm going to answer'.

unfolding is a term which implies the gradual revelation of an aspect of a text as an extract or the whole work progresses or 'unfolds'.

unloading information is when a candidate writes everything s/he can possibly think on a text regardless of whether or not it has relevance and is *answering the question*.

use of: a phrase employed in examination questions to ask about the *function* of a particular aspect of a text within the whole.

what contribution does...? invites a candidate to *consider* the essential *importance* of one aspect of a work in relation to the whole.

what do you find of interest...? is a genuinely open question inviting you to *consider* the proposed subject in any way you find interesting. There is no hidden agenda to this kind of question: it is genuinely trying to draw out your responses and enthusiasms (see AS/A level AO4 in Appendix 3), and the main thing which you must remember is to root everything you say firmly in a close consideration of the text (see AS/A level AO3 in Appendix 3).

what do you take to be...?: another way of saying '*what do you consider...?*'. The use of 'you' in all these kinds of formulation is a prompt for AO4 (see Appendix 3).

what do you make of...?: a similar prompt to *what impressions...* or *your reading*.

what have you found...?: this phrase is an invitation to AO4 (see Appendix 3).

what impressions...: as with *your reading*, this phrase in a question is designed to draw out AO4 (see Appendix 3).

what do you consider the significance of...? see *discuss* and *significance/importance*.

with this comment in mind is similar to *taking as a starting point....*

write a commentary: see *commentary*.

write a critical appreciation: see *appreciation*.

APPENDIX 2
HINTS FOR EXAMINATION SUCCESS

PREPARING FOR THE EXAMINATION

assessment objectives: it is essential that you have an awareness of which assessment objectives (see Appendix 3) are being targetted by each examination paper and by each of the questions on the paper.

critics: it is important to read a range of critical introductions and commentaries about the texts you are studying, as they will set you thinking, give you ideas which you can accept or reject, and help to you realise that there is no one or 'right' way of reading and understanding a *text*. However, see also *secondary opinion* under the following section.

question papers ensure that you see the previous years' or other specimen question papers so that you can study the type of questions you will be asked, how many you have to do, whether there are compulsory or optional questions, and any other *rubric* or instruction.

quotations, use of: the best kind of quoting is when brief, apt words from the text are woven into a candidate's own sentences. The learning of lengthy quotations (do not use 'quotes', which is a verb) for *closed text examinations* (see Appendix 1) is not an appropriate preparation as:

- candidates will tend to *twist* a question (see Appendix 1) in order to display such learning whether or not it is relevant to the question in hand
- it is unlikely that more than a word, phrase or brief piece of *text* will serve to illuminate a particular point.

See also under *quoting* in the following section.

training over the distance: athletes train over the distance which they are going to run in competition: so should examinees. The examination will require that you answer a number of questions in a given time, and it is vital for you to accustom yourself to this pressure. Find out how long you will have to write each essay in the examination. Then sit down in a quiet place, choose a title for a test essay, and do whatever reading and note-taking you think necessary by way of preparation. When you are ready, put all books and notes away, get out pen and paper, set an alarm for ten minutes less than your allotted time, and commence writing your essay. When the alarm goes, you have five minutes to draw the essay to a conclusion, and five minutes to check it through for mistakes. Leave the essay and come back to it later. How does it read? Did you say what you meant to? Did you leave anything out? Did you include anything which seems irrelevant and better left out? Ask a teacher or lecturer to assess your essay. After a couple of attempts at this exercise you may feel strong enough to write two essays consecutively. There is no point in the exercise unless you create examination room conditions for yourself. Write entirely uninterrupted: no background music and no getting up to take a drink in the middle.

IN THE EXAMINATION ROOM

In a literature examination questions are asked in the spirit of debate to see how well you can organise your ideas based upon your knowledge and understanding of the texts. They are not framed to see if you know the 'correct' answer as there is no such thing. You should present all sides of an answer within the terms of the question, and not merely the one which you favour. Give a structure to the way you display your knowledge and opinions, and support what you say with close reference to the text. Be disciplined: never allow yourself to get away with vague, general statements without referring to an appropriate part of the text in order to substantiate what you say. Quote where necessary, bearing in mind the things said elsewhere in this Appendix. You should take the initiative and provide focus where a question is general: this kind is usually more difficult than one on a specific aspect of the text, and it is easy to lose your way. See also advice on *passage-based questions* in Appendix 1.

drama texts:
- when writing on them refer to 'the play', never 'the book'
- never refer to a character as an 'actor', which refers to the person who is playing the character, not to the character her/himself.

essay plan: it is always a good idea to spend five minutes creating a skeleton plan for an answer before beginning to write. A line should be put through this so that examiners do not mistake it for a part of the answer proper.

generalisation: often an introductory or summative statement which, on its own, lacks illustration from the text to validate it. A general statement is reasonable at the opening of an essay, and in places during it, provided that close support follows. It rarely adds much as a final paragraph.

handwriting: be as neat as you can. It is obvious that in this and all other respects you should make your examination script user-friendly for the examiner, who probably has several hundred examination scripts to read in a limited time.

implicit relevance: while examiners are always on the look-out for implicit relevance in an answer, the onus is on the candidate to make explicit, with as much clarity as possible, the direction of her/his answer.

mechanical accuracy means good spelling, punctuation and grammar, and the lack of it is often commented upon by examiners as damaging an otherwise good essay. In reporting on the overall work of candidates in a recent A level English Literature module one Principal Examiner commented: 'As regards the presentation of material… even very good candidates misspell words, show grammatical inaccuracy, and do not punctuate properly'. Another noted an increasing tendency to omit words in a kind of email shorthand which is inappropriate in formal examination answers.

narrative in the sense of recounting the story of a text should be avoided except when a sharply focused brief account is necessary in order to illustrate an argument. Merely to tell the story as an answer is usually worthless.

paragraphing: a paragraph is a section of writing which deals with one idea or point, or one coherent aspect thereof. While paragraphs may be of any length, a good guideline for a writer is to avoid using a very long one, and to avoid using a very short one, unless s/he really means to do so for a particular effect. In general:

- opening paragraphs may be of various kinds, but the best address the question immediately. One good way to tackle an opening paragraph is to imagine that you have only one paragraph in which to answer the question. There may well be some *generalisation*, but you should 'set out your stall' by clarifying what you take to be the key words (see *questions*) in the essay title, making one or two direct and relevant references to the text, and showing as clearly as possible the line of argument you intend to pursue in the ensuing paragraphs. After writing the paragraph, put down your pen; read what you have written; check that your essay plan will still work; and then calmly proceed. Examiners really like it if by the end of the opening paragraph they can see where your essay is going
- concluding paragraphs should not merely repeat in brief what you have already said at length. Only use one if you have loose ends to tie up, final points to make, or the need to stress a conclusion. When you have said what you have to say, stop (even if your ending seems abrupt).

plagiarism, even of a minor kind, will lead to a candidate's disqualification from the whole examination and possibly any other examinations being sat in the same session; and may have an impact on the standing of any past or future examinations which the candidate has or will take. See *plagiarism* in Appendix 1 and under P in main entries.

questions:

- how many? – check how many questions you are required to answer on the paper as a whole (see *rubric*)
- choice – if there is a choice, consider carefully which will suit you best; but do not take too long to decide
- key words – when deciding whether to answer a question, the first task is to consider carefully which are the key words in the essay title, as the successful direction of an essay will depend upon this. If there are any which need clarifying, do that in the opening *paragraph* of your answer
- two (or more) elements to a question – when this is the case, try to divide your time equally between the constituent parts unless the question indicates or you can show in your answer that one aspect is more important than another
- write in the margin at the beginning of each answer the question and option (if applicable) – it is irritating for an examiner not immediately to know which question you are attempting. In this, as in *handwriting* and all other respects, you should do everything to keep the examiner well disposed towards you
- answer the question asked – this may seem obvious, but it is remarkable how often candidates are so keen to display all their knowledge that they unload everything they know about a text regardless of whether it is relevant or not. Relevance over-arches all the other Assessment Objectives laid out in Appendix 3. However good your ideas, they are worth little if misapplied. An

art examiner was once asked: 'If a candidate is asked to paint an oak tree and s/he paints a perfect cedar tree, what is the painting worth as an examination piece?' The reply was 'Nothing'.

quoting: do not quote too freely in *open text examinations* (see Appendix 1) simply because you have the text in front of you. The following are methods for laying out quotations:

- if you are quoting less than a line, try to embed the words in your own sentence
- if you are quoting more than a line of verse, lay it out as in the original, thus:
  It seemed that out of battle I escaped
  Down some profound dull tunnel...
- or, if you wish to embed the words of more than one verse line in your own sentence, use a forward slash to mark the end of the lines, thus:
  By opening his poem 'It seemed that out of battle I escaped / Down some profound dull tunnel...' Owen creates a sense of..., etc.
- if you wish to indicate foot (see *metre* under M in the main entries) divisions in a line of verse, use a forward slash between the feet and an accent over the stressed syllable, thus:
  It seémed / that oút / of bát/tle Í / escáped

  (Owen's STRANGE MEETING)

- when leaving a quotation in the middle of a sentence (in prose) or a line (in verse), trail off using three dots as in the examples above.

See also under *quotations, use of* above.

read through: try to leave time to read through your answer, particularly if you know that you are prone to make slips.

rubric: this is the list of instructions on the front of the paper. It is a terrible waste if you go well prepared into the examination and then answer the wrong number of questions, or contravene the instructions in some other way. However well you think you know the instructions for a particular paper, read again the rubric on the front before commencing to write.

secondary opinion is a phrase sometimes used to mean 'the critics'. While it is important to have read some critical opinion on your set texts (see *critics* in the previous section), it is most important to have digested that opinion and to have decided how far you accept it. Use critics in order to help in shaping your own opinions, and do not let them take over your mind. Your personal reaction is essential and the examiner wants to read about it, as indicated by the frequency with which questions contain the phrases '...do you find...', '...do you consider...', '...in your opinion...' and so forth. It is inappropriate to learn quotations from critics for use in *closed book examinations* (see Appendix 1).

style: keep your writing style clear and direct. Use critical and literary jargon only when strictly appropriate; your own personal and fresh choice of vocabulary will often serve you well. Avoid impressive-sounding but long-winded and empty phraseology.

technical terms: there is no point in spotting and listing all the technical devices, conventions and stylistic features of a writer or a particular passage, without considering to what effect a writer is using them. Content and the form of it should be discussed side by side. Architects have a phrase 'Form follows function'; that is, the form of a building is dictated by its intended function. With most writing the same is true. See *mechanic form, organic form.*

time planning: it is essential that you note the advice printed on the examination paper concerning the number of marks awarded for each question, and this will indicate to you the proportion of time that you should spend on each question. To give the most simple of examples, say you are confronted with a paper where you are required to answer two essay questions in two hours, with each essay worth the same number of marks: it is very foolish if you spend far in excess of an hour on the first question, giving yourself not enough time to do justice to your second answer. Even if the second answer looks promising, an examiner cannot reward apparent potential, but only what is actually there on the paper. By keeping ruthlessly relevant to the question you will make the best use of your time. If you do run short of time, resort to clear notes which make as many relevant points as possible and show the shape of the essay which you had hoped to write.

APPENDIX 3
ASSESSMENT OBJECTIVES

assessment objectives (AOs) is the collective name given to the stated aims of the English Literature AS/A and International Baccalaureate Standard and Higher level courses. They are as follows:

AS/A LEVEL

- AO1 – communicate clearly the knowledge, understanding and insight appropriate to literary study, using appropriate terminology and accurate and coherent written expression
  See *expression* in Appendix 1
- AO2i – respond with knowledge and understanding to literary texts of different types and periods
- AO2ii – respond with knowledge and understanding to literary texts of different types and periods, exploring and commenting upon relationships and comparisons between literary texts
  See *intertextuality, post-structuralism* in main entries
- AO3 – show detailed understanding of the ways in which writers' choices of form, structure and language shape meanings
  See *close reading, intrinsic attitude, New Critics, objective criticism* in main entries
- AO4 – articulate independent opinions and judgements, informed by different interpretations of literary texts by other readers
  See *death of the author, plurality, structuralism* in main entries
- AO5i – show understanding of the contexts in which literary texts are written and understood
- AO5ii – evaluate the significance of cultural, historical and other contextual influences on literary texts and study
  See *extrinsic attitude, contextuality, intrinsic attitude, literary/critical theory* in main entries (and the various cross-references listed thereunder, especially *post-structuralism*).
  AO2i and AO5i refer to AS level; AO2ii and AO5ii refer to A level.

INTERNATIONAL BACCALAUREATE

Standard level

Having followed the Language A1 programme at Standard Level (SL) candidates will be expected to demonstrate:

- an ability to approach works in an independent manner which reveals a personal response to literature
  See *death of the author, plurality* in main entries
- an ability to express ideas with clarity, coherence, conciseness, precision and fluency in both written and oral communication
  See *expression* in Appendix 1
- a command of the language appropriate for the study of literature and an

- appreciation of the need for an effective choice of register and style in both written and oral communication
  See *expression* in Appendix 1

- a sound approach to literature through consideration of the works studied
- a thorough knowledge both of the individual works studied and of the relationships between groups of works studied
  See *intertextuality* in main entries

- an appreciation of the similarities and differences between literary works from
- different ages and/or cultures
  See *intertextuality, contextuality* in main entries

- an ability to comment on the language, content, structure, meaning and significance of both familiar and unfamiliar pieces of writing
  See *close reading, intrinsic attitude, New Critics, objective criticism* in main entries

- an awareness of the effects of structure, technique and style as employed by authors
  See *close reading* in main entries

- an ability to structure ideas and arguments, both orally and in writing, in a sustained and logical way, and to support them with precise and relevant examples
  See *expression* in Appendix 1.

Higher level

Having followed the Language AI programme at Higher Level (HL) candidates will be expected to demonstrate:

- an ability to engage in independent literary criticism in a manner which reveals a personal response to literature
- an ability to express ideas with clarity, coherence, conciseness, precision and fluency in both written and oral communication
  See *expression* in Appendix 1

- a command of the language appropriate for the study of literature and a discriminating appreciation of the need for an effective choice of register and style in both written and oral communication demonstrating a sound approach to literature through consideration of the works studied
  See *expression* in Appendix 1

- a thorough knowledge both of the individual works studied and of the relationships between groups of works studied
  See *intertextuality* in main entries

- an appreciation of the similarities and differences between literary works from different ages and/or cultures
  See *intertextuality, contextuality* in main entries

- an ability to engage in independent textual commentary on both familiar and unfamiliar pieces of writing
  See *close reading* in main entries

- a wide-ranging appreciation of structure, technique and style as employed by authors, and of their effects on the reader
See *close reading, intrinsic attitude, New Critics, objective criticism* in main entries
- an ability to structure ideas and arguments, both orally and in writing, in a logical, sustained and persuasive way, and to support them with precise and relevant examples
See *expression* in Appendix 1.

APPENDIX 4

TIME-LINE

It is suggested that you use the white space on the time-line to write in additional writers, movements, periods and/or contexts which emerge as important in your particular areas of study.

AMERICAN TIME LINE

ENGLISH TIME LINE

1250	1300	1400	1410	1420	1430	1440	1450	1460	1470	1480	1490	1500	1510	1520	1530	1540	1550	1560	1570	1580	1590

MIDDLE ENGLISH PERIOD — **RENAISSANCE** — **Elizabethan age**

Dante

Petrarch

Boccaccio

Chaucer

Caxton

Erasmus

More

Wyatt

Surrey

Spenser

Sidney

Chapman ↑

Bacon ↑

Marlowe

Shakespeare ↑

Donne ↑

Jonson ↑

Tourneur ↑

Webster ↑

↑

↑

Key:

▭ — the period during which the author lived

↑ — continued on the next page

● — the year the author was born

COLONIAL PERIOD

RENAISSANCE

NEOCLASSICAL

| Jacobean Age | Caroline Age | Commonwealth Age | The Restoration | Augustan Age | Age of Sensibility |

1600 1610 1620 1630 1640 1650 1660 1670 1680 1690 1700 1710 1720 1730 1740 1750 1760 1770 1780 1790

Scott
Austen
Hazlitt
Byron

Chapman
Bacon

Shakespeare
Donne
Jonson
Tourneur
Webster
Herbert
Ford

Dryden
Behn

Defoe
Vanburgh
J. Swift
Congreve
Farhquar
Pope
Richardson
Fielding
Johnson
Sterne
T. Gray
Smollett
Goldsmith
Cowper
Sheridan
Crabbe
Blake
Wordsworth
Burns

Bradstreet

Milton
Marvell

National Period | American Renaissance | Post Colonial Realistic

Neoclassical/Romantic period | **VICTORIAN PERIOD**

1800 1810 1820 1830 1840 1850 1860 1870 1880 1890 1900

Scott
Austen
Hazlitt
Byron
Percy Shelley
Keats
Mary Shelley
Hawthorne
Elizabeth Barrett Browning
Poe
Gaskell
Thackeray
Robert Browning
Dickens
Trollope
Whitman
Melville
Twain
Wharton
Chekov
Yeats
Kipling
Wells
Pirandello
Crane
Synge
Frost
Cather
E. Thomas
Forster
Sheridan
Crabbe
Blake
Wordsworth
C. Bronte
E. Bronte
A. Bronte
O'Casey
Carlos Williams
Sassoon
Lawrence
Pound
Arnold
Swinburne

1800 1810 1820 1830 1840 1850 1860 1870 1880 1890 1900

Hardy

James

Hopkins

Wilde

Schreiner

Shaw

Conrad

Wilkie Collins

Dickinson

D.G. Rossetti

C. Rossetti

Meredith

Tolstoy

Ibsen

T.S. Eliot

O'Neill

Mansfield

Leavis

Brecht

Wilder

Faulkner

Owen

Cummings

Fitzgerald

MODERN PERIOD

MODERN PERIOD

ı Harlem Renaissance ı

ı Edwardian period ı

1900 1910 1920 1930 1940 1950 1960 1970 1980 1990 2000

Twain

Chekov

• Miller

Wharton

Yeats

• Gordimer

Kipling

Wells

Pirandello

Synge

• Lessing

Frost

Campbell

Cather

E. Thomas

Lowell

• Murray • Eagleton

• Churchill • Barker

Chatwin

• Ngugi • Shepard

• Duffy

• M. Amis

Desai

Larkin

Saro Wiwa

• Armitage

• McGough

• Barnes

• Dabydeen

K. Amis

Steinbeck

Forster

Stead

Orwell

Waugh

O'Casey

Carlos Williams

Sassoon

• Winterson

• Okri

Lawrence

• Harrison • Walker

Pound

Greene

Empson

Swinburne

Corso

1900 1910 1920 1930 1940 1950 1960 1970 1980 1990 2000

Hardy
James

Schreiner

Shaw

Conrad

● Rich ● Adcock ● Atwood ● Rushdie
● Walcott ● Proulx ● Coetzee ● Edgar
Beckett
Betjeman
● Achebe ● Stoppard ● MacEwan
● Pinter ● Soyinka ● Armah ● G.Swift
Auden
Williams
Golding
White

Meredith
Tolstoy
Ibsen

● Ginsberg ● Ayckbourn
● Shaffer ● Fugard ● Heaney
● Albee ● Drabble
T.S. Eliot

O'Neill

Mansfield

Plath
Leavis
Brecht
Wilder
Faulkner
Coward

Bradbury

cummings
Fitzgerald
Carter

Owen

D. Thomas
Berryman
Farrell

Chaudhuri

Further *Complete A–Z Handbooks* are available from Hodder & Stoughton. Why not use them to support your other A levels and Advanced GNVQs? All the *A–Zs* are written by experienced authors and Chief Examiners.

0 340 65467 8	*The Complete A–Z Business Studies* Third Edition £9.99
0 340 65489 9	*The Complete A–Z Geography Handbook* Second Edition £9.99
0 340 64789 2	*The Complete A–Z Leisure, Travel and Tourism Handbook* £9.99
0 340 65832 0	*The Complete A–Z Sociology Handbook* Second Edition £9.99
0 340 65490 2	*The Complete A–Z Psychology Handbook* Second Edition £9.99
0 340 66985 3	*The Complete A–Z Economics and Business Studies Handbook* Second Edition £9.99
0 340 66373 1	*The Complete A–Z Biology Handbook* Second Edition £9.99
0 340 68804 1	*The Complete A–Z Physics Handbook* Second Edition £9.99
0 340 68803 3	*The Complete A–Z Mathematics Handbook* Second Edition £9.99
0 340 67996 4	*The Complete A–Z 20th Century European History Handbook* £9.99
0 340 69131 X	*The Complete A–Z Media and Communication Handbook* £9.99
0 340 68847 5	*The Complete A–Z Business Studies CD-ROM* £55.00 + VAT
0 340 69124 7	*The Complete A–Z Accounting Handbook* £9.99
0 340 67378 8	*The Complete A–Z 19th and 20th Century British History Handbook* £9.99
0 340 72513 3	*The Complete A–Z Chemistry Handbook* Second Edition £9.99
0 340 70557 4	*The Complete A–Z Health & Social Care Handbook* £9.99
0 340 71220 0	*The Complete A–Z Law Handbook* £9.99
0 340 77213 1	*The Complete A–Z Physical Education Handbook* £9.99
0 340 80289 8	*The Complete A–Z Business Studies Coursework Handbook* Second Edition £6.99
0 340 80291 X	*The Complete A–Z Sociology Coursework Handbook* Second Edition £6.99
0 340 79063 6	*The Complete A–Z Psychology Coursework Handbook* £6.99
0 340 78954 9	*The Complete A–Z Economics Handbook* £9.99
0 340 80277 4	*The Complete A–Z ICT and Computing Handbook* £9.99

All Hodder & Stoughton *Educational* books are available at your local bookshop, or can be ordered direct from the publisher. Just tick the titles you would like and complete the details below. Prices and availability are subject to change without prior notice.

Buy four books from the selection above and get free postage and packaging. Just send a cheque or postal order made payable to *Bookpoint Limited* to the value of the total cover price of four books. This should be sent to: Hodder & Stoughton Educational, 39 Milton Park, Abingdon, Oxon OX14 4TD, UK. EMail address: orders@bookpoint.co.uk. Alternatively, if you wish to buy fewer than four books, the following postage and packaging costs apply:

UK & BFPO: £4.30 for one book; £6.30 for two books; £8.30 for three books.
Overseas and Eire: £4.80 for one book; £7.10 for 2 or 3 books (surface mail).

If you would like to pay by credit card, our centre team would be delighted to take your order by telephone. Our direct line (44) 01235 827720 (lines open 9.00am - 6.00pm, Monday to Saturday, with a 24 hour answering service). Alternatively you can send a fax to (44) 01235 400454.

Title _____ First name _____ Surname _____

Address _____

Postcode _____ Daytime telephone no. _____

If you would prefer to pay by credit card, please complete:

Please debit my Master Card / Access / Diner's Card / American Express
(delete as applicable)

Card number _____ Expiry date _____ Signature _____

If you would not like to receive further information on our products, please tick the box ☐